AF241662

SEA RANCH IMPRESSIONS

SEA RANCH IMPRESSIONS

KAREN CAIRN KREISEL

A collection of botanical impressions from Sea Ranch

and the Northern California coast

© 2026 Karen Cairn Kreisel

Flooding Island Press

ISBN: 978-1-961882-00-3

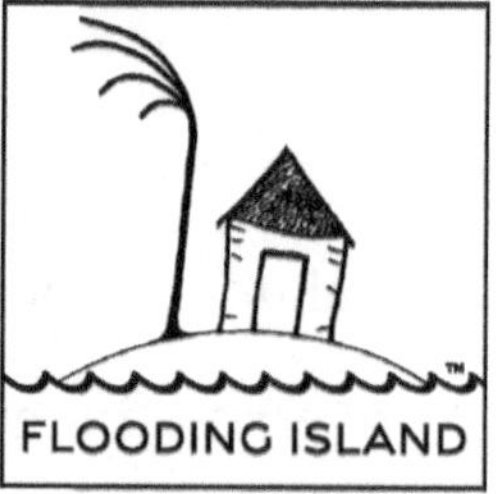

First printing March, 2026

Great effort was made to correctly identify the plants that were collected and printed in this book; however, mistakes are possible. This book should not be used as a source for identifying plants that will be consumed.

All plant imprints in this book are by Karen C. Kreisel

Cover design and back cover photo by S. Saroff

Thank you to the friends who have walked and explored with me.

Thank you to the authors of the botany books that fill my shelves; I will never tire of holding physical books or of the joy of turning pages. Thank you to the creators and users of iNaturalist software, who have taken some of the complexity out of plant identification. Thank you also to Suzanne Saroff for her artistic encouragement and for sharing her multifaceted expertise, including her help with InDesign.

Special thanks to Karen Wilkinson and Mike Petrich for inspiring joy and curiosity in our many biotic surveys, river ramblings, and walks, and for their encouragement to observe, create, and share. Thank you to Julia Larke for kindly sharing of her decades of wisdom and observation.

And finally, thank you to my partner, Steve Saroff, who has always encouraged me to do what I love and who agrees that kitchen tables are the brightest and best places to work on projects.

CONTENTS

INTRODUCTION

I am happiest when I am outside. Over the years, as I have explored the forests, streams, woodlands, and meadows of Sea Ranch in Northern California, I have often tried to share what I see and feel with others. I have done this by taking walks together, where we talk and point out to each other whatever is capturing our attention. Sometimes those are big things: the sky going wild before storms; the whales, on their seasonal migrations, blowing and breaching close to shore; and flocks of amazing birds that sing and swoop past. But mostly, it is smaller things that I often try to share my enthusiasm for: the gentle, quiet plants that have been growing here, year after year, long before any of us walked along this coast.

This book project began in the fall of 2024, when the coastal rain and fog hung over the ocean horizon, and most of the bright flowers were gone. I set out to walk, look closely, and "discover" as many native plants as I could. Finding and identifying each new plant was a small adventure. As I inked and then carefully pressed leaves and stems onto paper, over and over again, the shape and texture of these wild plants kept surprising me with their simple beauty.

You will see the actual size of each plant's leaves and stems on these pages. However, though the plants in this book are correctly identified, it is not a complete plant identification book. I have not tried to include every possible plant found at Sea Ranch, nor have I included plants that made uninteresting prints. Rather, I have included only prints of plants I found both lovely and fascinating — the ones that made me happy, and that is what I hope to share with you.

These pages are loosely organized into four general environments found at Sea Ranch: Forest, Streamside, Woodland, and Meadow. I have also written a few notes about each plant. Sometimes a detail, sometimes an interesting fact; most often a feeling or noticing from the day I collected and then made the plant's print.

I hope the prints in this book will remind you to take some time and connect with our natural surroundings as often as you can. I invite you to touch, smell, inspect, and notice the plants that grow nearby.

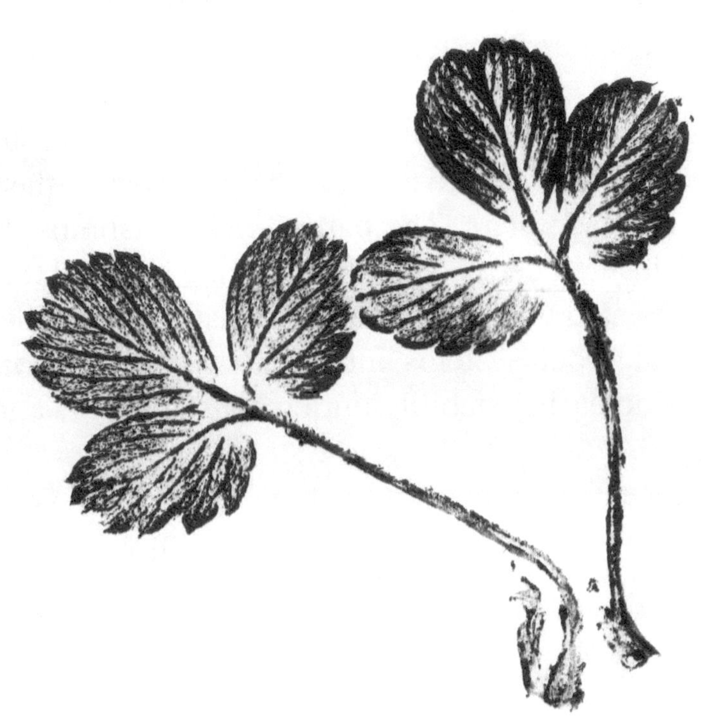

FOREST

Coast Redwood
Sequoia sempervirens

We are lucky to be able to walk among these giants. They are the heartbeat of the forest. Visit on a foggy morning and look up. Silence. Then the song of a Pacific Wren…

Redwoods are the tallest tree species on Earth. Native to a narrow strip along the Pacific Coast from southern Oregon to central California, some grow more than 300 feet tall. Yet these impressive sentinels begin from a tiny seed; redwood cones are only about an inch long.

Redwoods absorb moisture directly through their needles from coastal fog, helping sustain them during dry summers. The bark is rich in tannins that resist insects, decay, and fire, allowing survival through repeated wildfires. The trees' shallow but wide-spreading root systems interlock with neighboring trees, increasing stability during coastal storms and winds.

Redwoods are resilient; where they have been cut down, others often grow back in a circle. We can learn by visiting. Come with me…

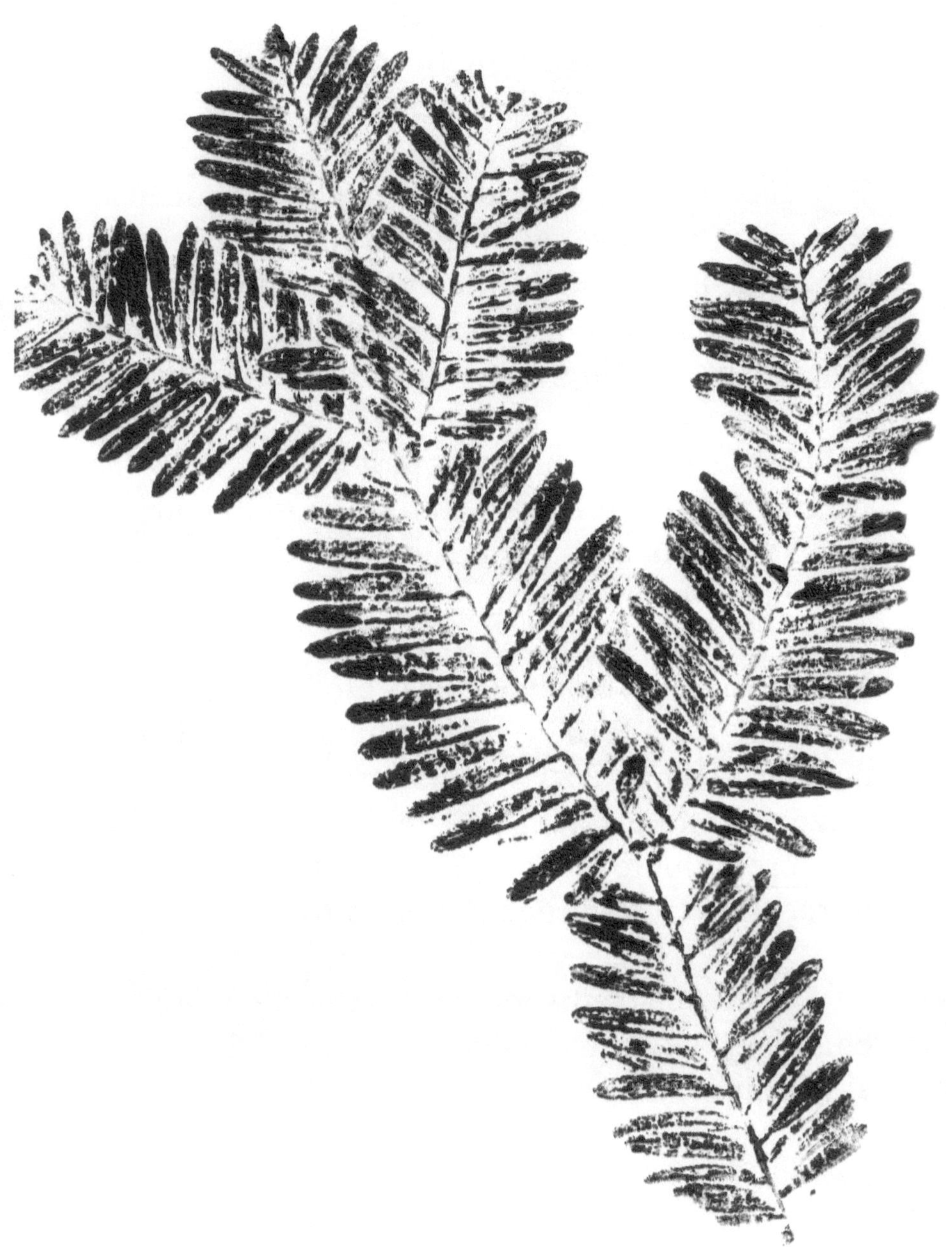

FOREST

Redwood Sorrel
Oxalis oregana

Beneath the redwoods, in patches, a soft carpet. One day, as I was searching for an elusive four-leafed bit of green luck, I noticed that the leaves seemed to close as sunbeams reached where I was sitting. They open on lucky days...

When the sun is shining or rain is falling, the fragile leaves fold down like closed umbrellas. Scientists call this behavior nyctinasty. The movement happens within minutes.

Symbol of luck, balance, and protection, it thrives in acidic soils formed by decomposing redwood needles. Dense sorrel mats, rising from scaly rhizomes, help retain soil moisture by shading the forest floor. It is often among the first plants to recolonize disturbed redwood forest soils.

At Sea Ranch, redwood sorrel carpets mark the boundary between persistent fog and drier coastal openings.

Redwood sorrel leaves have a high concentration of oxalic acid and are mildly toxic.

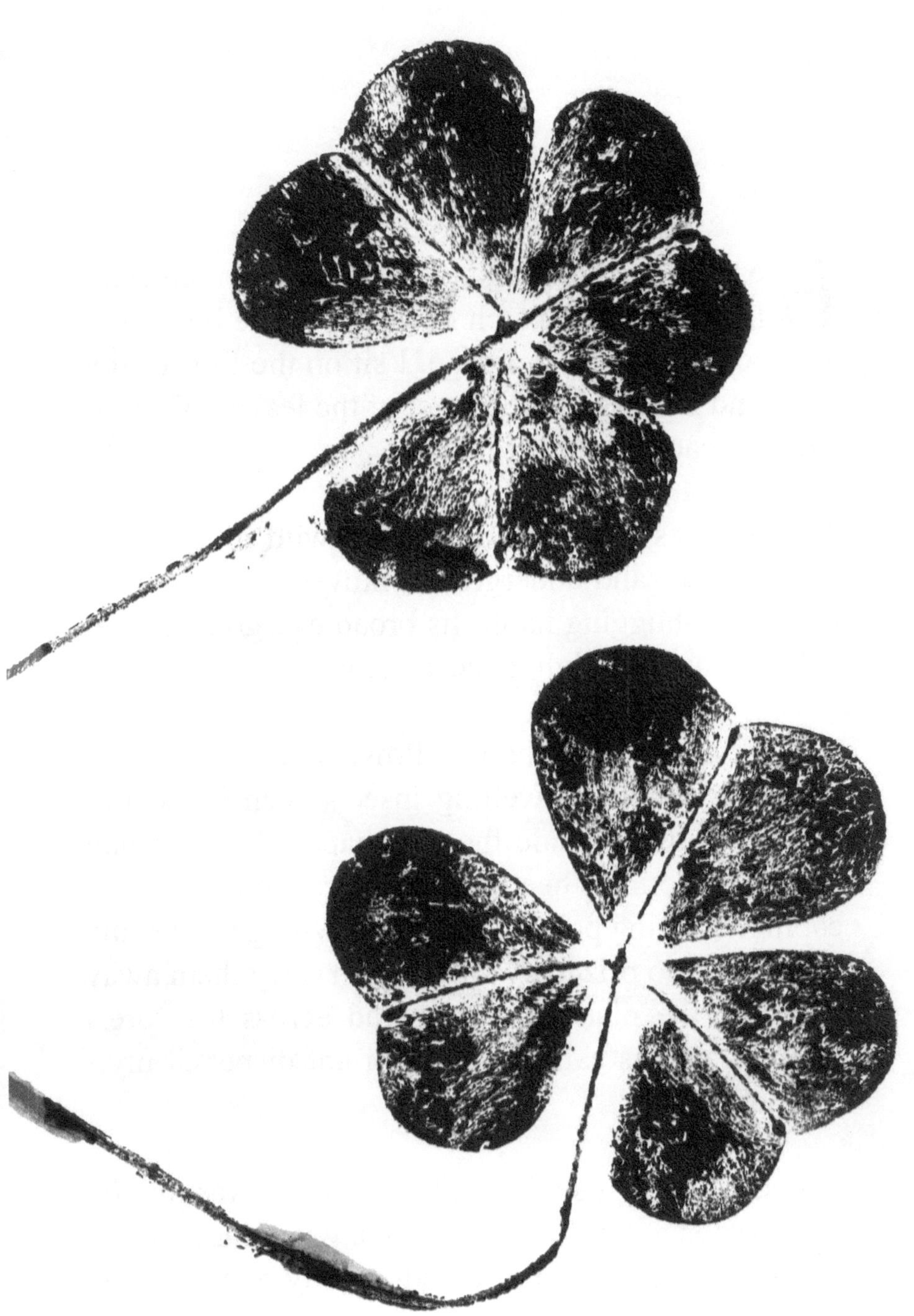

FOREST

Wild Ginger
Asarum caudatum

Heart-shaped leaves and gentle, hidden tentacles hint at love. A patch of ginger at the bottom of a wooded redwood drainage. I sit on the forest floor and bend my head to the level of the leaves. There is a dark, beautiful flower…

The ancients and wise associated wild ginger with hidden paths and underground movement, reflecting its ground-hugging habit. Its broad evergreen leaves help capture dim light beneath dense forest canopies.

Wild ginger's jug-shaped flowers are pollinated mainly by ground-dwelling insects such as beetles and small flies. Inside the jug-shaped flower, small insects sometimes become briefly trapped before escaping, carrying pollen with them. Wild ginger's tiny seeds are also prized by ants, which carry them away and help the plant slowly spread across the forest floor. Scientists call this form of ant dispersal myrmecochory.

Found from British Columbia through Washington and Oregon to northern California, wild ginger forms long-lived colonies and spreads slowly by rhizomes.

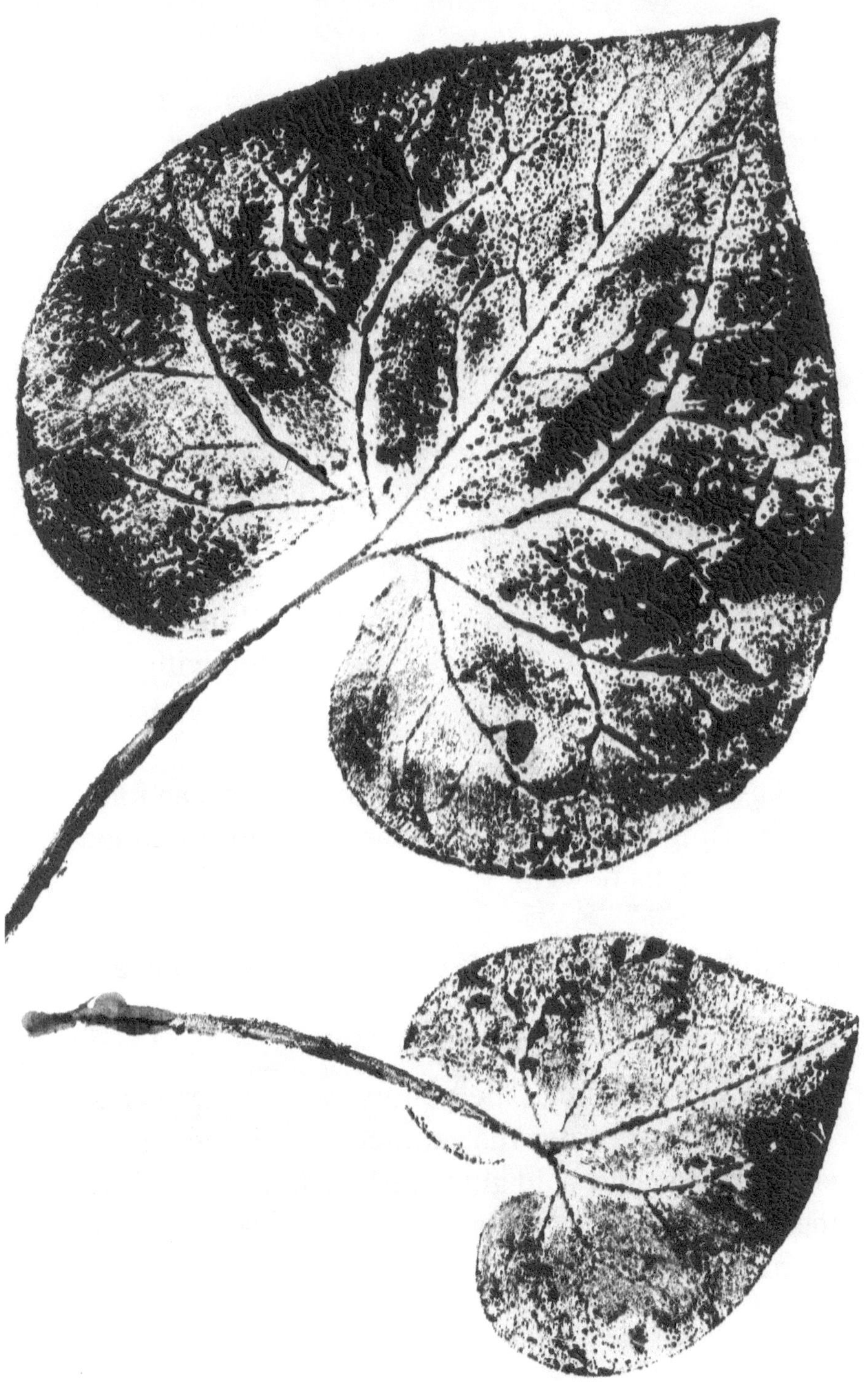

Redwood Violet
Viola sempervirens

Sweet with its heart-shaped leaves and yellow flowers carpeting the forest. A happy plant. Its flowers remind me of a childhood rhyme, even if the flower is not blue…

Redwood violet is native to coastal California and southern Oregon and is closely associated with redwood forests, blooming in early spring.

When pollinators are scarce, redwood violet can form seeds using hidden, self-pollinating flowers called cleistogamous flowers.

The Latin name, *Viola sempervirens*, means "always green" or "always living."

Its flowers are often pale yellow with darker veins. They produce nectar that attracts small bees, flies, and ants. As with wild ginger, ants carry the seeds to their nests. This ant-assisted seed dispersal is called myrmecochory.

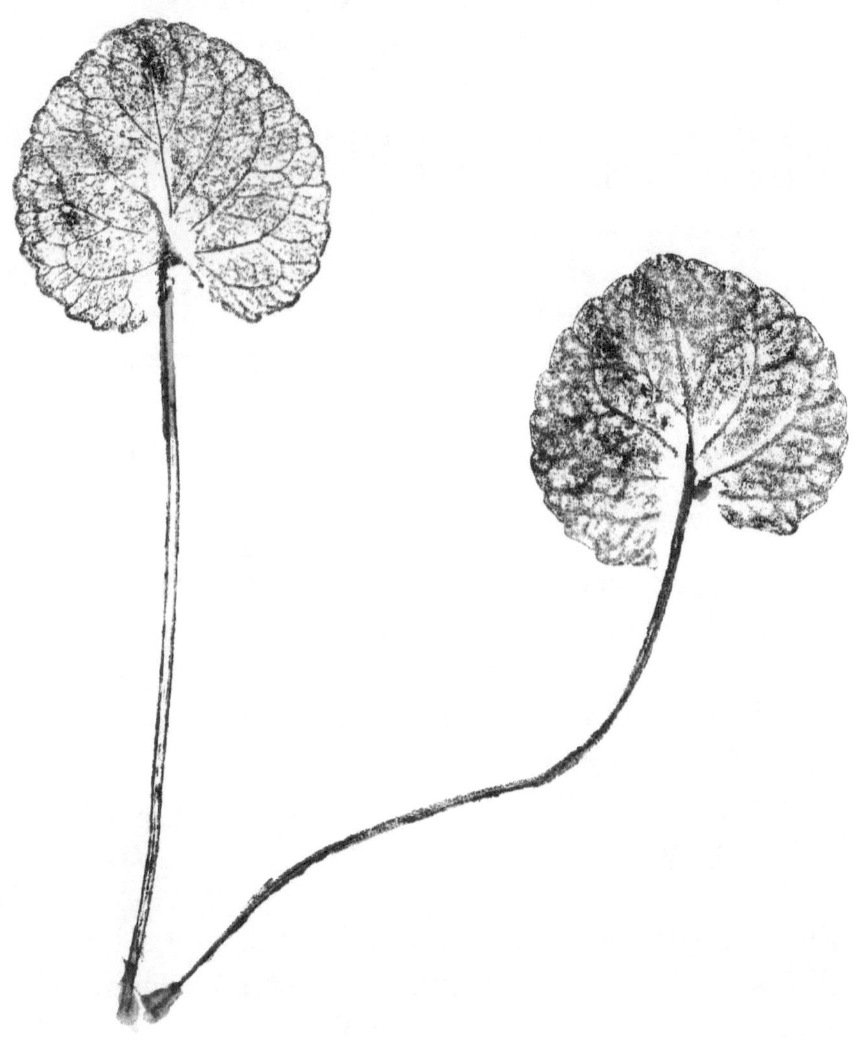

FOREST

Star-flowered Lily-of-the-Valley
Maianthemum stellatum

Repeated shapes and small patches near stream banks, with puffs of white flowers opening like stars…

Star-flowered lily-of-the-valley is a native woodland perennial found across much of North America.

It grows in forests, along streambanks, and in moist meadows, often in partial shade.

In spring, slender stems rise from creeping rhizomes and bear several alternate leaves along their length.

The leaves are oval to lance-shaped with parallel veins, typical of many forest monocots. At the tip of each stem, a small cluster of delicate white flowers opens in late spring.

Each flower has narrow, star-like petals and a light fragrance. Blooming typically occurs from May into June, depending on elevation and latitude.

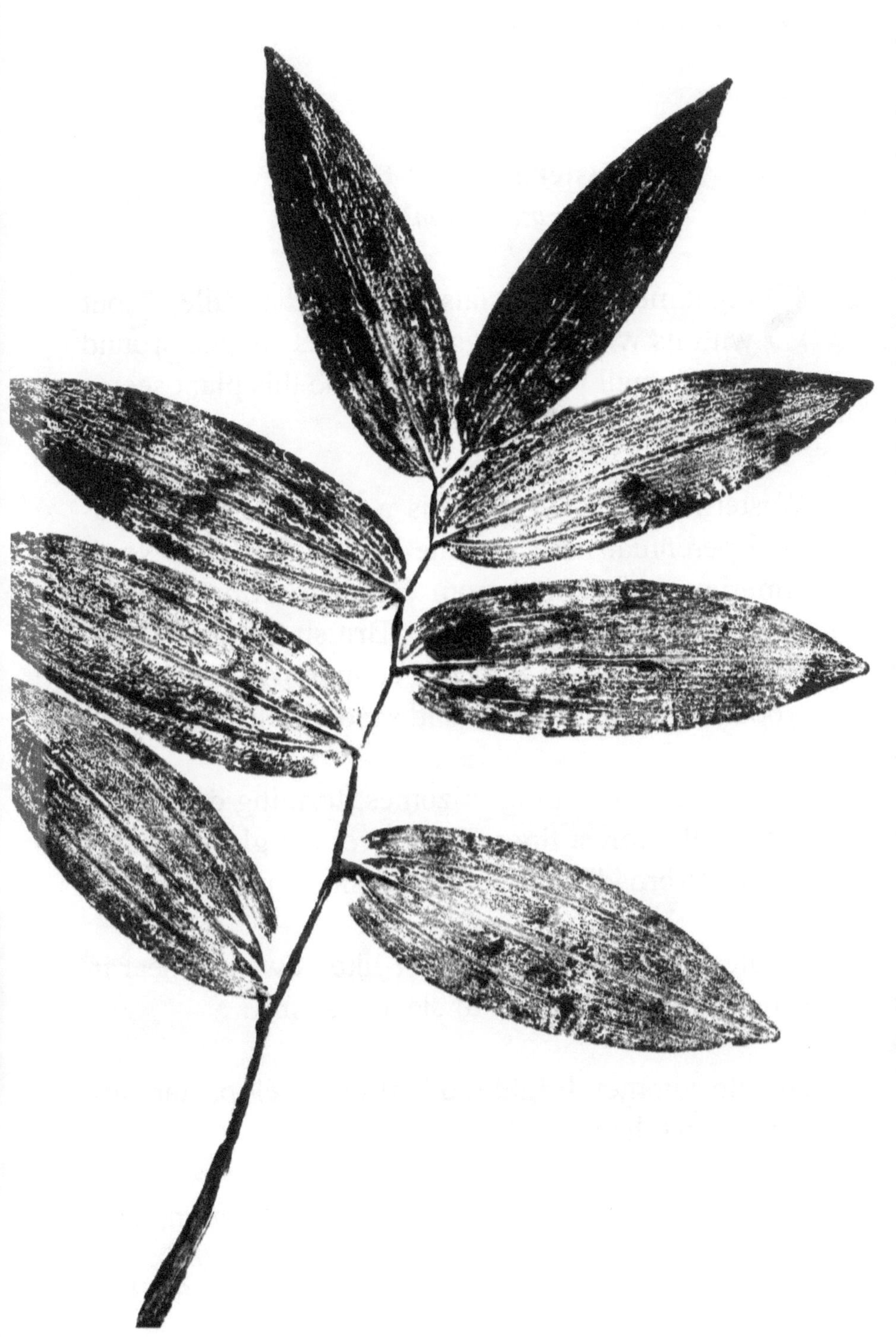

FOREST

Western Lily-of-the-Valley
Maianthemum dilatatum

Sometimes called "false lily of the valley," but with its wide, bright green leaves cupped around a stem of small white flowers, to me this plant seems true like a protective parent…

Western lily-of-the-valley is a low-growing woodland perennial native to the Pacific Coast of North America. It is found from central California north through Oregon, Washington, British Columbia, and into Alaska. At Sea Ranch it commonly carpets redwood forest understories and shaded coastal ravines.

It spreads by creeping rhizomes, forming dense carpets on the forest floor. The leaves are glossy, heart-shaped to broadly oval, with prominent parallel veins.

In late spring, small white star-like flowers appear in short clusters at the top of slender stems.

By late summer, bright red berries develop, standing out against the green leaves.

The berries are eaten by birds and small mammals.

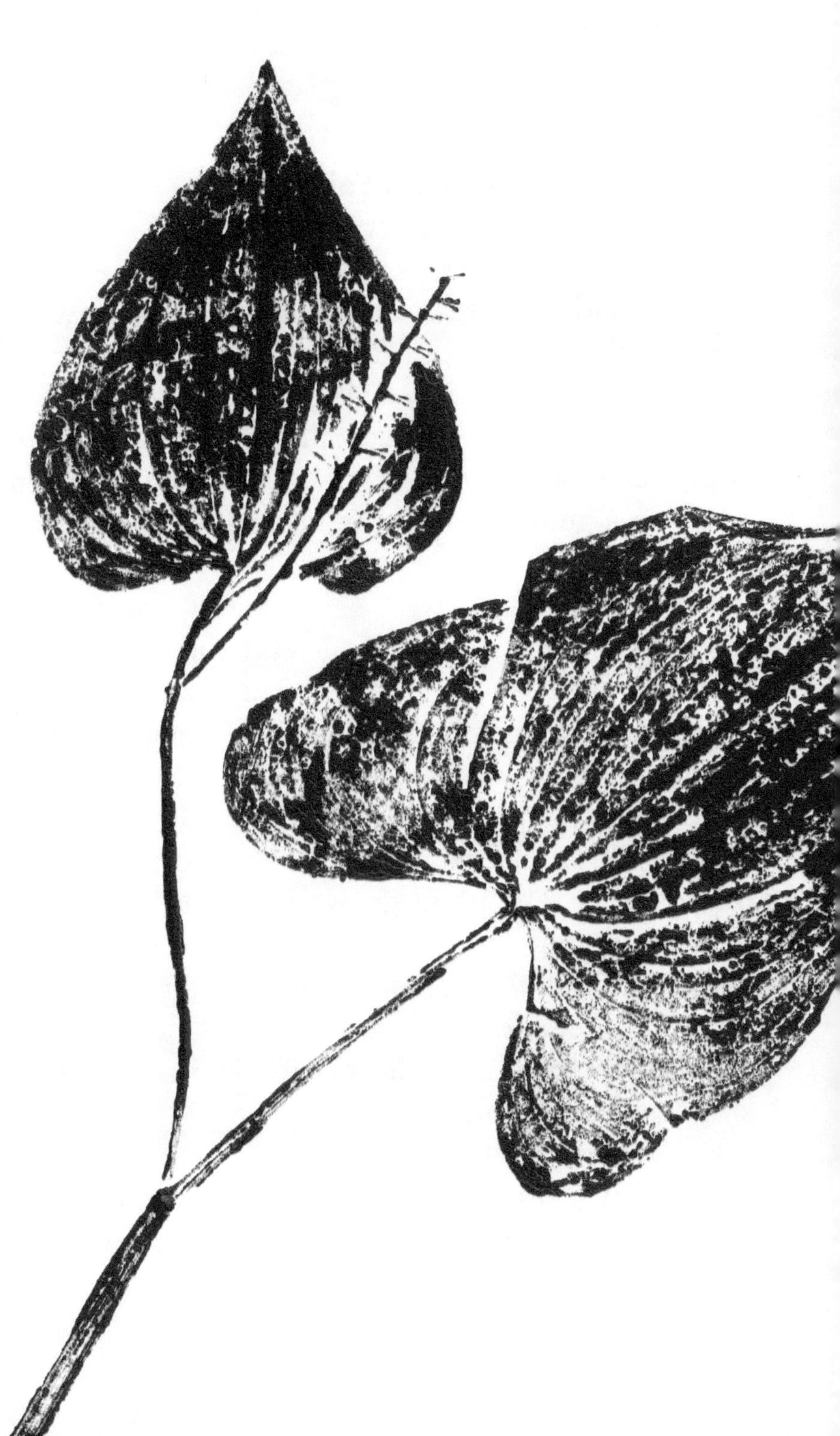

FOREST

Hooker's Fairybells
Prosartes hookeri

The native bees visiting fairybells' flowers are the smallest of dancers...

Nodding flowers protect pollen from rain in moist coastal climates. The slender stems often grow in a gentle zigzag, bending slightly at each leaf.

The flower has six tepals (petal-like parts that are not differentiated into sepals and petals). There are six stamens inside, often extending beyond the creamy tepals.

It is most abundant in stable, shaded forest environments. The plant grows from rhizomes and spreads slowly over time. Its bright red berries provide food for forest birds and small mammals. The berries ripen quickly after flowering, making them one of the earlier fruits available on the forest floor.

Fairybells bloom early in spring, before the forest canopy fully closes and the understory returns to deep shade.

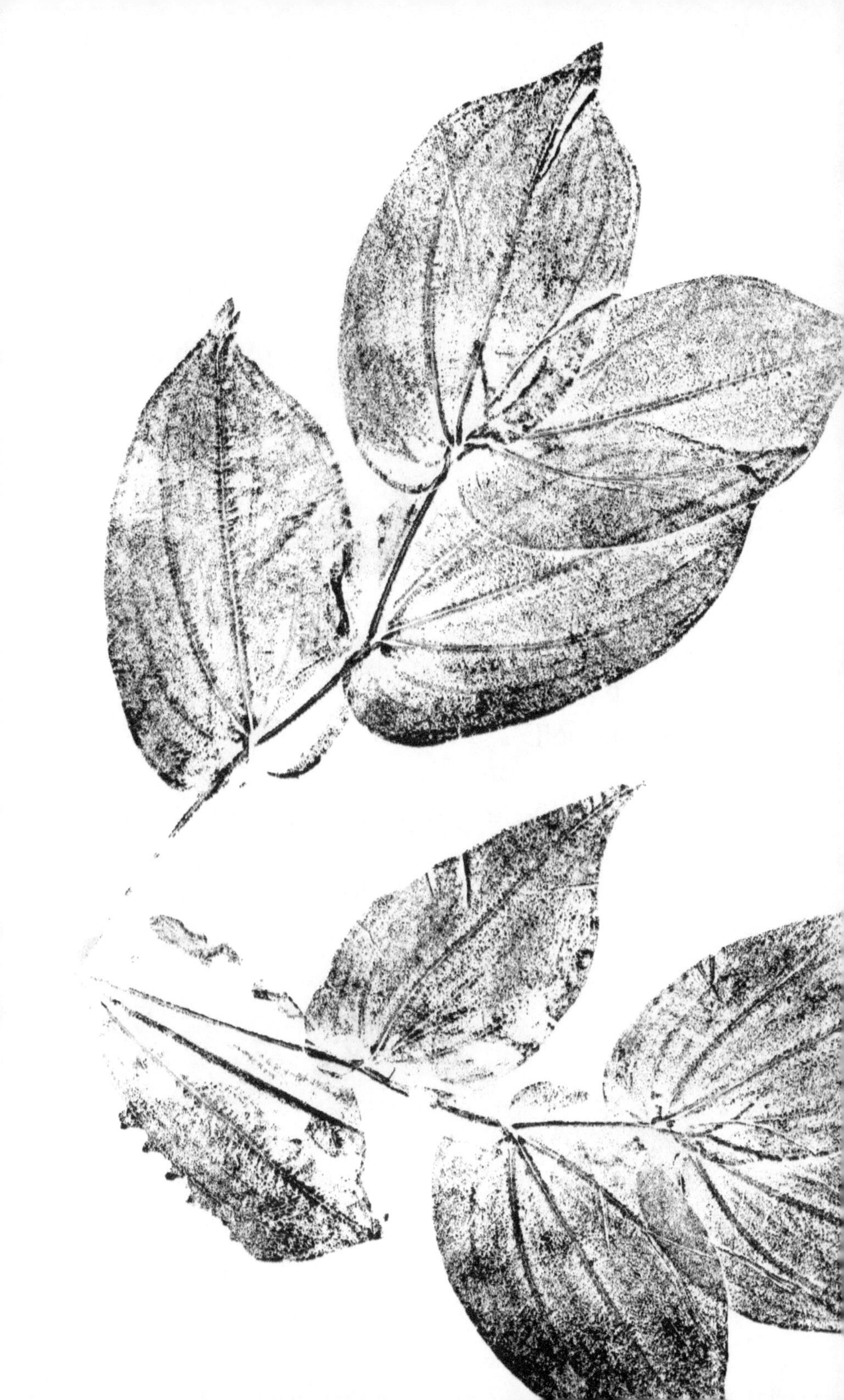

FOREST

Goldenback Fern
Pentagramma triangularis

Small and surprising. When I first found this fern, the triangular shape was distinctive and helped me remember its name. Turn the frond over, and you will see…

The underside of its fronds is coated with a yellow or white powder that reflects sunlight.

This powder helps reduce water loss and heat stress. Goldenback fern grows on rocky slopes and outcrops with minimal soil.

It tolerates drier conditions than many forest ferns.

The species increases plant diversity in otherwise sparsely vegetated rocky habitats.

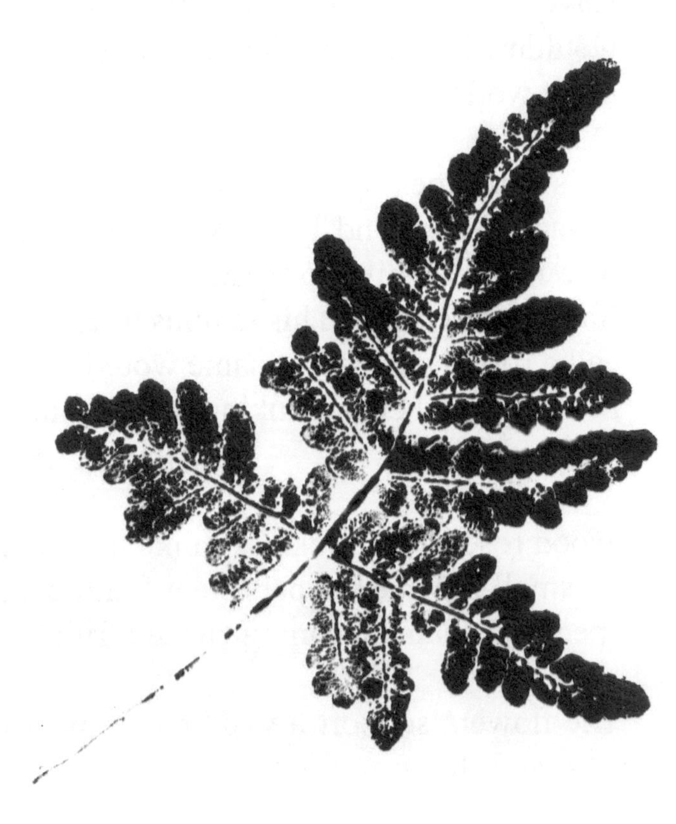

FOREST

Wood Rose
Rosa gymnocarpa

Once, when I worked watching birds in a dark hemlock forest, wood roses grew in the understory. One rainy day, I picked a few delicate rose leaves to put on my face so that the mosquitoes wouldn't be able to bite. You might have laughed, but it worked!

This rose goes by many names, including Baldhip, Dwarf, Wood, and Little Wild Rose. Although this rose is only native to western North America, when Shakespeare penned his famous line, "That which we call a rose by any other name would smell as sweet," he could have been thinking of a cousin to this sweet beauty.

Wood rose lacks prickles, unlike most native roses. Its small hips lack a persistent floral cup, giving the species its name meaning "naked fruit."

The flowers support a wide range of insect pollinators, and the hips are eaten by birds and mammals, aiding seed dispersal.

It typically grows along shaded woodland edges.

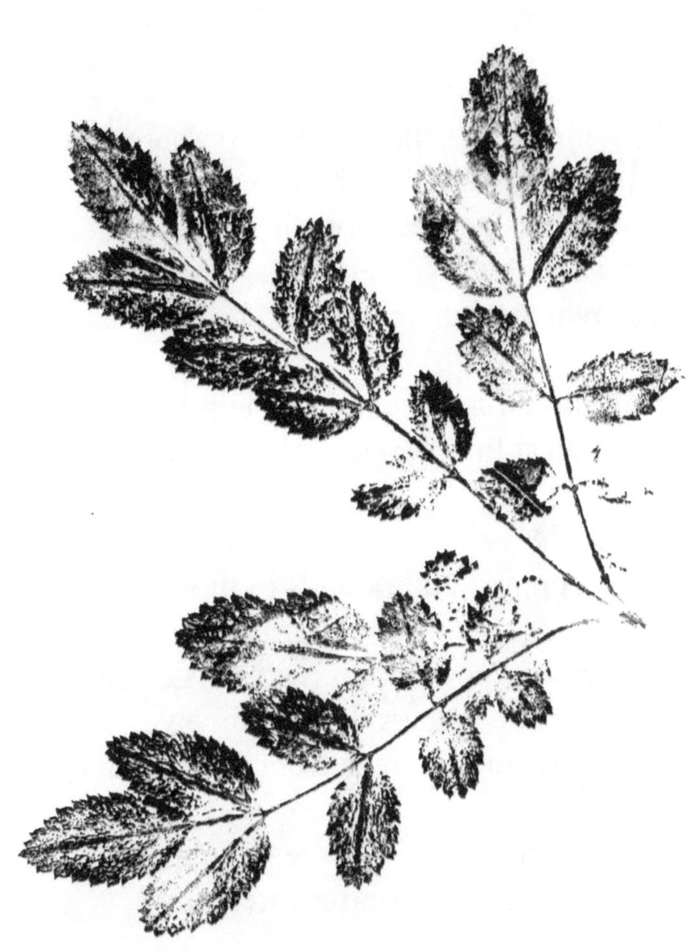

FOREST

Grand Fir
Abies grandis

Wind is not their friend, perhaps because they reach so high, which may be a price of being too grand. When the forest is calm, listen for the quiet honks of Pygmy Nuthatches that like to walk head-first down the trunks looking for insects.

Grand fir can grow over 250 feet tall, making it one of the tallest fir species in North America.

The needles release a citrus-like scent when crushed due to aromatic compounds in the foliage.

The bark is smooth with resin blisters when the tree is young but becomes deeply furrowed with age, distinguishing mature trees from younger individuals.

Grand fir contributes to deep shade and cool temperatures in mixed conifer forests.

Its fallen needles decompose relatively quickly, enriching forest soils with organic matter.

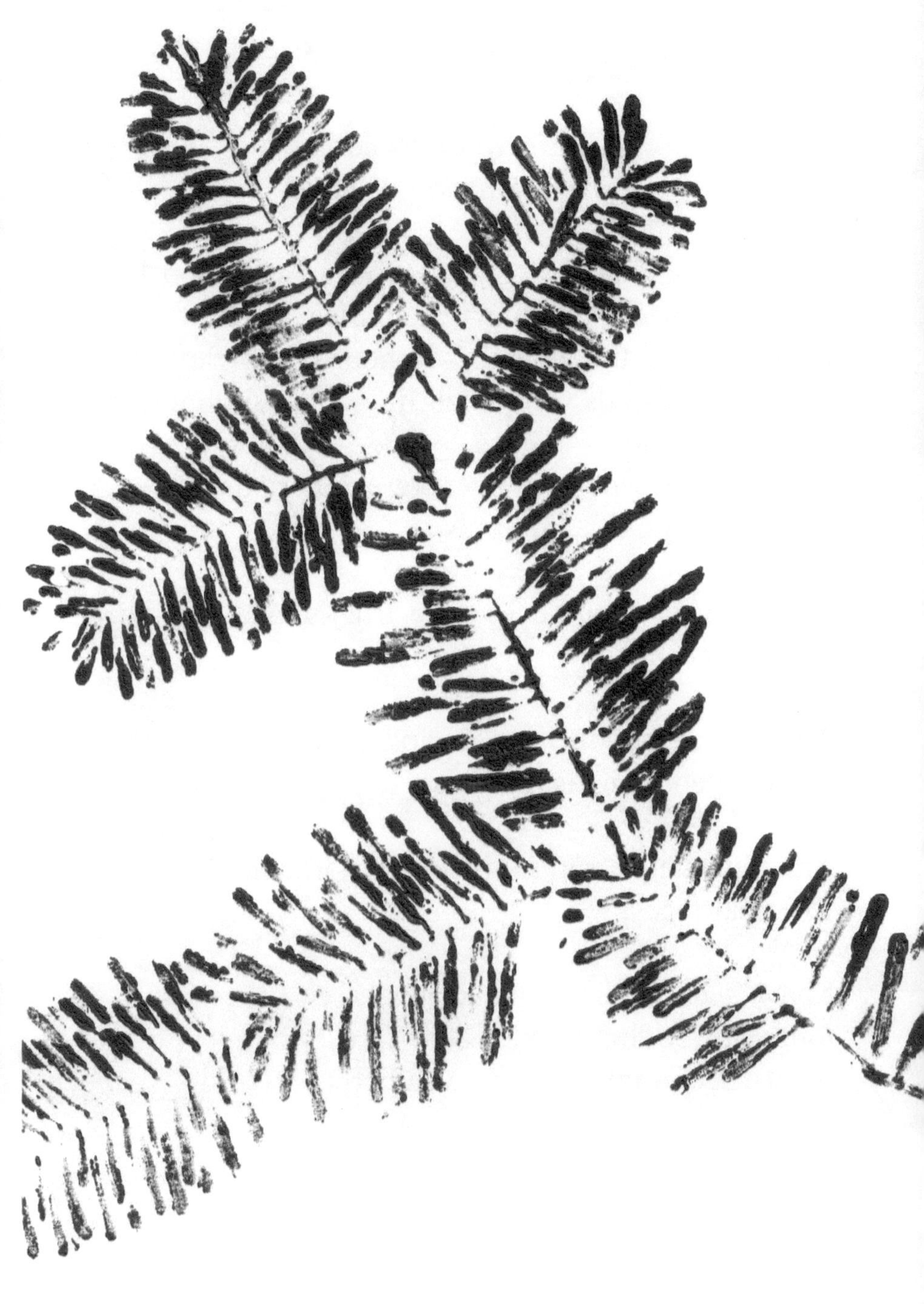

FOREST

California Polypody
Polypodium californicum

Look for this fern growing out of redwood logs near sorrel. Not long after sunrise, I passed small, tightly curled fiddleheads. An hour later, when I returned, the fronds were uncurling in the sunlight…

California polypody is an evergreen fern that remains green through dry summers.

It often grows on rocks, tree trunks, and decaying logs rather than directly in soil.

The fronds curl inward during drought and unfurl again when moisture returns.

This fern helps trap moisture and organic debris on forest surfaces.

I have seen yellow banana slugs, six or seven inches long, slowly sliming along the forest floor near these plants, seemingly without a care in the world.

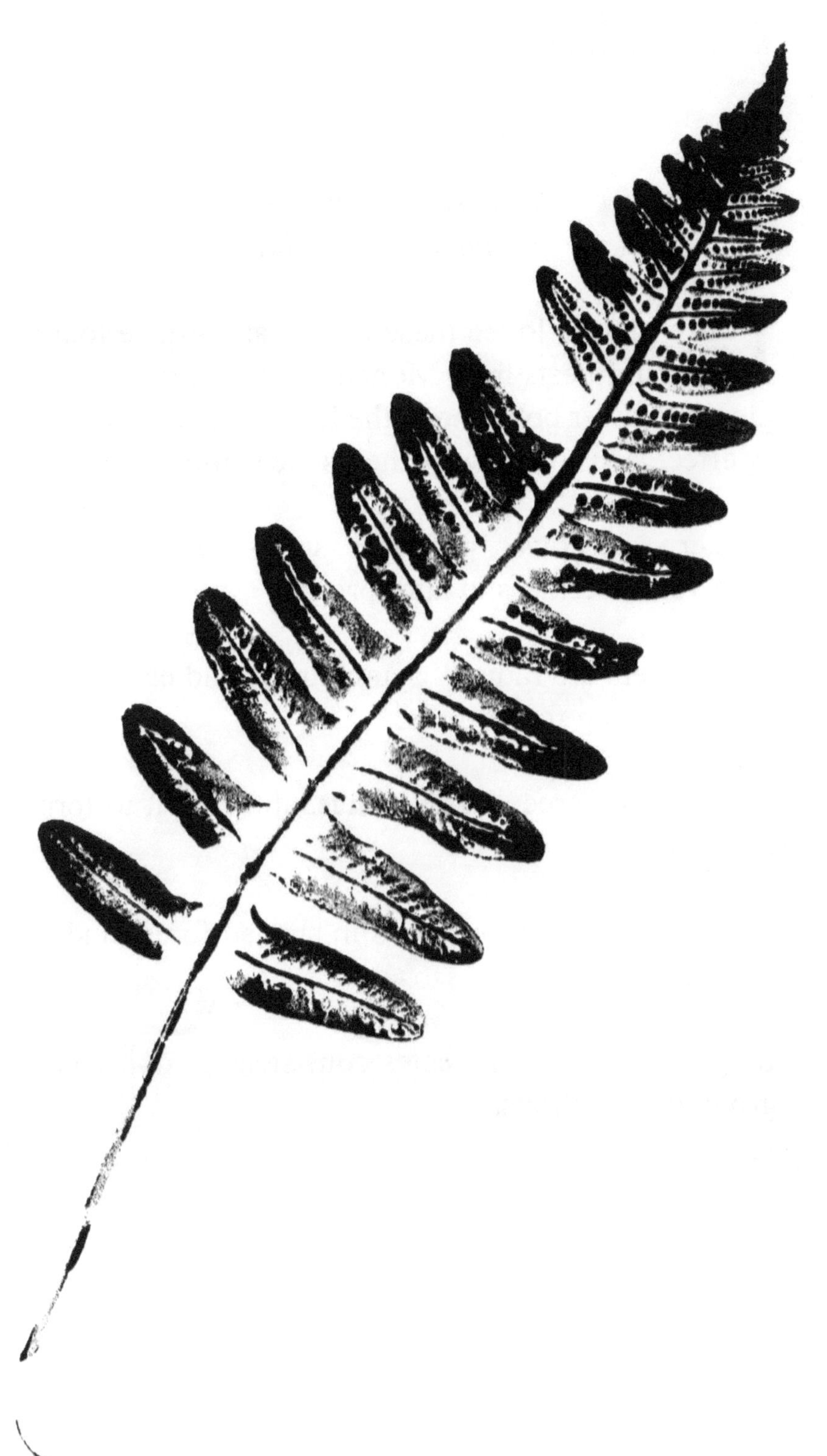

FOREST

Western Starflower
Lysimachia latifolia

I have always loved these plants, and I have found them in forests from Montana to California. A single tiny flower bobs above the leaves, creating a starry effect. This one always helps me smile…

Western starflower produces small white flowers with yellow centers in late spring.

The flowers are radially symmetrical and easily recognized along forest trails.

It spreads by creeping rhizomes, allowing it to form loose colonies.

The plant favors moist soils in shaded forest understories.

Its presence often indicates consistently cool, damp growing conditions.

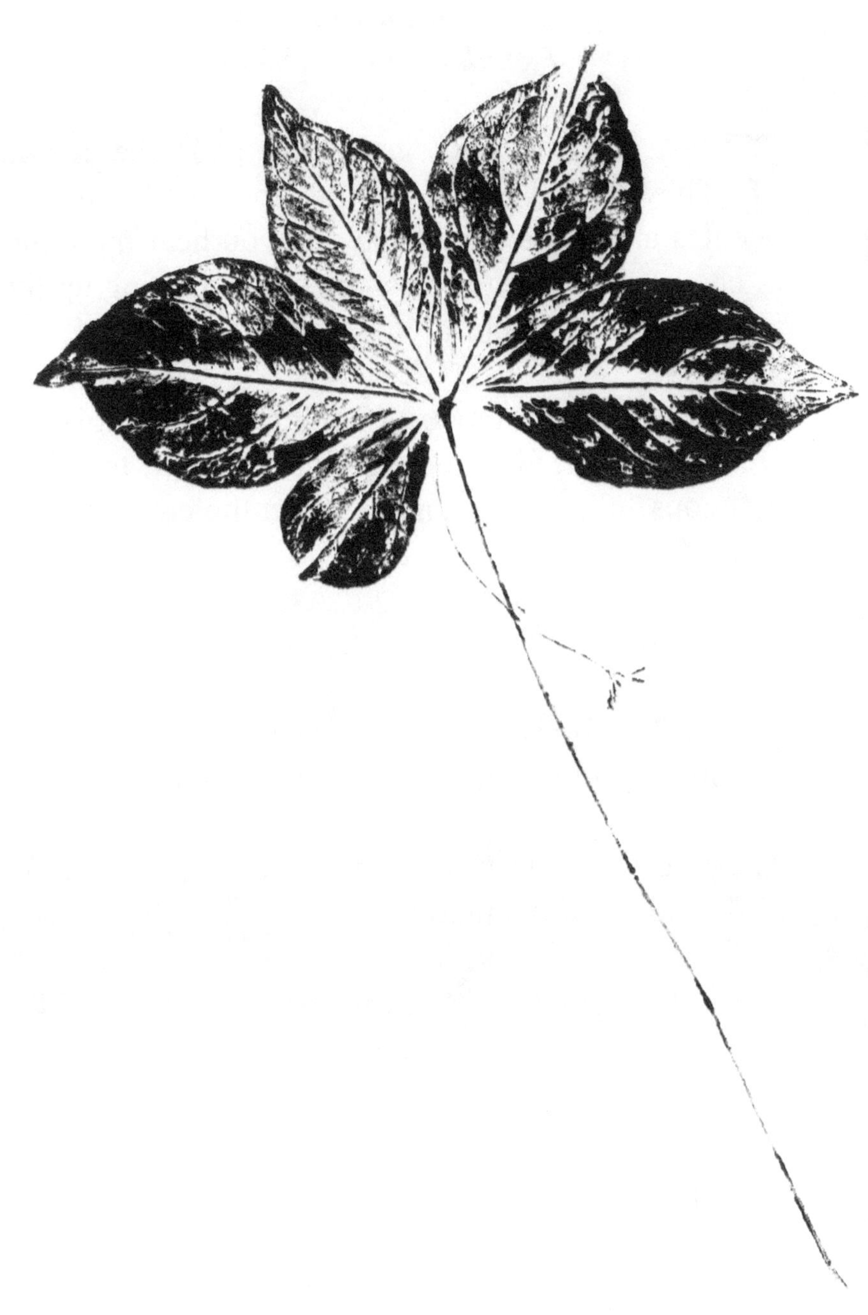

FOREST

Douglas Fir
Pseudotsuga menziesii

These are the gray grandfathers of the forest. They are the gentle, waiting greeters. Even their needles are soft to the touch. Do you hear the high-pitched call from the brown creeper spiraling up the tree trunk? Listen closely…

The three-pointed bracts emerging from Douglas-fir cones resemble tiny mouse hind legs and tails. Indigenous folklore says mice hid in the cones during forest fires, leaving their bodies visible.

Douglas-fir is not a true fir, despite its common name.

Douglas-fir forests support diverse understory communities by allowing filtered light to reach the ground.

The trees provide nesting and roosting habitat for birds and small mammals.

John Muir called it "a great forest monarch of the West."

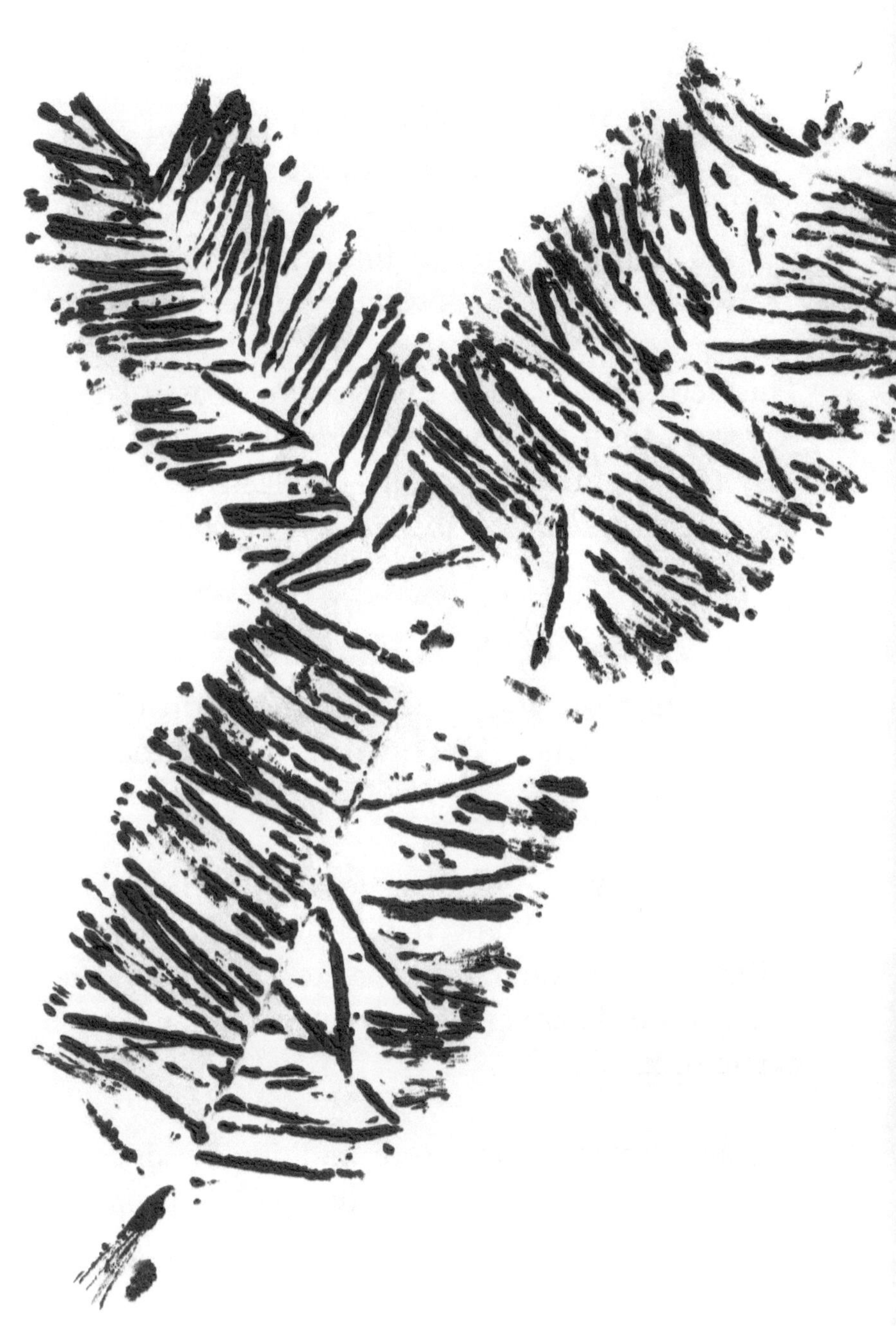

FOREST

Western Maidenhair Fern
Adiantum aleuticum

This fern is special to find, light and thin as it waves its fronds in even the gentlest breeze…

This fern grows along the western coast of North America, from Alaska down through California. It is easy to recognize by its polished black stems, which hold light green, fan-shaped leaflets along gently arching fronds.

The fronds move readily with air. It grows in shaded ravines, north-facing slopes, and along riparian corridors at Sea Ranch. You often see water beading on the fronds.

The genus name *Adiantum* derives from the Greek adiantos, meaning "unwetted," referring to the fronds' ability to shed water. The species epithet *aleuticum* refers to the Aleutian Islands, reflecting the northern extent of its range.

The shiny black stems were traditionally dried and split into narrow strands by Indigenous peoples of the Pacific Coast and woven into baskets to create dark, contrasting lines and borders.

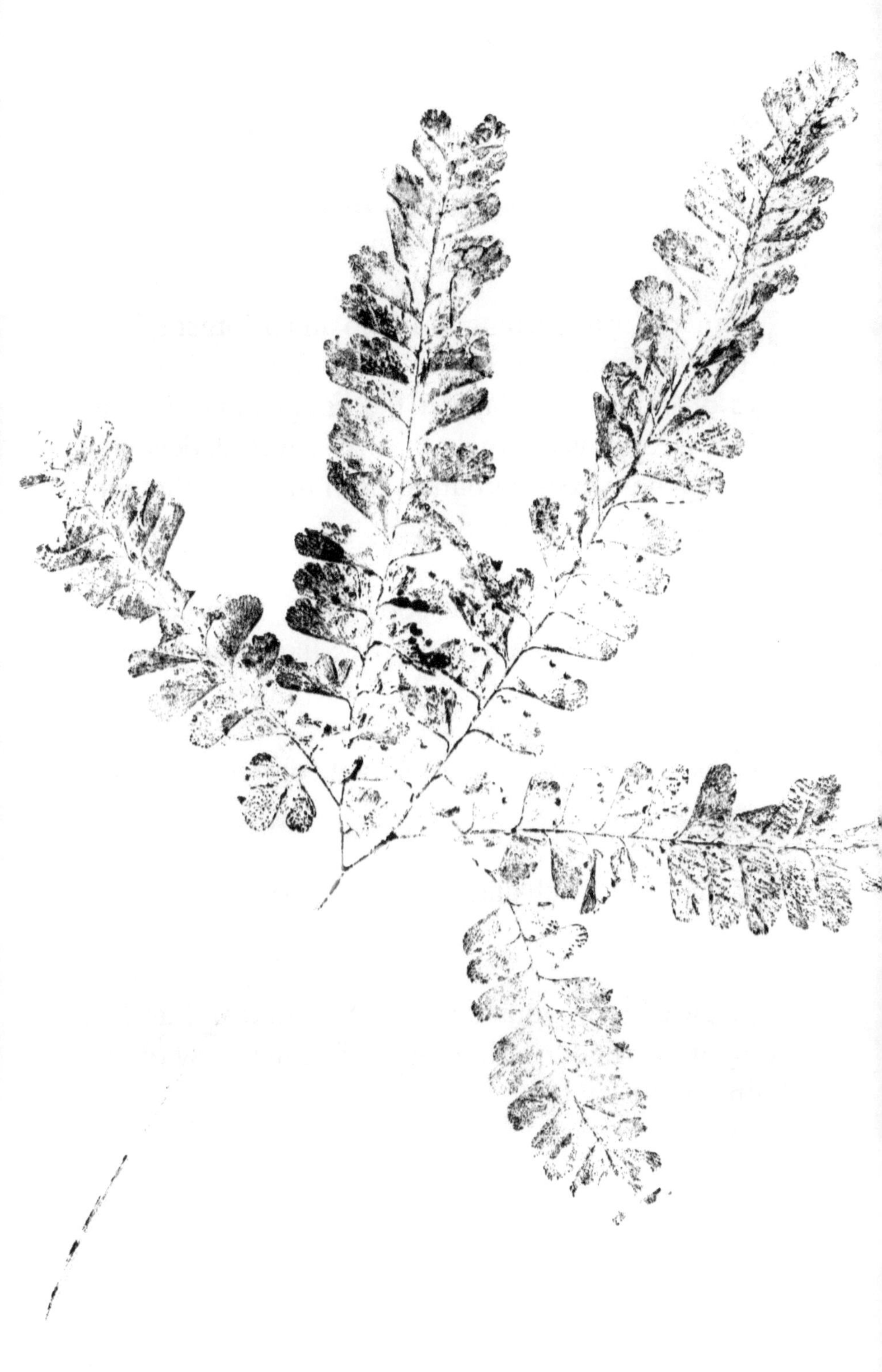

FOREST

Western Hemlock
Tsuga heterophylla

I remember a morning in Idaho and a forest of old-growth hemlocks. It was just after sunrise, with rays of light coming under the boughs and lighting spider webs covered in dew. Moss-covered, decaying logs had new trees sprouting from them. In that moment, birth and death felt accepted…

Western hemlock has droopy, lazy tops, and its branches slouch in a relaxed way, like an old friend. Even the needles are friendly to the touch.

It is one of the most shade-tolerant conifers in coastal forests.

The cones are small and hang downward from branch tips.

If you are lucky, you may hear the ethereal flute-like song of a varied thrush, or get a fleeting view of one flying in the canopy.

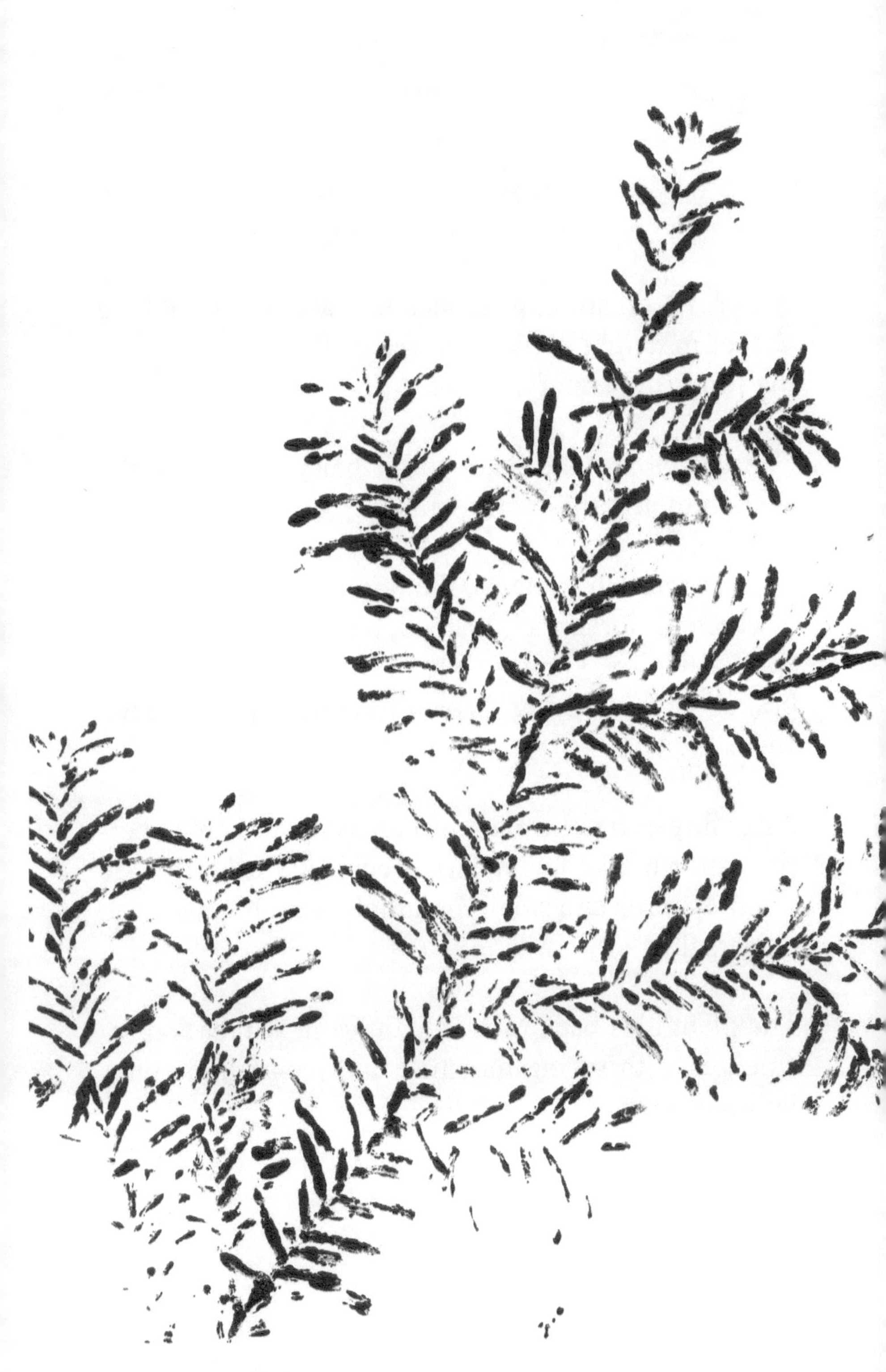

FOREST

Largeflower Fairybells
Prosartes smithii

It grows on arching stems and reaches two to three feet in height, making it one of the taller herbs of the forest understory.

The leaves are alternate, softly hairy, and clasp the stem at their base, partly wrapping around it.

Hidden under the leaves, the flowers are pale yellow to cream-colored, bell-shaped, and often streaked or spotted within. One to seven flowers hang from the branch tips in spring, typically from April through June.

After flowering, the plant produces red to orange berries, often marked with dark speckles. The berries are eaten by birds and small mammals, which aid in seed dispersal.

The plant dies back to its rhizomes in winter and re-emerges with spring moisture and lengthening daylight.

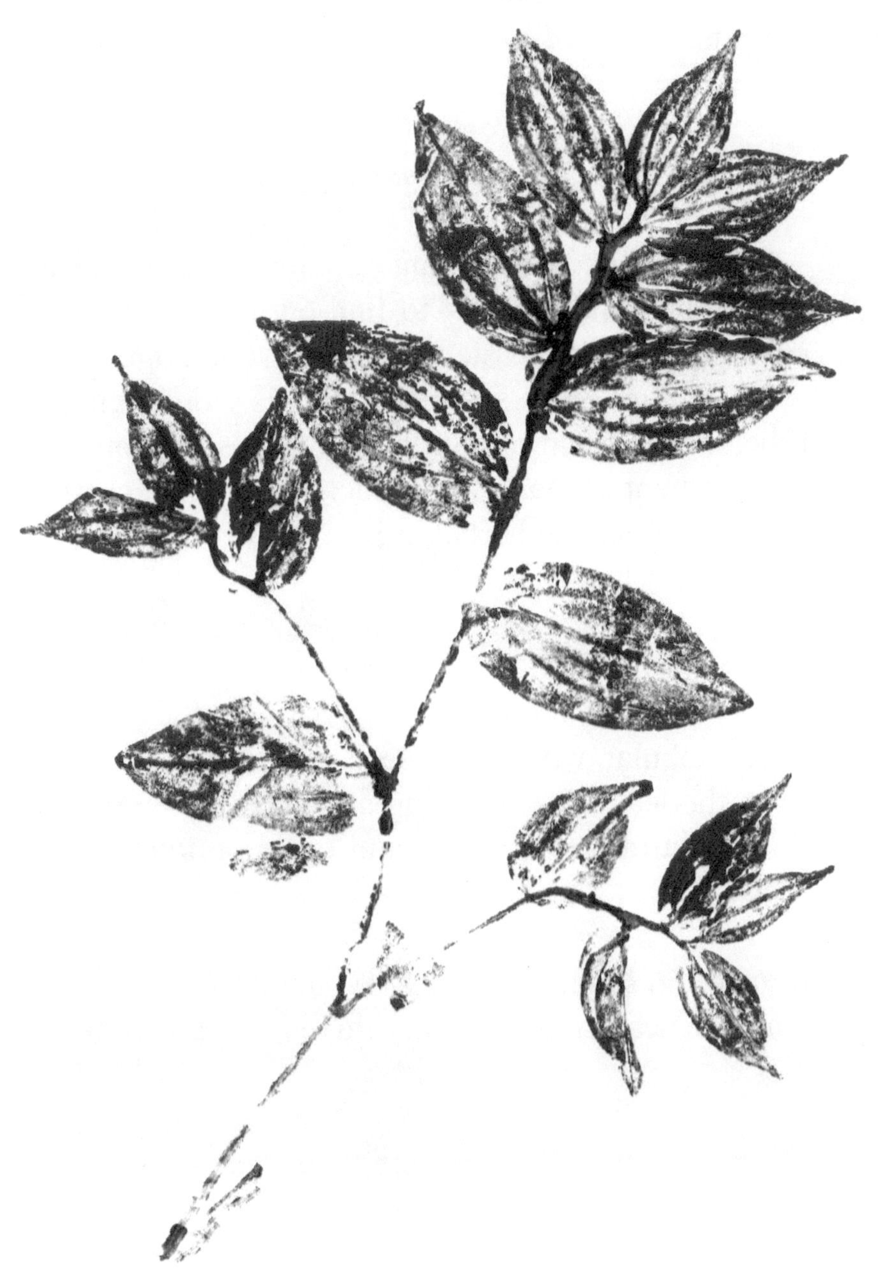

FOREST

Yerba Buena
Clinopodium douglasii

At Sea Ranch, this plant remains evergreen year-round and is a joy to find on any gray winter day. Gently roll the stem between your fingers and feel the edges of the square stem. This is one sign that it belongs to the mint family; another is the opposite arrangement of leaf pairs at each node. Then crush a leaf and notice the herbal, mint-like scent…

It spreads by slender creeping stems that root at the nodes, forming loose mats across the forest floor.

Small tubular white to pale lavender flowers arise from the leaf axils in spring and early summer. The flowers attract small bees and other pollinating in-sects.

It grows in shaded, moist forest understories, partic-ularly beneath redwood and mixed evergreen cano-pies.

"Yerba Buena" is Spanish for "good herb." The com-mon name was historically applied to several fragrant mints in California used by Indigenous peoples and early settlers.

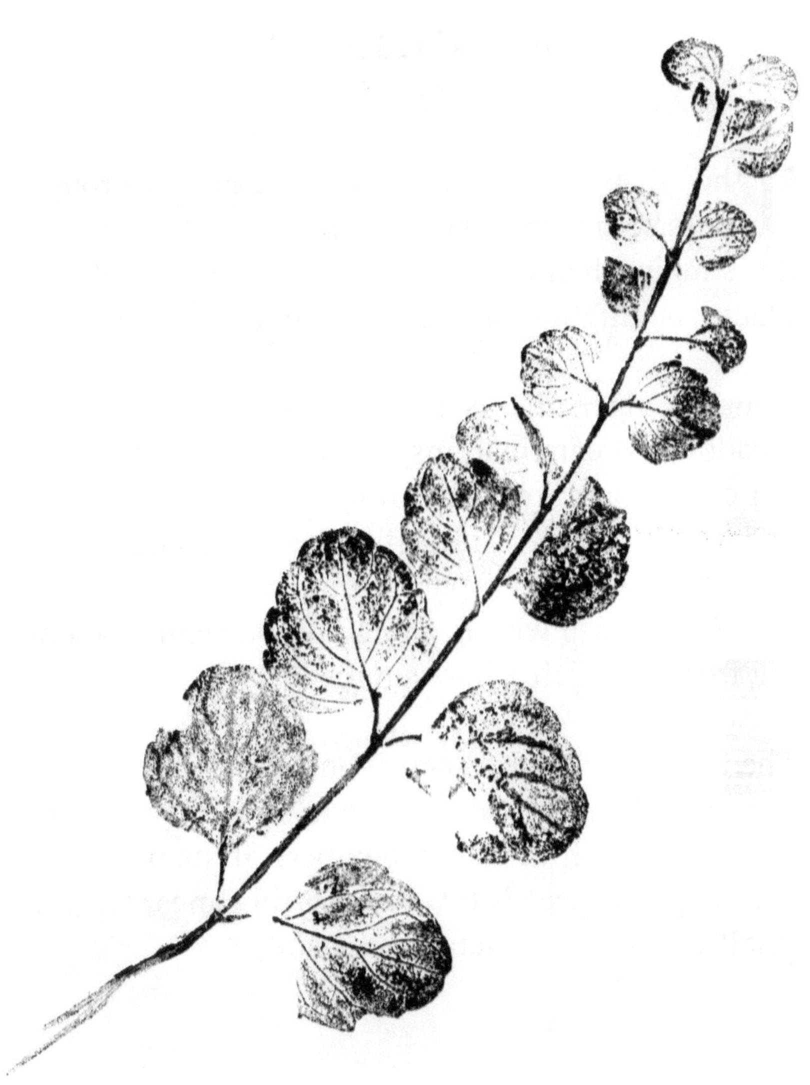

FOREST

Rough Hedgenettle
Stachys rigida

Though called a nettle, it does not sting; its roughness comes from non-glandular hairs rather than the stinging hairs of true nettles. If you touch this plant, you might think you have touched sandpaper.

Rough hedgenettle is a perennial native to moist meadows, stream margins, and forest edges throughout coastal and interior California. Its square stems and opposite leaves identify it as a member of the mint family. Pink to purple tubular flowers are arranged in dense whorls along upright stems, blooming from late spring into summer.

The flowers are rich in nectar and attract native bees, especially bumblebees adapted to prying open the tubular blooms. Like many members of the mint family, the plant spreads by creeping rhizomes, forming small colonies in suitable moist soils.

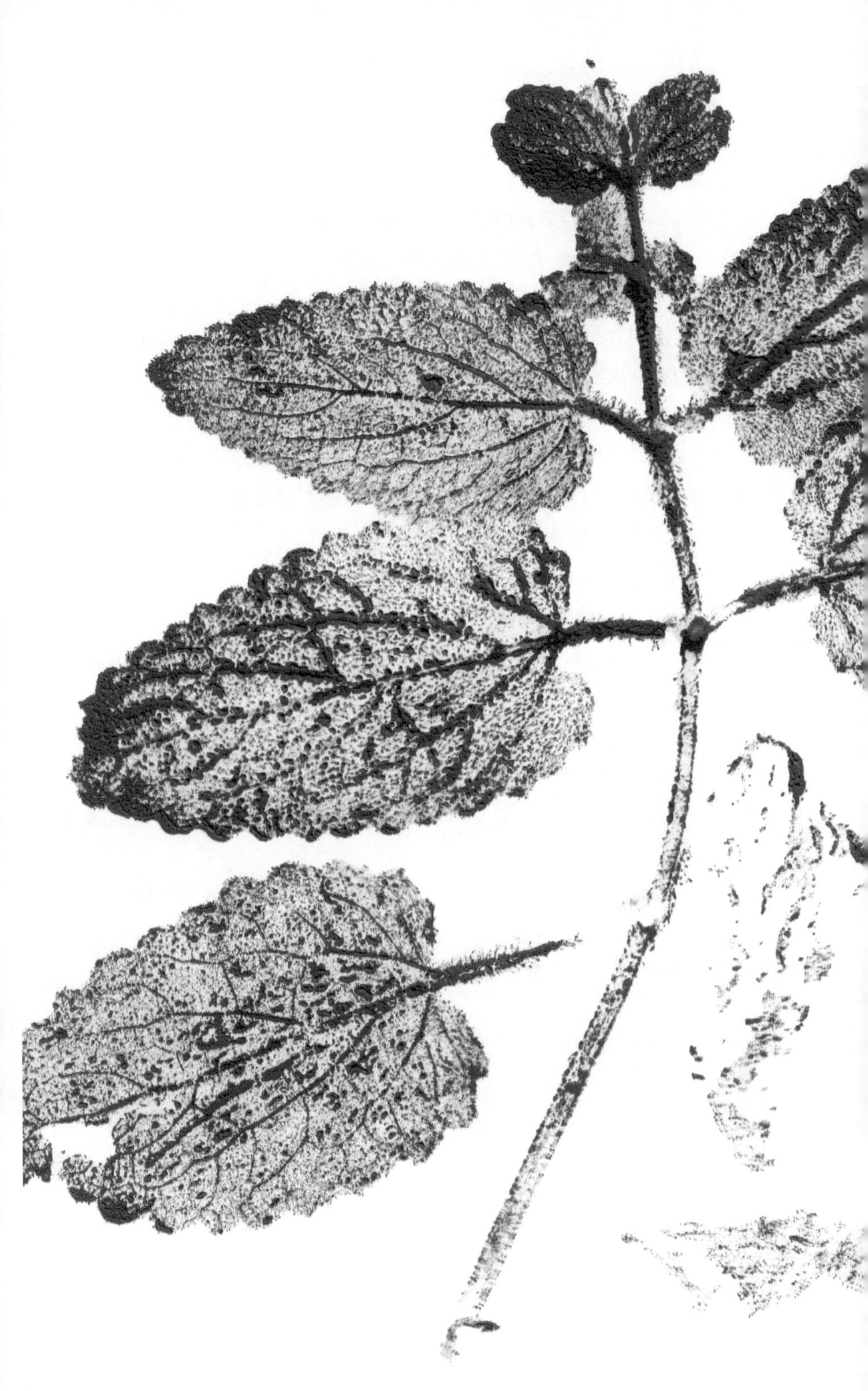

FOREST

Dwarf Oregon Grape
Berberis nervosa

It marks the start of winter for me when the leaves turn reddish or bronze in colder weather…

It has sharp, holly-shaped leaves, waxy and well protected, more compact and pointed than those of the tall Oregon grape.

In early spring, it produces clusters of bright yellow flowers that stand above the foliage. The flowers are fragrant and provide nectar and pollen for early-season bees and other insects. Blue to purple berries follow in summer, coated with a pale bloom or powder. The berries are edible but very tart.

At Sea Ranch, dwarf Oregon grape grows beneath redwood and mixed evergreen canopies, especially on north-facing slopes with consistent moisture.

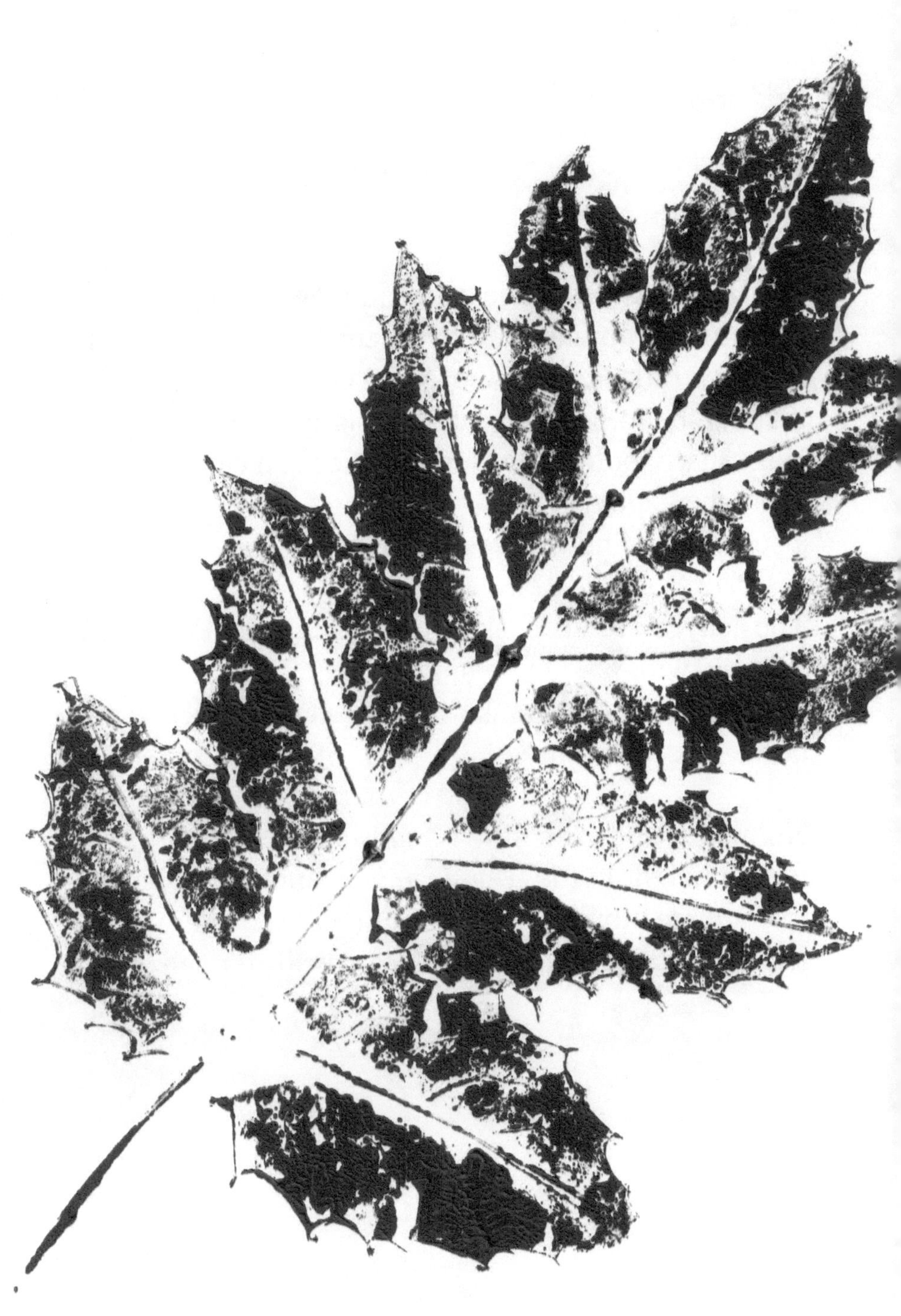

FOREST

Nutmeg Tree
Torreya californica

The seeds resemble true nutmeg in appearance but are unrelated and are toxic if consumed in quantity (all parts of the plant contain compounds that can be toxic if ingested in significant amounts). With sharp, pointed leaves, this tree can cause injury if brushed against carelessly. Even so, it is a joy and a surprise to find in a coastal forest.

The leaves are stiff, sharply pointed, and arranged spirally, with a strong resinous scent when crushed. The species is dioecious, with male and female cones borne on separate trees.

Nutmeg tree grows slowly and may reach 30 to 60 feet in height but is usually much smaller in shaded forest understories. It thrives in cool, shaded ravines and north-facing slopes with deep, well-drained soils.

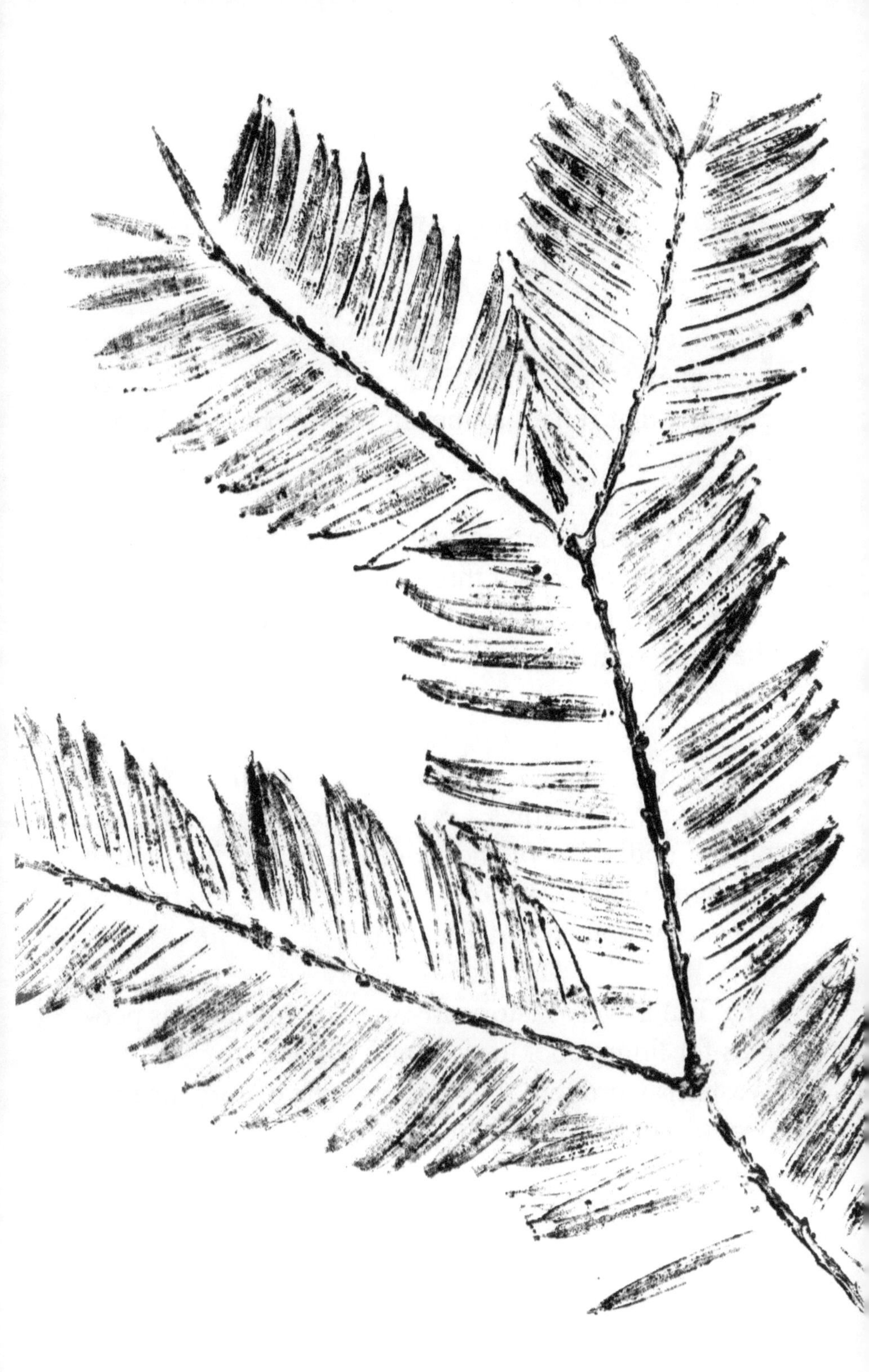

FOREST

Western Sword Fern
Polystichum munitum

Covering the humus under redwoods, this fern shapes the forest floor with ancient, repeated patterns that reflect a lineage dating back to the age of dinosaurs.

Western sword fern produces large, arching fronds that commonly reach three to five feet in length and can exceed five feet in ideal conditions. It is one of the most common ferns along the Northern California coast.

The genus name *Polystichum* comes from Greek, meaning "many rows," referring to the rows of sori on the underside of the fronds. The species epithet *munitum* means "armed" or "defended," referring to the sharp-toothed leaflet margins.

The fronds were historically used by Indigenous peoples for lining cooking pits and baskets.
Western sword fern tolerates periodic disturbance but declines in prolonged drought or heavy soil compaction.

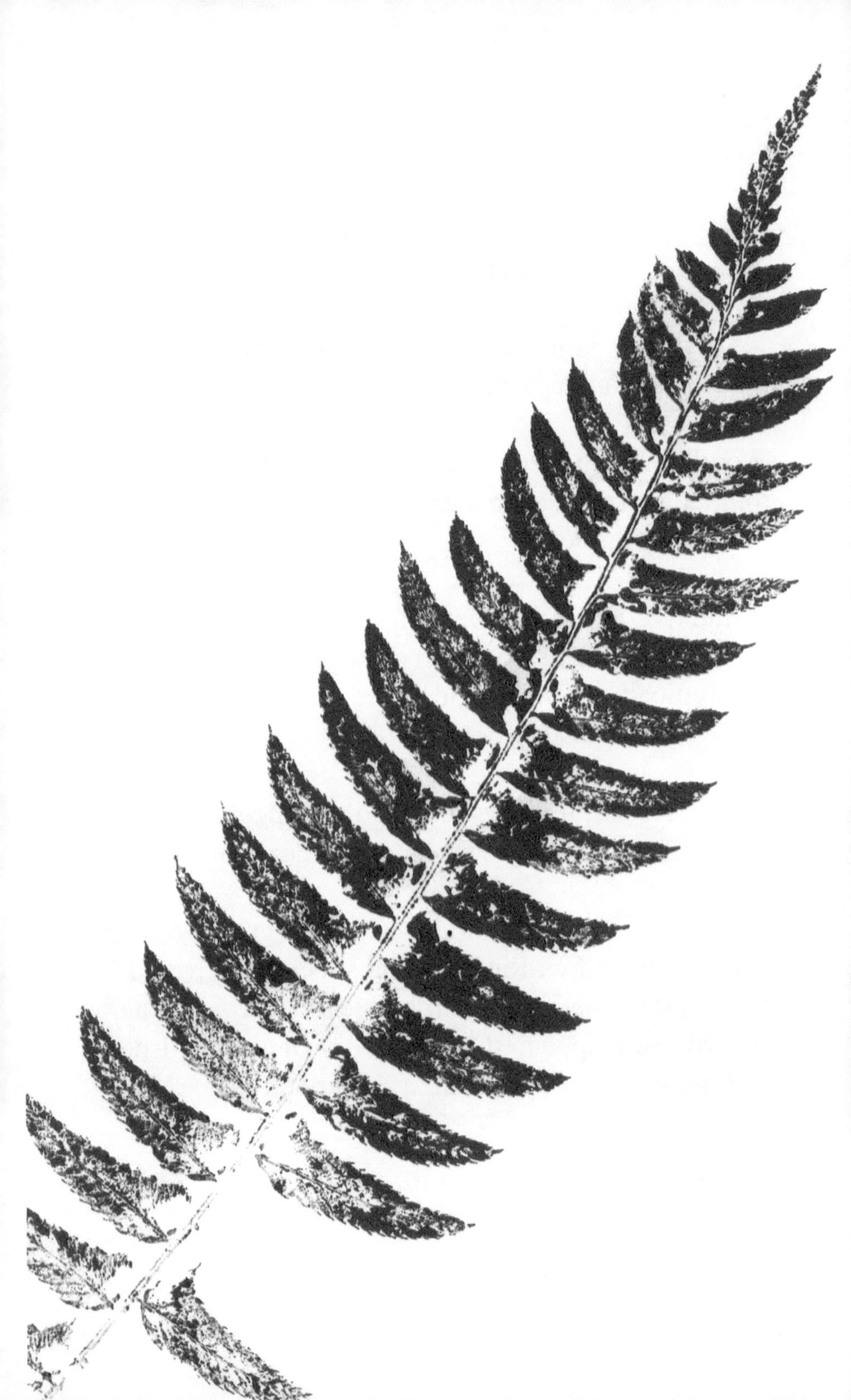

FOREST

Woodland Strawberry
Fragaria vesca

A sweet, familiar friend that you want to visit again and again…

Woodland strawberry produces trifoliate leaves with toothed margins, each leaflet arising from a long petiole at ground level.

White five-petaled flowers bloom in spring, followed by small red fruits borne on slender stalks. The fruits are typically smaller and more intensely aromatic than cultivated strawberries.

At Sea Ranch, it grows along forest edges where filtered light and sandy soils provide ideal conditions.

The same woodland strawberry that grows quietly along trails at Sea Ranch is the species cultivated in medieval Europe and recorded in early herbals, where strawberries appeared as symbols of righteousness and humility in devotional art and poetry.

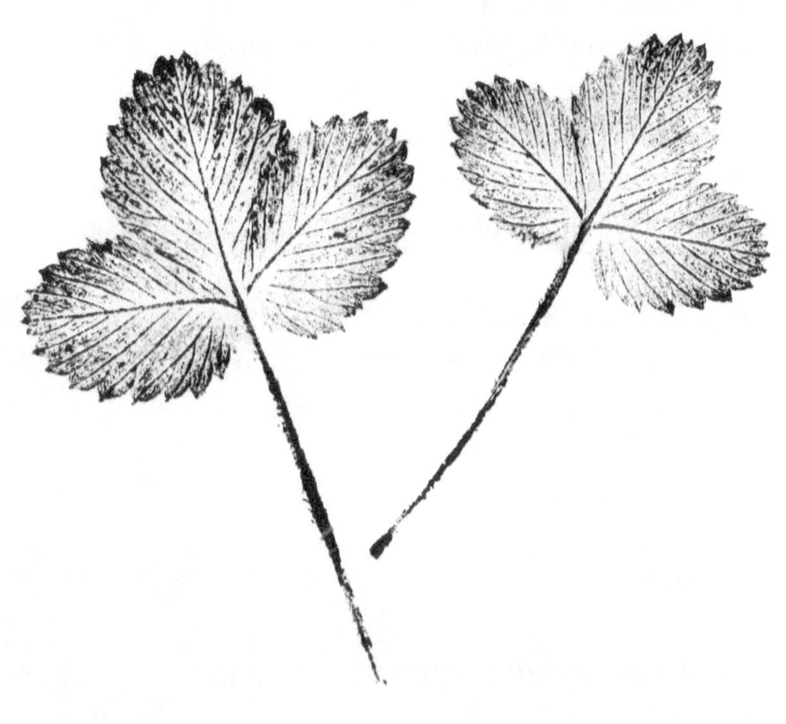

FOREST

Bracken Fern
Pteridium aquilinum

I sometimes feel small when I walk among these ancient wonders…

This fern differs from many others by rising on a single stalk that branches into a broad, triangular frond. It often appears in unexpected places—under trees and along meadow trails. Bracken fern is one of the most widespread fern species in the world, occurring on every continent except Antarctica.

It produces large fronds that rise singly from underground rhizomes and can reach three to six feet in height.

At Sea Ranch, bracken appears along meadow edges, forest margins, and trails where light reaches the ground.

Its dense summer growth can suppress competing vegetation and alter plant succession. The plant contains the carcinogenic compound ptaquiloside and is considered toxic, particularly with repeated consumption.

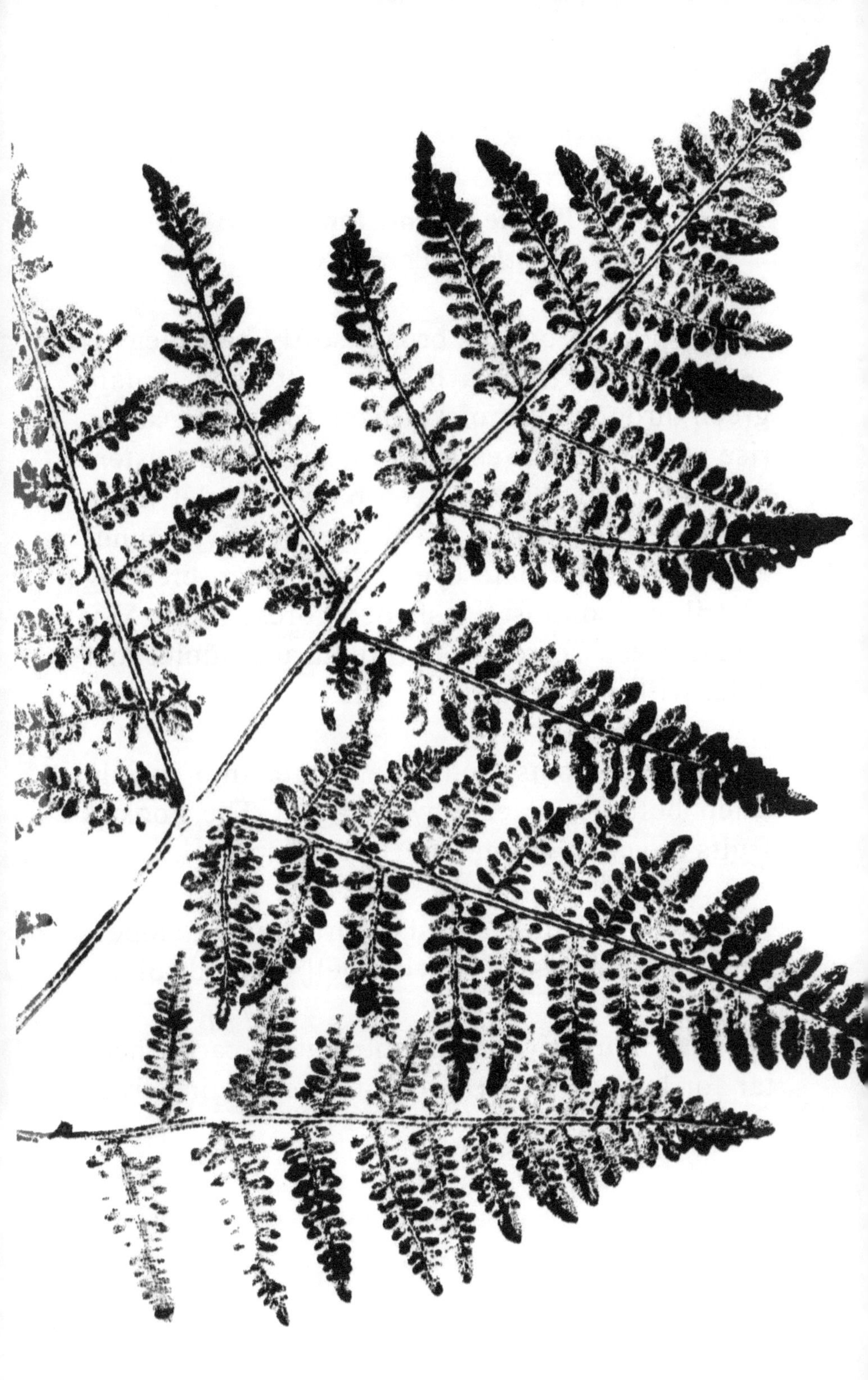

FOREST

Pacific Houndstongue
Adelinia grandis

The plant produces broad, softly hairy leaves that arise from a basal rosette and remain green through the moist season. Flowering stems rise above the leaves and bear drooping clusters of small, bell-shaped, deep blue to violet flowers in early spring. Each flower has five rounded petals and a pale eye at the center, creating a striking contrast in shaded forest light. You might see a secretive hermit thrush, quiet and pale, with rust-colored wings...

The plant blooms from late winter into spring, often before full canopy leaf-out. The hooked fruits attach to animals for seed dispersal.

It grows in shaded forests, north-facing slopes, and moist understories with well drained soils.

Pacific houndstongue contributes early nectar for hungry forest pollinators emerging from winter.

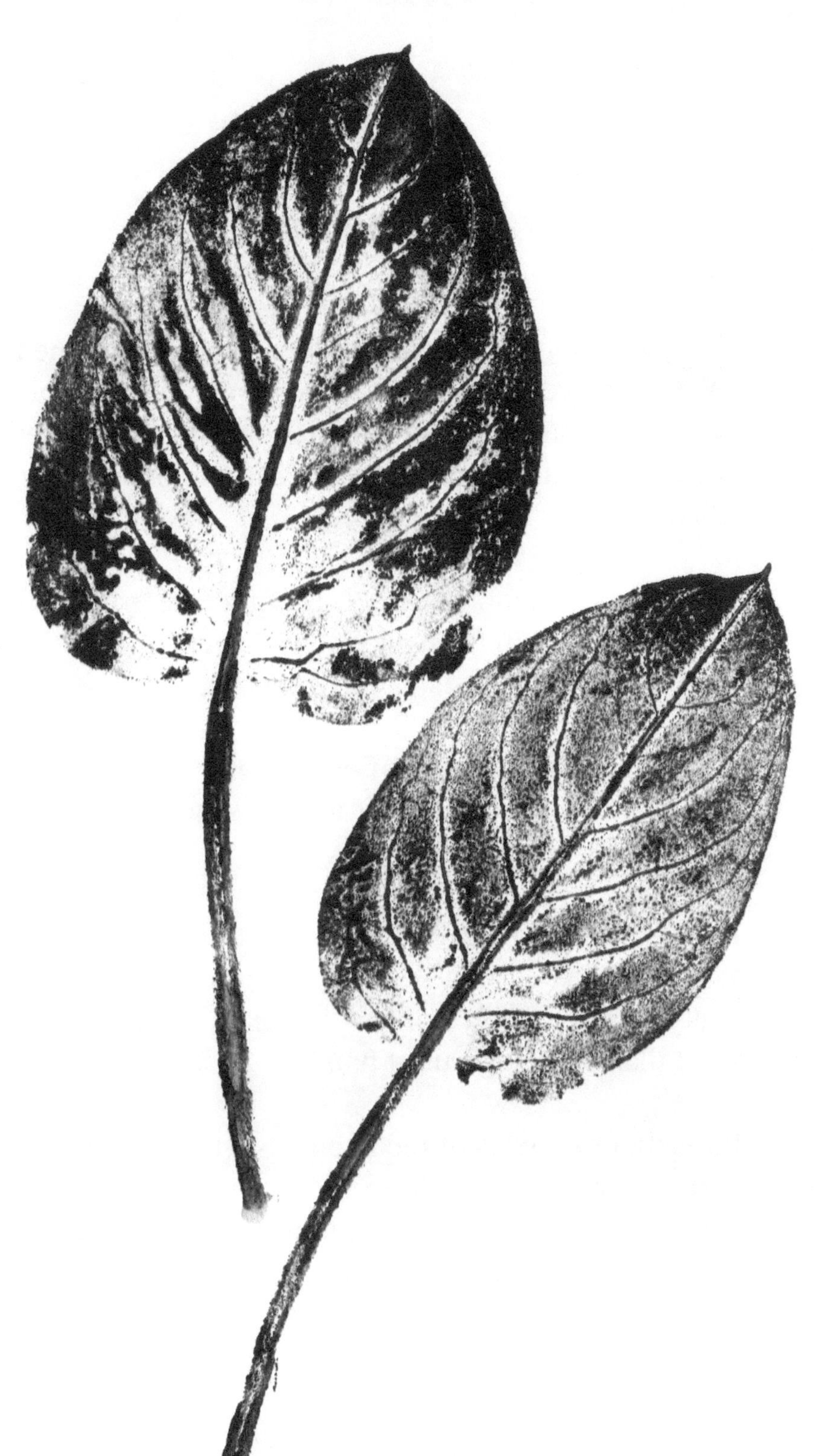

FOREST

Oregon Grape
Berberis aquifolium

With its holly-shaped leaves — glossy, spined, and evergreen — Oregon grape holds its place in the understory through all seasons. Before sunset, when the light softens, the leaves can shine as if polished.

Despite its common name, it is not a true grape; the name comes from the dusky blue clusters of fruit that hang like small grapes in early summer.

In spring, upright sprays of bright yellow flowers rise above the foliage, carrying a faint scent that draws early bees.

By late spring to early summer, the flowers give way to berries coated in a soft, silvery powder. The fruit is edible but sharply sour — better suited to jelly or wine than to eating out of hand.

Indigenous peoples of the Pacific Northwest used the berries for food and the roots and bark for dye and medicine. The inner bark contains berberine, a bright yellow compound known for antimicrobial qualities.

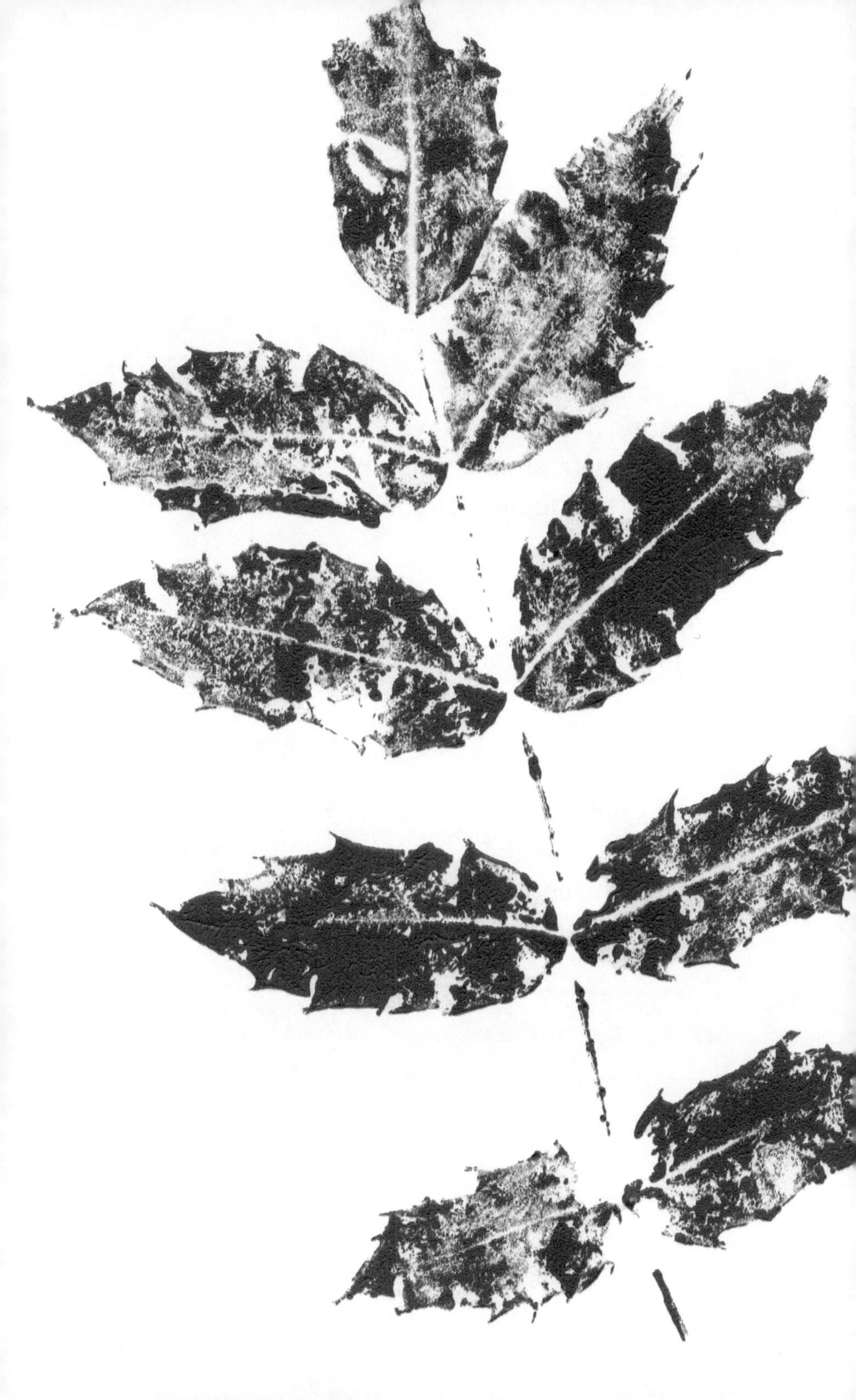

FOREST

American Trailplant
Adenocaulon bicolor

Along the trails, these look like true arrows, suggesting a "Go this way." But with their distinctly contrasting green tops and white undersides, when the wind blows, the directions change…

In summer, slender stems rise above the leaves bearing small, nodding, discoid flower heads. But unlike many members of the sunflower family, it lacks showy ray petals; the flowers are subtle and easily overlooked.

It grows small fruits which are sticky and cling to clothing and animal fur, spreading the plant along trails. Thus the common name.

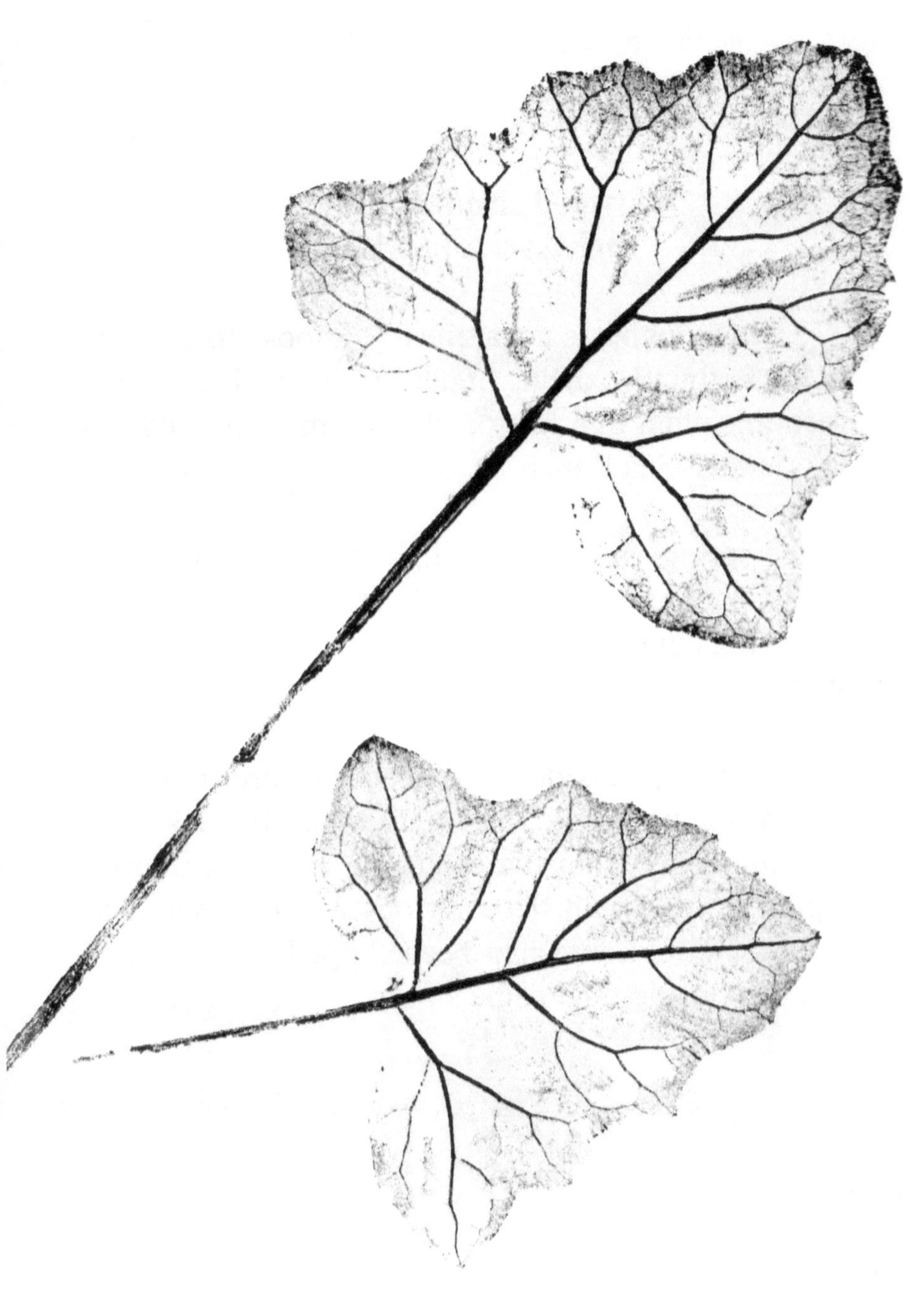

FOREST

Redwood Inside-out Flower
Vancouveria planipetala

Even though it is not a true ivy, it looks like an ivy. It is found growing under redwoods. I have only seen this plant in a few patches by the sag ponds on the ridge at Sea Ranch.

In the spring, look for small, pale flowers that seem lightly caught in motion, their petals swept back like tiny wings in the filtered light of the redwood understory.

But the five petals do not spread outward in a typical open cup. Instead, they curve sharply backward, bending away from the center of the flower, forming an inverted cup. To early observers, it looked as though the blossom had been flipped "inside out," and the "inside-out" name stuck.

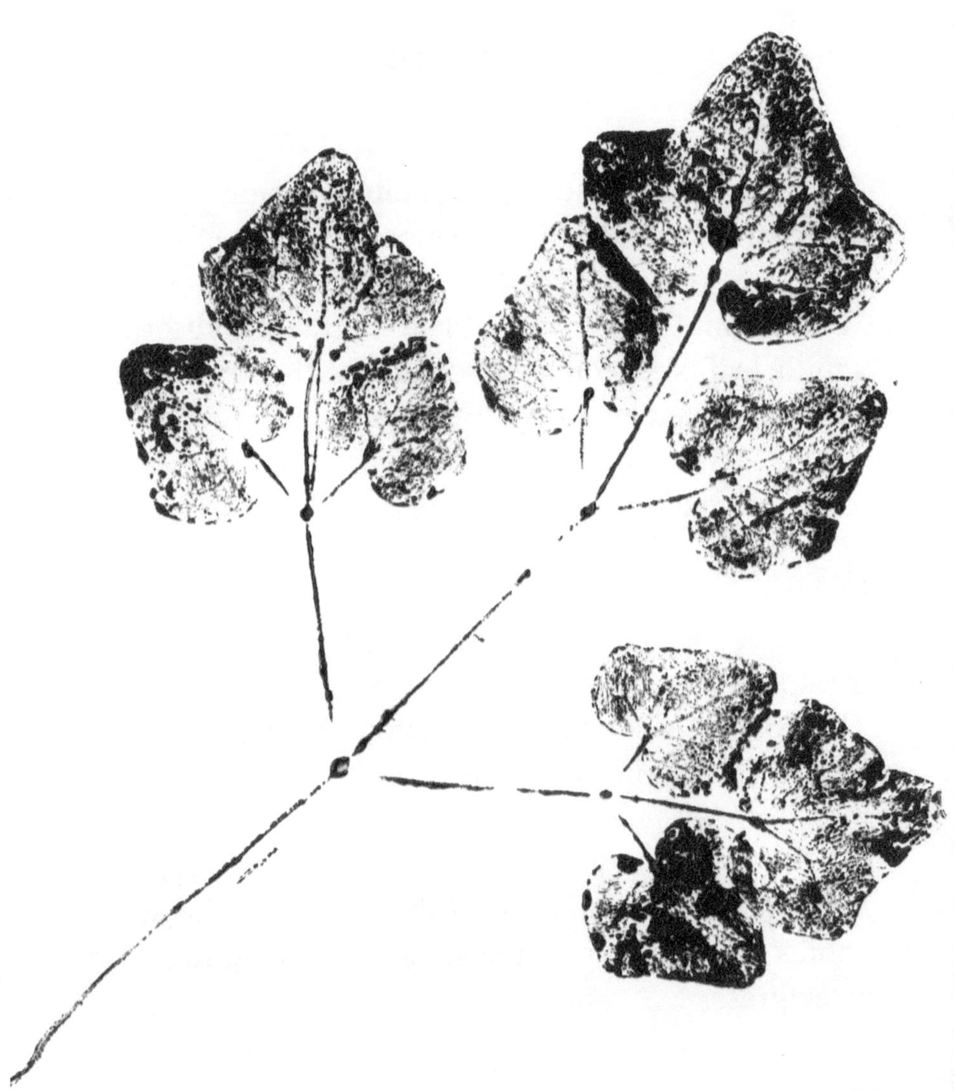

FOREST

Vanilla Leaf
Achlys triphylla

Like an open hand waving hello, bold and yet simple, it is wonderful to chance upon in the forest…

Found from British Columbia to northern California, vanilla leaf is especially associated with redwood forests and mixed evergreen woodlands, where it forms quiet colonies in cool, shaded understories beneath redwoods and Douglas-firs.

Its leaves are distinctly trifoliate — three broad, fan-shaped leaflets arising from a single point — giving the species name *triphylla*, meaning "three-leaved." The flowers lack petals, their exposed stamens forming soft, pale spikes in early spring.

As the leaves dry, they release a sweet fragrance reminiscent of vanilla or freshly cut hay. The scent comes from coumarin, the same compound found in sweetgrass.

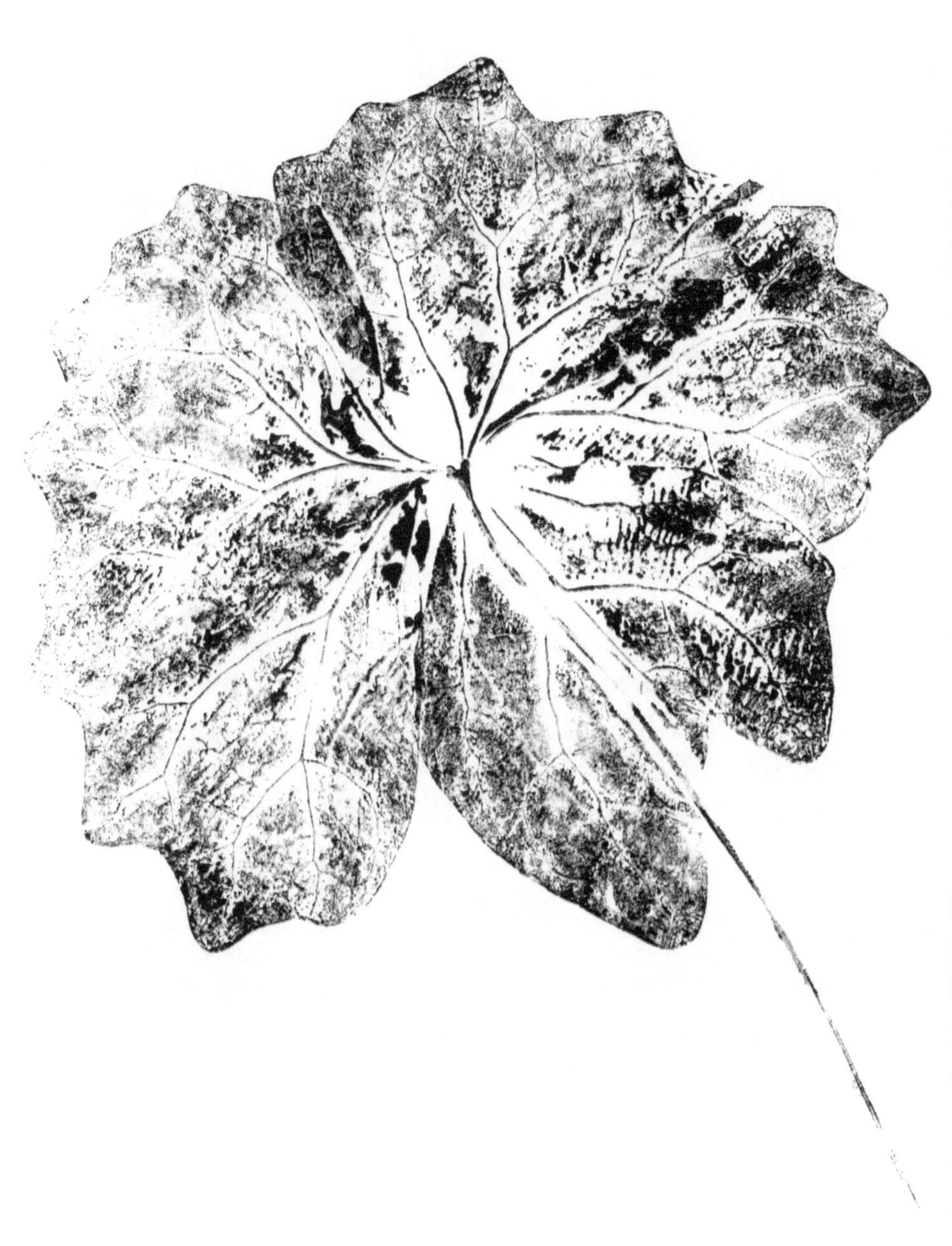

FOREST

Modesty
Whipplea modesta

Along the side of the trail, modesty grows in quiet clumps. Easily overlooked, it brightens the dim redwood understory each spring when in bloom.

Spreading slowly, it forms soft groundcover beneath taller shrubs and trees.

Its leaves are opposite, oval to lance-shaped, softly textured, and remain green year-round.

In late spring to early summer, small clusters of tiny flowers are surrounded by larger, petal-like white bracts — leaf-like parts that grow around a flower — often mistaken for petals and giving the plant a delicate, star-like appearance. The true flowers are small and inconspicuous at the center of the bracts.

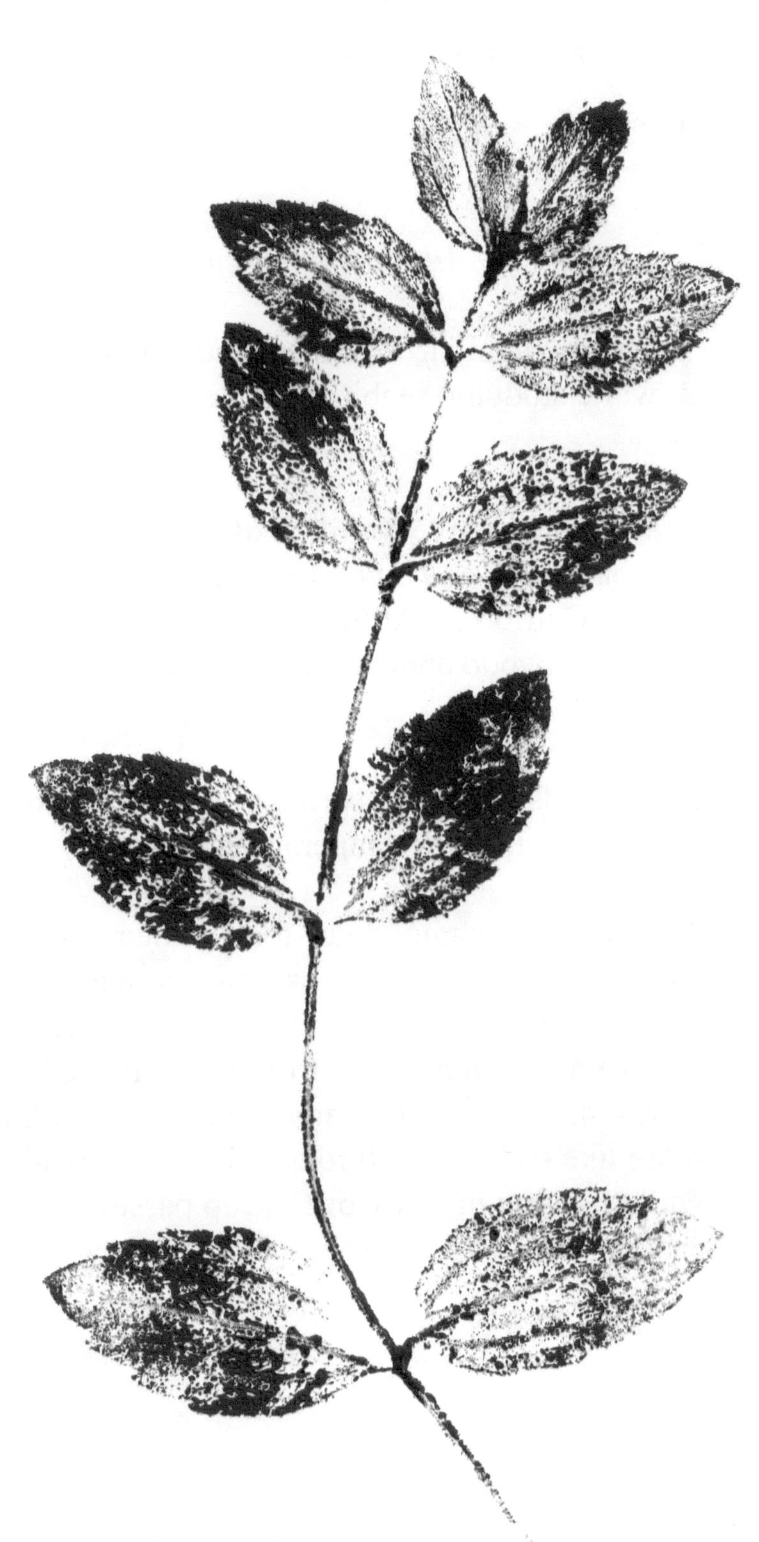

FOREST

Lady Fern
Athyrium filix-femina

I became familiar with these ferns on Buldir Island while studying seabirds on the Aleutians, in Alaska.

Lady fern is native to much of North America, Europe, and Asia, and is common in moist woodlands of coastal California. At Sea Ranch, lady fern is found in cool redwood understories and along shaded creek corridors.

New fronds emerge in spring as tightly coiled fiddleheads that unfurl as temperatures warm.

The common name "lady fern" reflects the stodgy Victorian-era botanical naming conventions that labeled finer-textured ferns as "female." If I were to give a common name to this one, I might call it "swimming fern," from my memories of hiking, or more like swimming, through six-foot tall lady ferns while fighting my way over steep passes and getting soaking wet from the water that those beautiful ferns held.

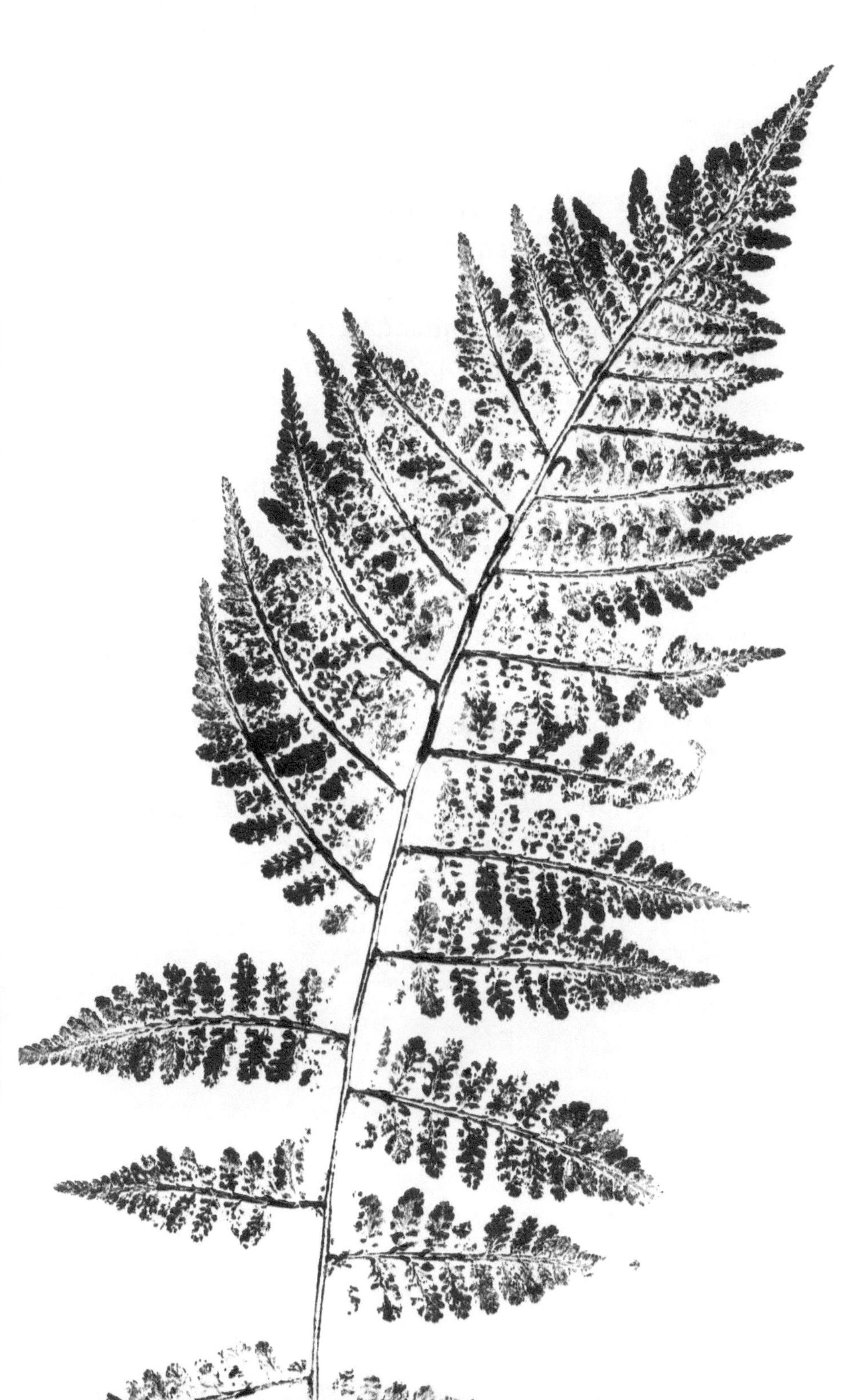

FOREST

Trillium
Trillium chloropetalum

Trillium makes a statement: "This is me. I am here and I am beautiful," proclaiming itself as one of the first signs of spring in the redwood forests.

Because each plant shows its parts in threes — petals, leaves, and sepals — it has often been linked with ideas of birth and renewal.

It can take several years for a plant to reach flowering age. Each plant then bears a single, striking flower atop a whorl of three leaves.

Flowers are pollinated by beetles and flies attracted to their subtle scent and dark coloration.

The above-ground growth usually disappears by late summer, though some trillium leaves may still be seen in the fall.

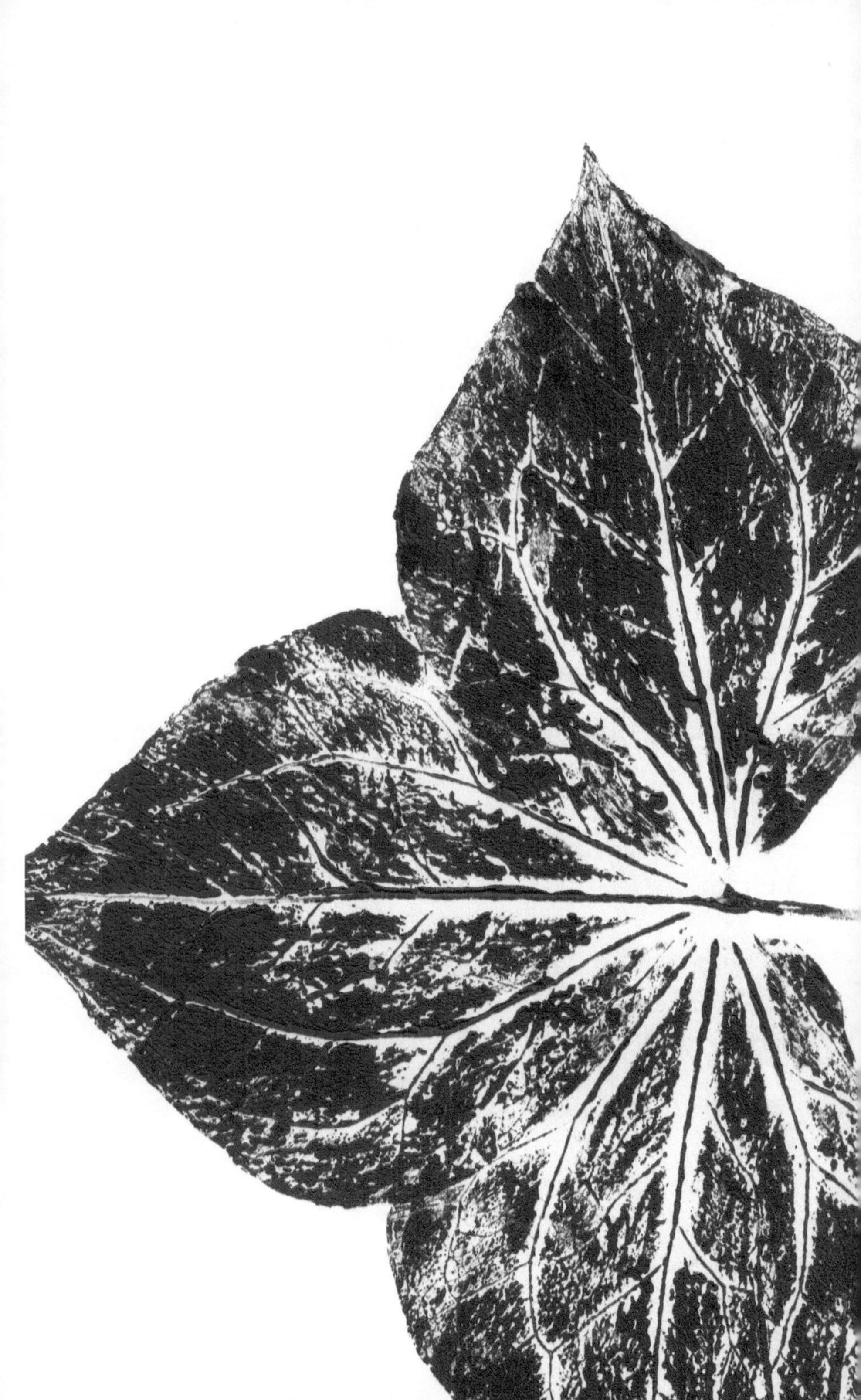

FOREST

Milkmaids
Cardamine californica

Milkmaids is one of the earliest wildflowers to bloom in California forests. Turning a leaf over, I was surprised to see that the underside was purple. Milkmaids often disappear by early summer and survive underground until winter rains return. Botanists call this a spring ephemeral. This print is of the first leaves that appeared in an ephemeral spring…

Later leaves are divided into rounded leaflets, typically three to seven per leaf. In late winter to early spring, clusters of four-petaled flowers bloom atop slender stems. The petals are usually white, sometimes blushed with pale pink or lavender.

The common name refers to the frothy white appearance of the flowers, much like the milk pails carried by dairy workers in early California.

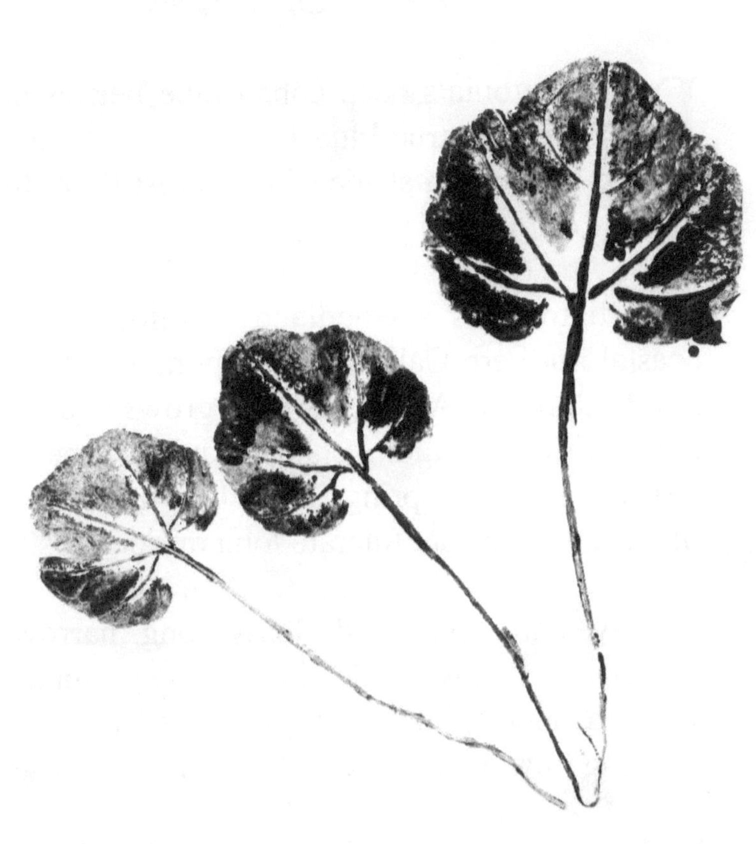

FOREST

Red Clintonia
Clintonia andrewsiana

Red clintonia's deep cobalt-blue berries are one of the rare true-blue fruits in North American forests. In the dim shade of the forest floor, they almost glow…

Red clintonia is a woodland wildflower native to coastal northern California, Oregon, and southwestern Washington. At Sea Ranch it grows in cool forest understories and along shaded ravines where moisture lingers into spring. It prefers moist soils and shade, and does not tolerate long dry periods.

Its leaves are broad and glossy, long, narrow ovals that grow in a low circle close to the ground. In late spring a slender stalk rises above the leaves, holding nodding flowers in shades of deep pink to rose.

By late summer the flowers mature into bright blue berries that stand out against the dark forest floor like small lanterns. Birds and small mammals eat the berries, though they are not edible for people. Red clintonia grows in stable soils and is often found in undisturbed forests.

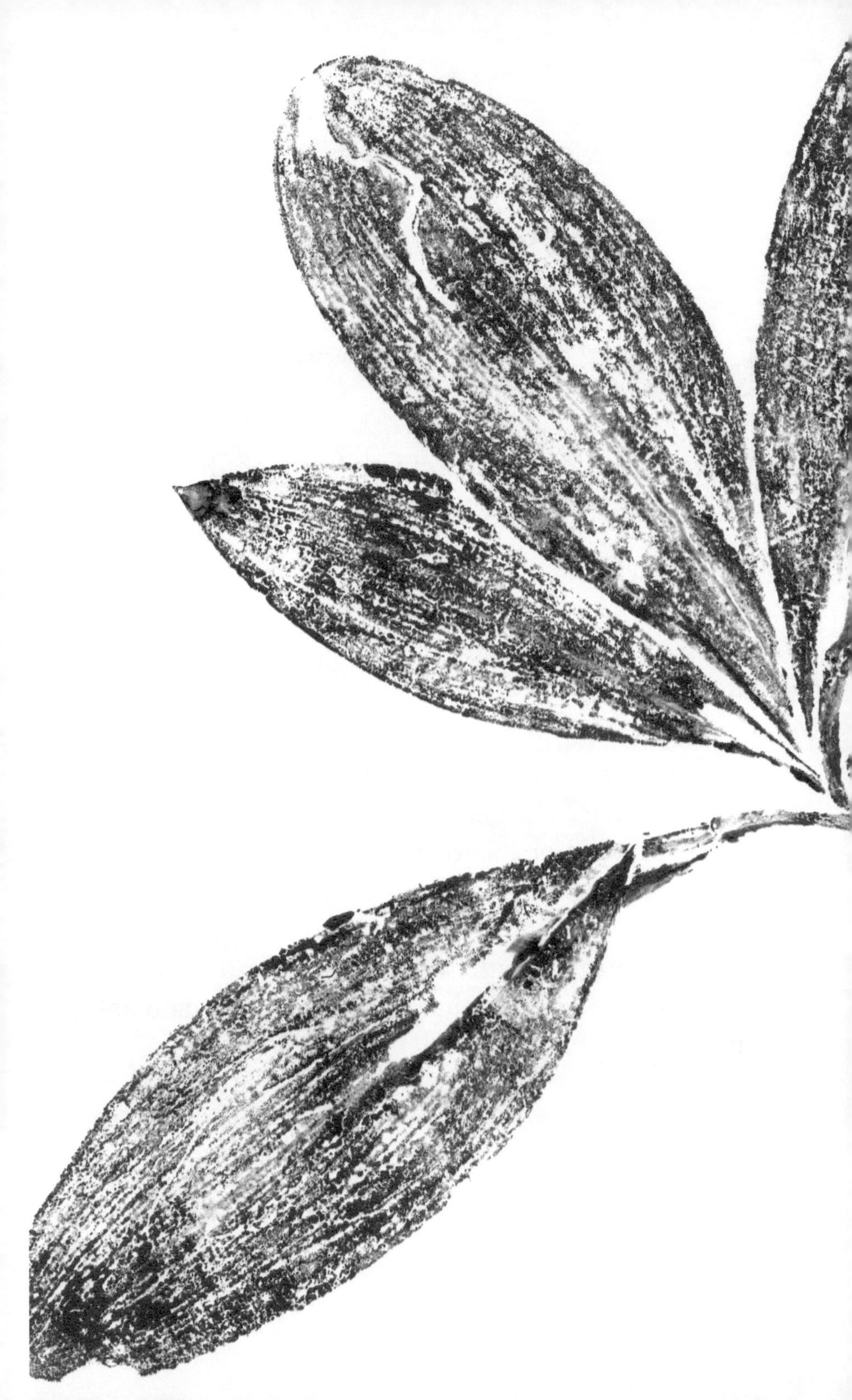

FOREST

Fragrant Bedstraw
Galium triflorum

Like an ornate necklace forgotten on the forest floor…

At Sea Ranch, it threads quietly through the understory, often weaving among ferns and beneath taller shrubs.

With slender, trailing stems, its leaves grow in circles around the stem, usually six to eight at a time, giving the plant a star-like pattern.

In late spring to early summer, tiny white flowers appear in clusters. The genus name *Galium* comes from a Greek word referring to milk, as some species were once used in cheese making.

After flowering, small round seeds form, covered with tiny hooked hairs that cling to clothing and animal fur.

The common name "bedstraw" comes from the historic practice of using dried stems and leaves to stuff mattresses, where their scent helped freshen bedding.

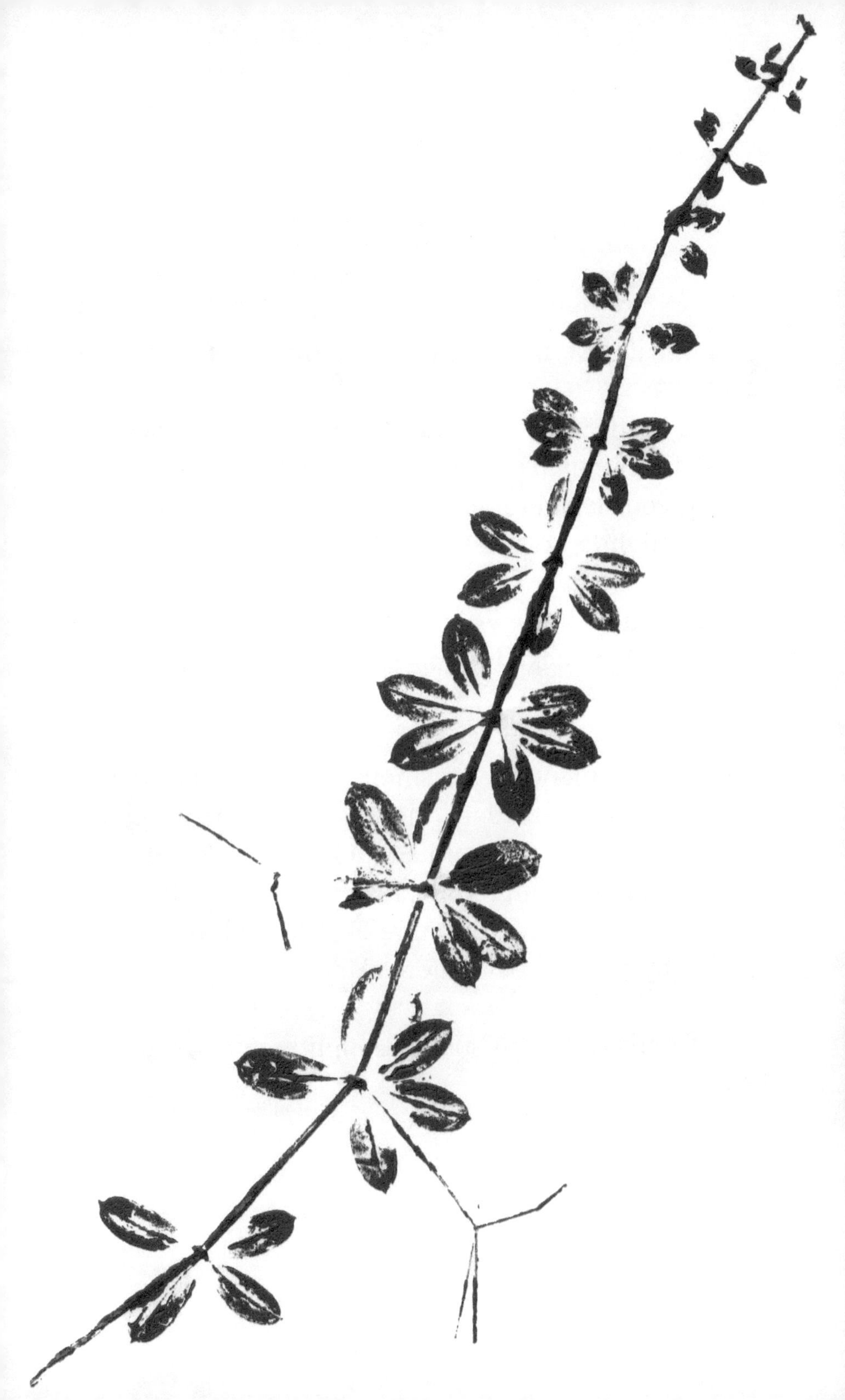

FOREST

Coastal Wood Fern
Dryopteris arguta

Delicate and intricate in the damp forest…

Unlike many ferns that die back in winter, coastal wood fern remains green year-round. Its fronds are dark green, leathery, and finely divided, giving the plant a slightly bold, textured look.

At Sea Ranch, it grows beneath redwoods and Douglas-firs, often tucked along shaded trails and damp ravines.

The leaf segments have small, sharp points along their edges, reflected in the species name *arguta*, meaning "sharp" or "pointed." On the underside of mature fronds, small round clusters of spores form in neat rows. These spores are released into the air and carried by wind to begin new plants.

New fronds uncurl in spring as tightly coiled fiddle-heads.

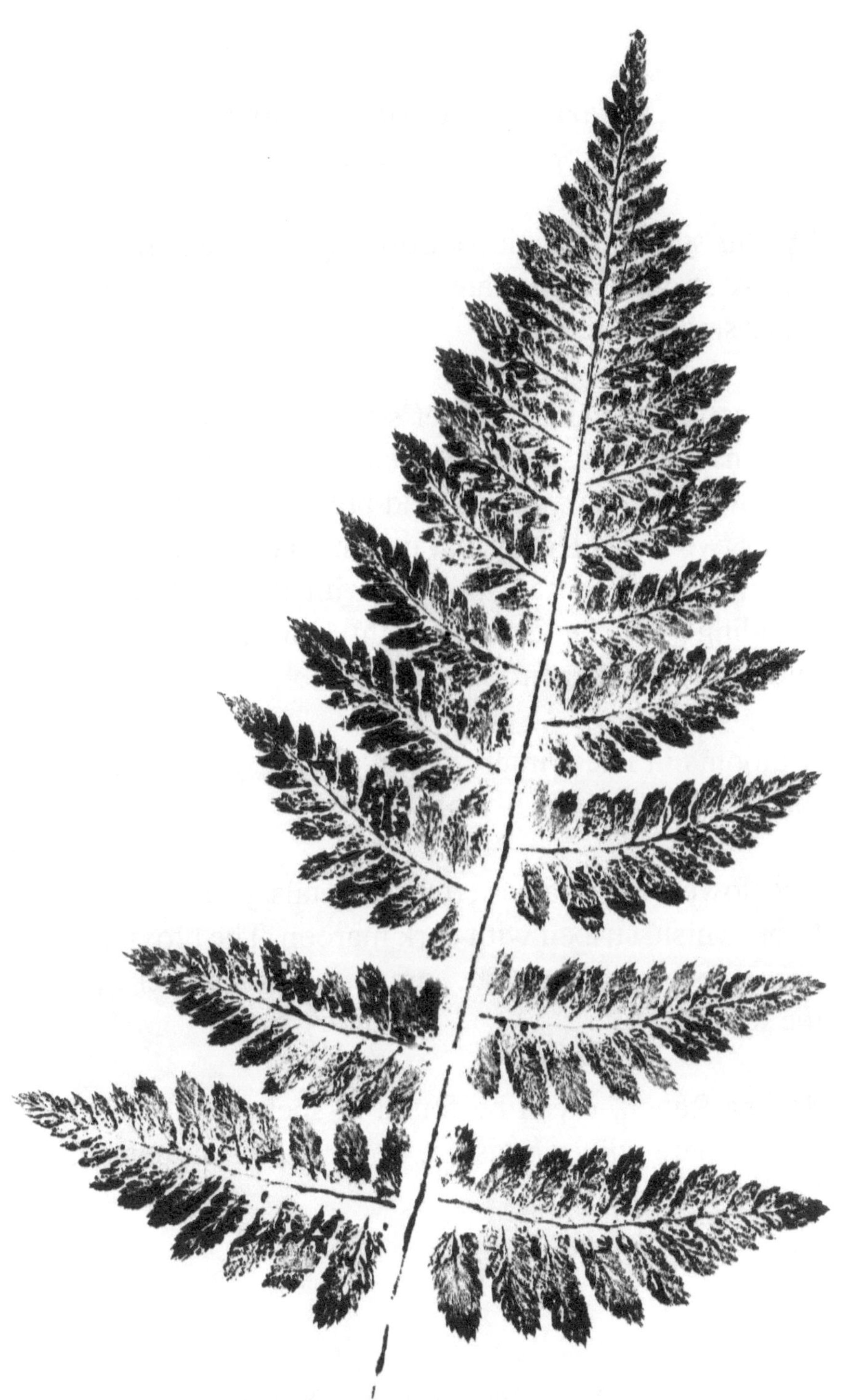

FOREST

California Fetid Adderstongue
Scoliopus bigelovii

This stinks! But it is a surprising treasure to find… A strong, unpleasant odor draws in gnats and other small insects.

The common name "Adder's-tongue" refers to the long, narrow petals, which resemble a snake's tongue. It grows from an underground bulb and usually produces two broad leaves that lie flat on the forest floor. The leaves are often mottled with darker patches, blending into the dappled light beneath redwoods and mixed evergreen forests.

It blooms in late winter to early spring, often before the forest canopy fully leafs out.

The flowers have narrow, twisted petals, yellow-green to brownish, striped with dark maroon. The blossoms grow close to the ground, sometimes hidden beneath the leaves.

At Sea Ranch, it can be found in sheltered forested areas where winter moisture lingers and summer fog keeps the soil cool.

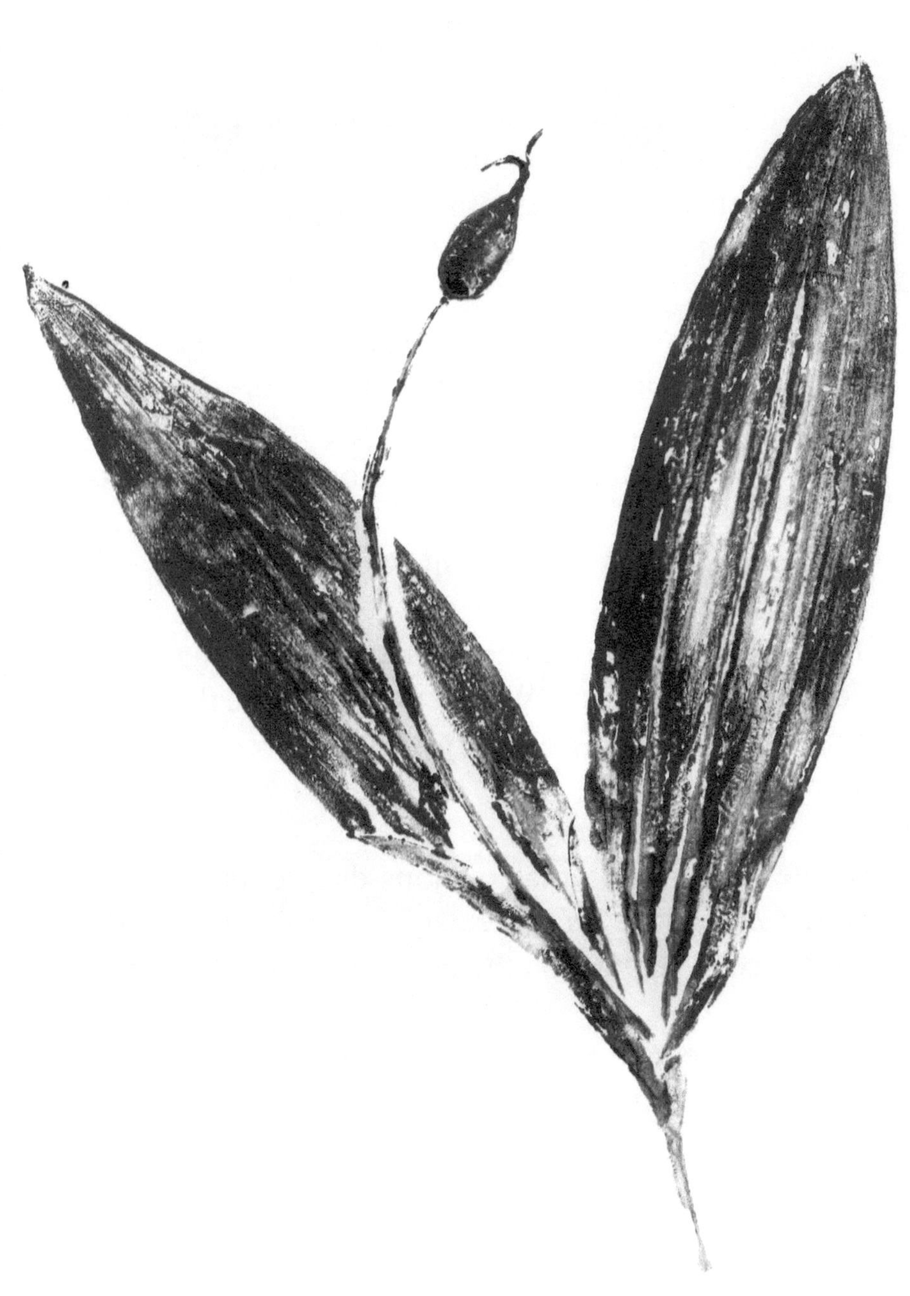

STREAMSIDE

Red Alder
Alnus rubra

Leaves fell and scattered across the trail. With each step, I caught the autumn-sweet scent of Red Alder. Then I caught the bright flash of a northern flicker flying away…

Red Alder is one of the few broadleaf trees in coastal forests that drops its leaves in winter. A fast-growing native of the Pacific Coast, it ranges from Alaska to northern California. It thrives in moist coastal forests and along streams and rivers. At Sea Ranch, it grows in sheltered draws where winter water collects.

The bark is smooth and gray when young, often mottled with pale lichens. When cut or scraped, the inner bark turns reddish-orange, giving the tree its common name.

In late winter, long male catkins dangle and release pollen before the leaves emerge. The small, woody female cones persist on the branches through winter.

Indigenous peoples of the Pacific Northwest used the bark for dye and medicine, and the wood for carving.

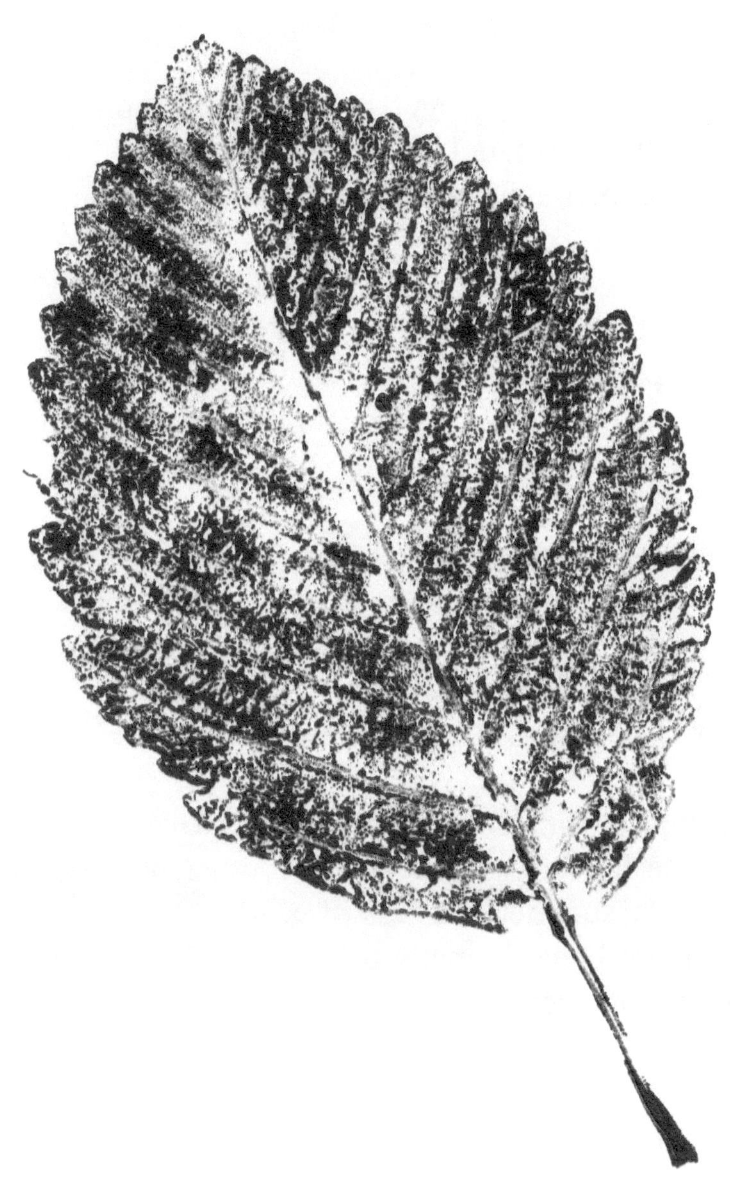

STREAMSIDE

California Blackberry
Rubus ursinus

This native blackberry is smaller and more delicate than the tangled thickets of invasive Himalayan blackberry, but it still has thorns. Dare yourself to pick the black, ripe sweets…

It grows from British Columbia through California and into parts of Baja. At Sea Ranch, it rambles along forest margins, creek banks, and sunny openings where fog and winter rain keep the soil moist.

Arching stems creep along the ground and root where they touch. Curved prickles help the plant scramble and protect it from browsing animals. Leaves are usually divided into three leaflets, though five may appear on vigorous shoots.

In spring, five-petaled flowers open white to pale pink. The flowers attract bees and other pollinating insects. By summer, clusters of glossy black berries ripen. Each berry is made of many small drupelets clustered together.

These patches provide shelter and nesting habitat for birds and small mammals.

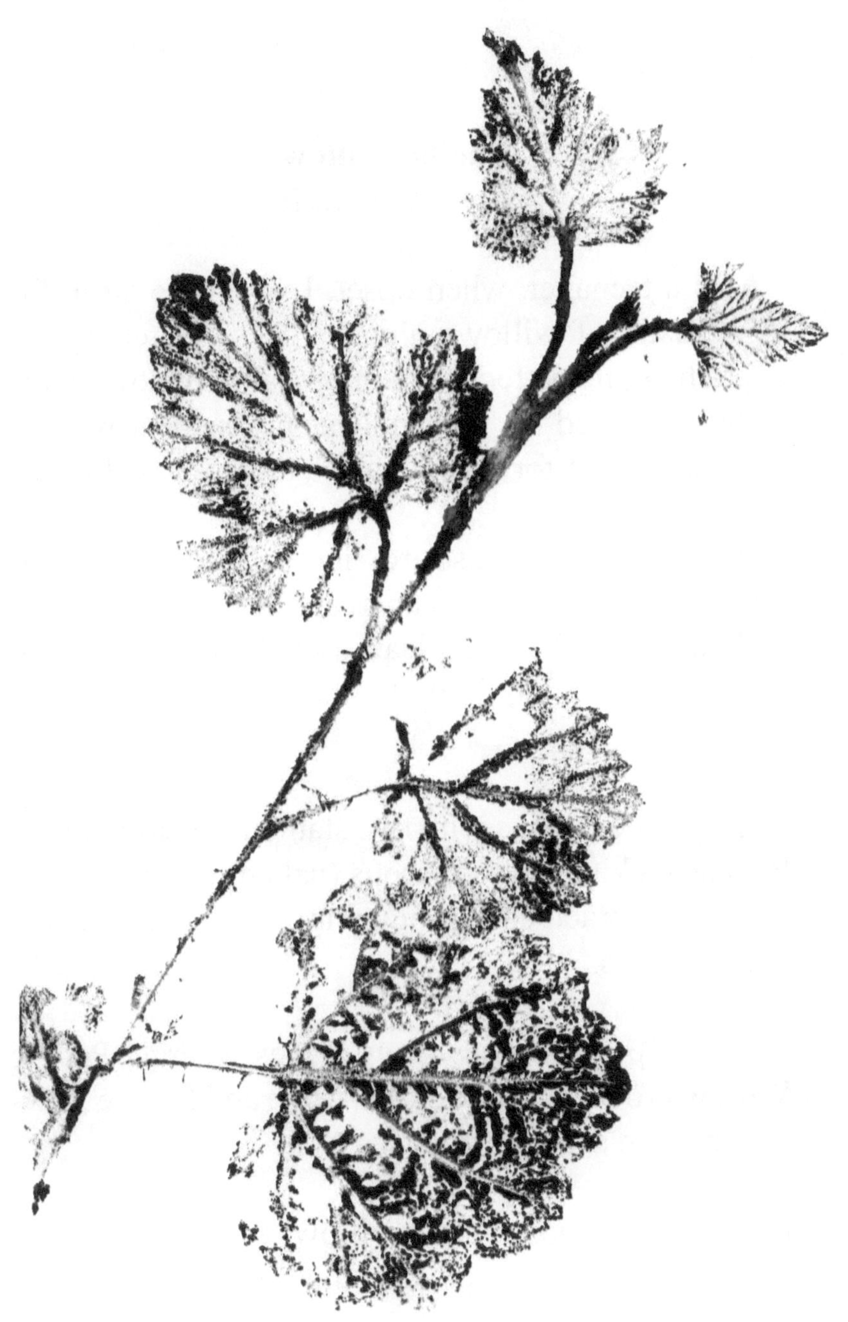

STREAMSIDE

Pacific Willow
Salix lasiandra

As a teenager, when upset, I would go sit in the shade of willows along creeks. Watching the ever-changing patterns of sunlight and shadow on the water reminded me that life was never the same and always moving forward. I have a thing for willows…

Pacific Willow is a fast-growing native tree of western North America. It can reach 30 to 60 feet tall and has brown bark. Its leaves are long, narrow, and glossy green, often finely toothed. They shine in the light.

Showy male catkins with five stamens release pollen. Female catkins have glabrous (naked) ovaries with a large silky bract, each producing a tiny seed attached to silky hairs.

In early spring, before or as leaves emerge, Pacific Willow produces soft catkins. Male and female flowers grow on separate plants.

Indigenous peoples used willow wood for basketry, tools, and fish traps, and the bark for medicinal preparations.

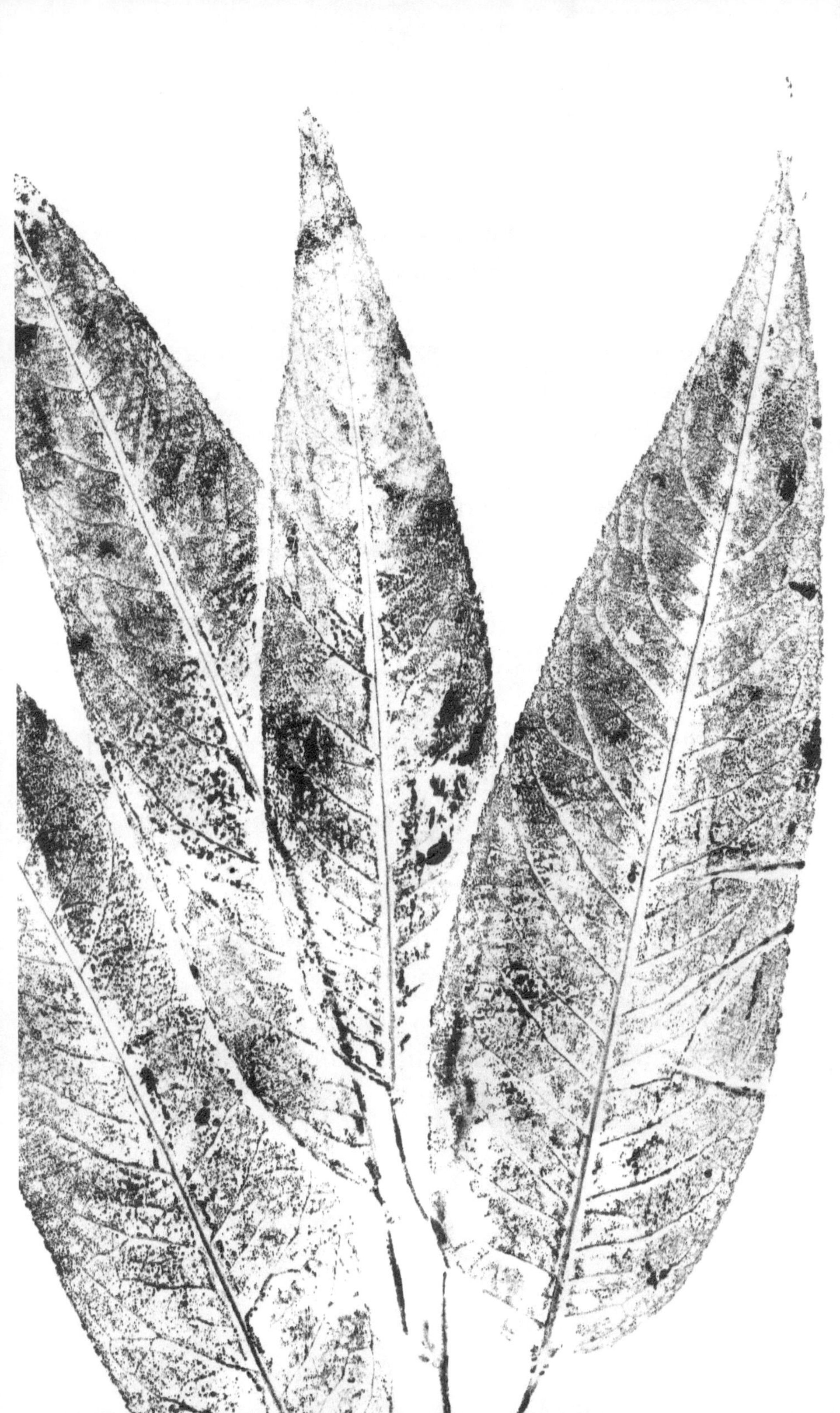

Thimbleberry
Rubus parviflorus

Thimbleberry has no prickles, but you are lucky when you find ripe fruit because birds will almost always beat you to the treat…

Thimbleberry is a native shrub of western North America. Its range extends from Alaska south through California and east into parts of the Rocky Mountains and Great Lakes region. It grows along forest edges, stream banks, roadsides, and in moist clearings.

At Sea Ranch, it may appear in sheltered woodland openings and along damp trails. Its leaves are large, soft, and maple-like, often five-lobed and velvety to the touch.

In late spring to early summer, it produces showy white flowers with five broad petals. By mid- to late summer, bright red berries ripen. The fruit is soft, hollow, and shaped like a tiny thimble, which gives the plant its common name.

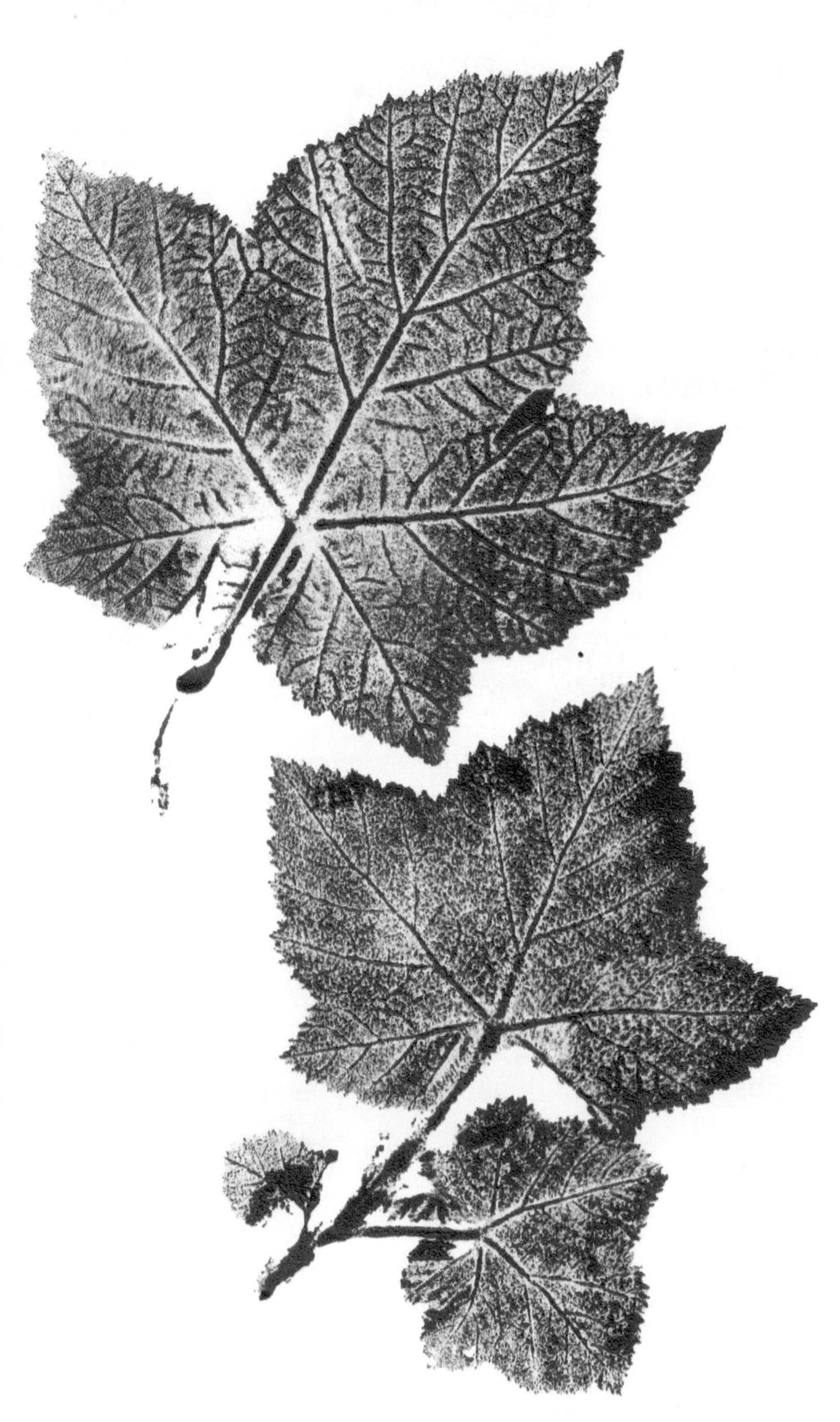

STREAMSIDE

Stream Violet
Viola glabella

Small heart-shaped leaves grow in patches, splashing color along creek sides and among the brown humus of fallen needles on the forest floor. Listen for the singing of a song sparrow, a few clear notes followed by a sweet melody…

Stream violet is a small perennial wildflower native to moist Pacific coast forests from northern California north through Oregon and Washington to British Columbia and southeastern Alaska. It thrives in damp ravines and along seasonal streams at Sea Ranch, where soils remain cool and saturated through winter and spring. Leaves arise from the base on slender stems, often forming colonies in wet ground.

In early to mid-spring, delicate violet to pale lavender flowers rise just above the foliage. Each flower has five petals, the lower often marked with faint darker veins that guide pollinators.

Native bees and other early-season insects visit the blooms.

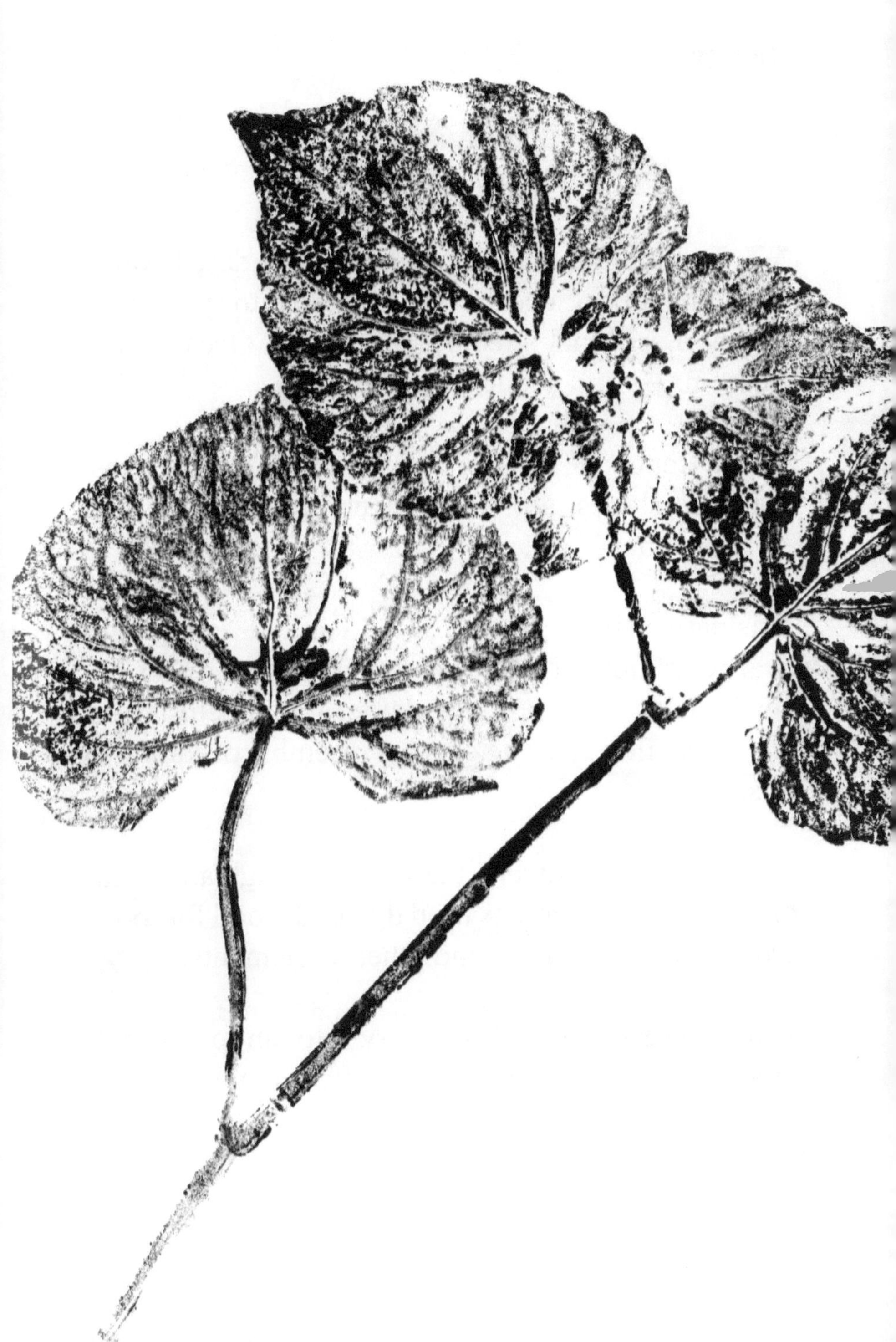

STREAMSIDE

Ocean Spray
Holodiscus discolor

Walking the bluff trail on a windy day, I watch the tops of ocean waves blown into spray. Following a seasonal stream inland, I see Ocean spray blossoms — and suddenly smile…

At Sea Ranch, Ocean Spray brightens forest margins, sheltered slopes, and bluff edges in late spring and early summer.

This native shrub grows 3 to 15 feet tall. Leaves are oval with toothed edges, green above and paler beneath. In bloom, it produces large, arching clusters of tiny white flowers. The clusters resemble ocean foam or sea spray.

Despite its airy flowers, the wood is tough and durable. Indigenous peoples used the hard wood for tools, arrows, digging sticks, and other implements.

After flowering, the clusters dry into tan to rust-colored seed heads that persist into late summer and fall.

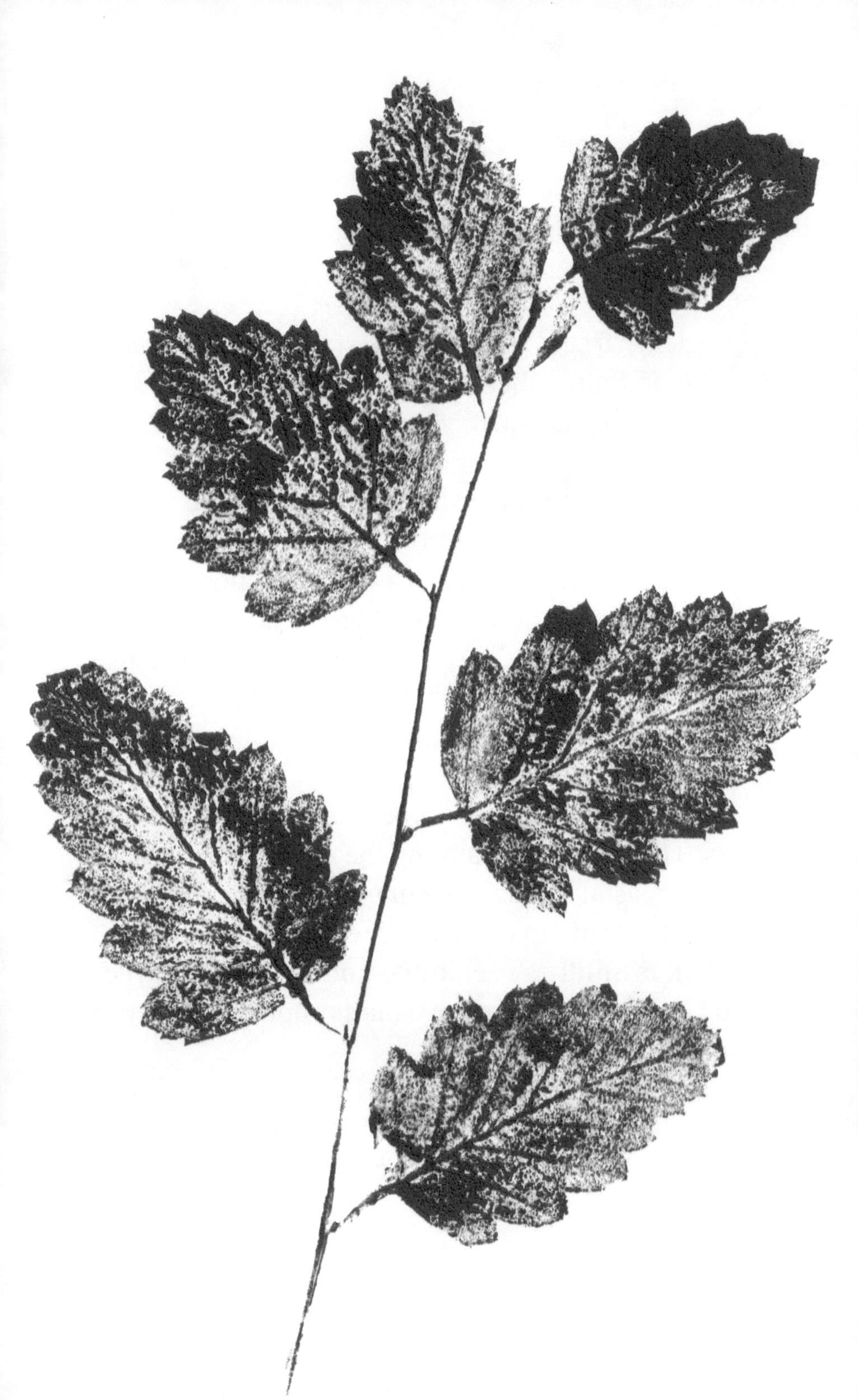

STREAMSIDE

Salmonberry
Rubus spectabilis

A prickly friend with bending stems near the creek. When Salmonberry is blooming, I look for warblers migrating north…

Salmonberry is a native shrub of the Pacific Coast of North America, ranging from Alaska south through California. At Sea Ranch, it appears along damp woodland edges and creeks where winter water lingers. It can grow 3 to 12 feet tall, forming dense thickets. Unlike Thimbleberry, it has fine prickles along its stems.

Leaves are divided into three leaflets with toothed edges. The flowers are among the earliest berry blossoms in coastal forests, opening deep pink to magenta. By late spring to early summer, the fruit ripens. The fruit is mildly sweet, often golden-orange or red. Each berry is made of many small drupelets clustered around a central core.

After logging or fire, Salmonberry is often one of the first shrubs to reappear. Birds, bears, and small mammals feed on the fruit.

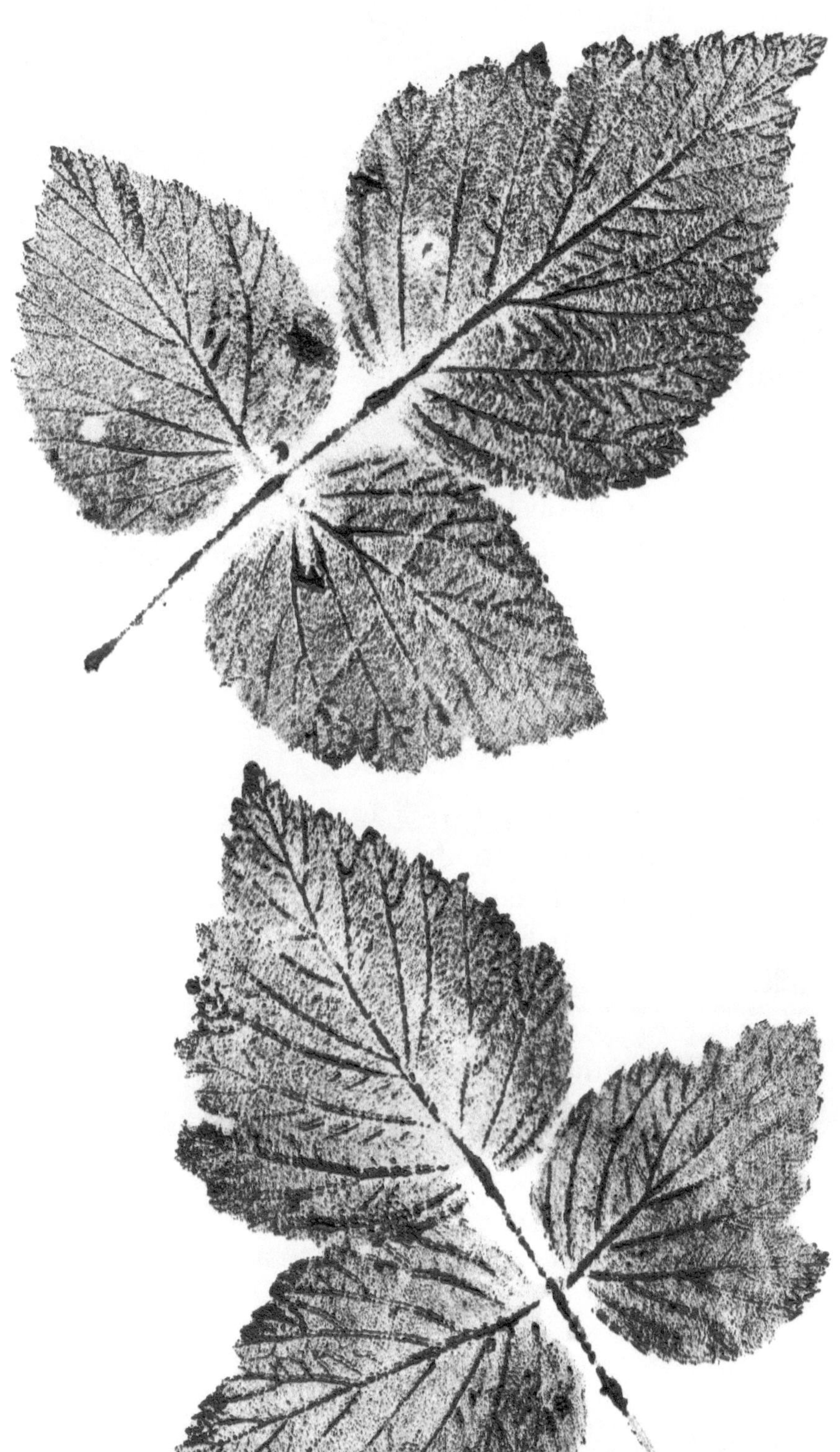

Snowberry
Symphoricarpos albus

Snowberry produces small pinkish flowers followed by distinct bright white berries, which are mildly toxic. Do not eat these!

Snowberry is a native shrub of western North America, ranging from Alaska south through California and east across much of Canada and the northern United States.

At Sea Ranch, it appears in woodland openings and along coastal trails, often near streams.

Snowberry typically grows 3 to 6 feet tall. Leaves are oval to rounded, smooth-edged or lightly toothed, and soft green. In late spring to early summer, small bell-shaped flowers bloom in shades of white to pale pink.

Birds may eat the white berries in late winter, but they can cause stomach upset in humans if ingested.

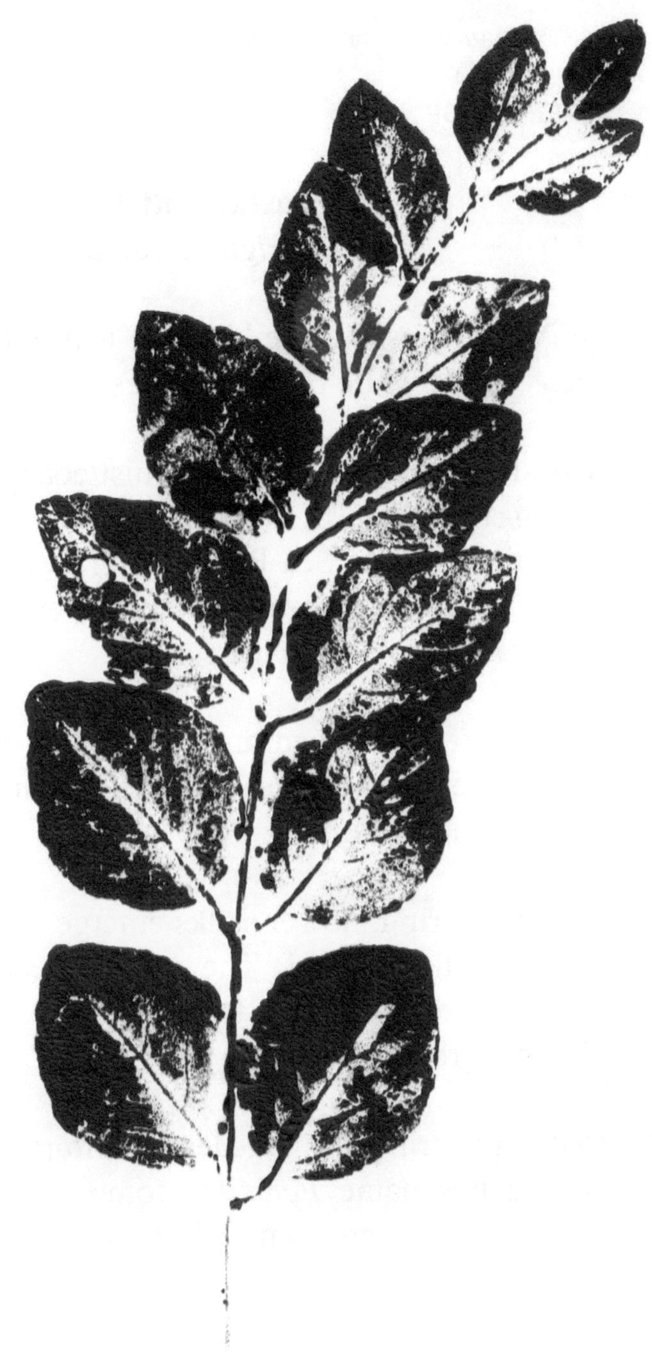

STREAMSIDE

Coastal Coltsfoot
Petasites frigidus var. *palmatus*

Once, I used these big, soft leaves to protect my hands while picking nettles…

Coastal Coltsfoot grows in moist coastal forests and along stream banks, from Alaska south through coastal California. At Sea Ranch, it grows near seasonal streams and damp ravines and often shows where water moves beneath the surface.

The leaves are broad and lobed, sometimes resembling oversized maple leaves. Their undersides are pale and felt-like.

In early spring, flower stalks emerge before the large leaves fully expand. The flower heads cluster in dense spikes, pale pink to purplish. Male and female flowers grow on separate plants.

After flowering, the large leaves unfurl on long stalks. The genus name *Petasites* comes from the Greek word for a broad-brimmed hat, referring to the size of the leaves.

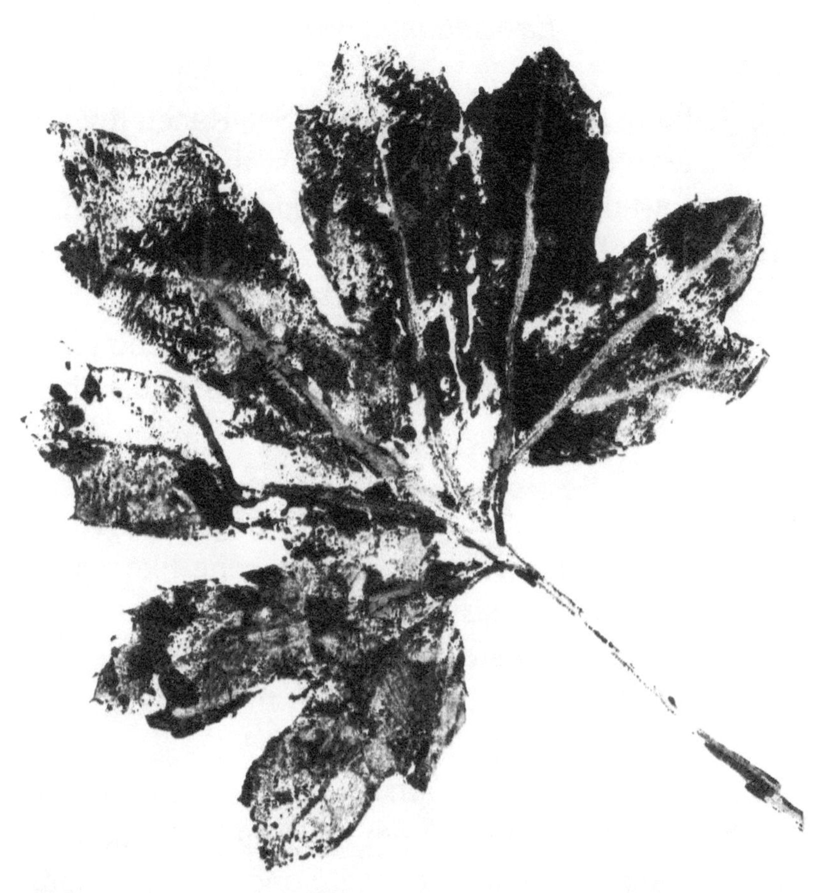

STREAMSIDE

Common Horsetail
Equisetum arvense

Walking the trail just north of Sea Ranch toward the river campground, we pass through a patch of six-foot-tall horsetails. These plants feel like visitors from another time…

Common horsetail is an ancient, non-flowering plant related to ferns. It reproduces by spores rather than seeds.

It has two types of stems. In early spring, pale brown fertile stems emerge, topped with cone-like spore structures. After releasing spores, the fertile stems wither. Later, green sterile stems grow, forming upright, jointed shoots with whorls of fine branchlets.

Silica in the tissues gives the stems a rough texture. Run your fingers along a stem and you will feel it — a faint sandpaper rasp. They were once used to scour and polish pots and tools.

Horsetails are living descendants of ancient plants that once formed vast forests during the age of the dinosaurs.

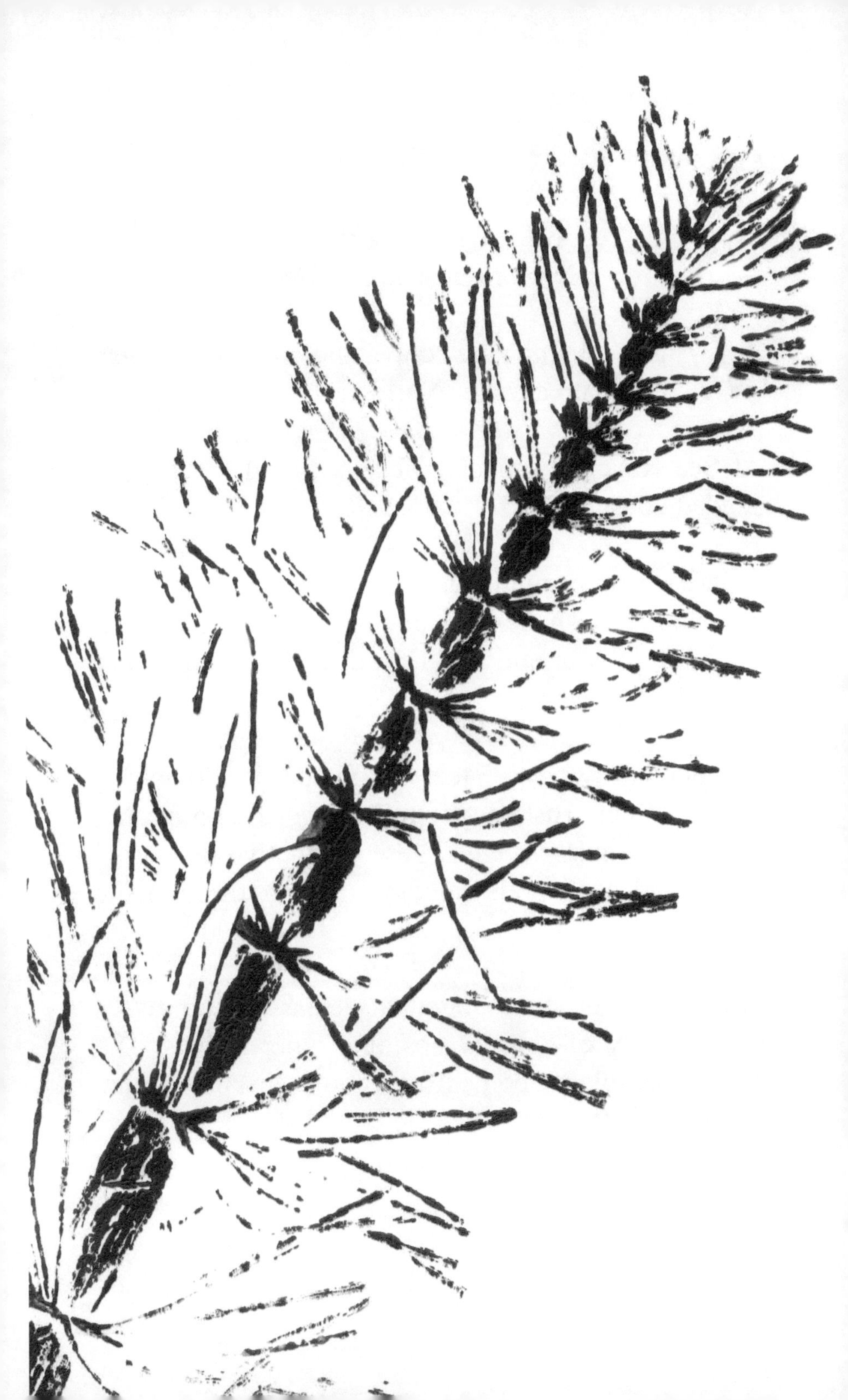

STREAMSIDE

California Bee Plant
Scrophularia californica

With a magnifying loupe, the smallest flowers open into another world…

At Sea Ranch, it appears near seasonal creeks and shaded coastal bluffs.

In late spring through summer, small, rounded flowers bloom in shades of reddish-brown to maroon. They are tubular and two-lipped, with a small upper lip and broader lower lip.

The plant grows 2 to 5 feet tall on upright, branching stems. When crushed, the foliage releases a strong, somewhat musky scent. These distinctive tall, dried stems and seed pods remain standing through the winter.

The flowers produce abundant nectar that attracts a wide variety of bees, wasps, and other insects. The name "bee plant" comes from the many pollinators that visit its flowers.

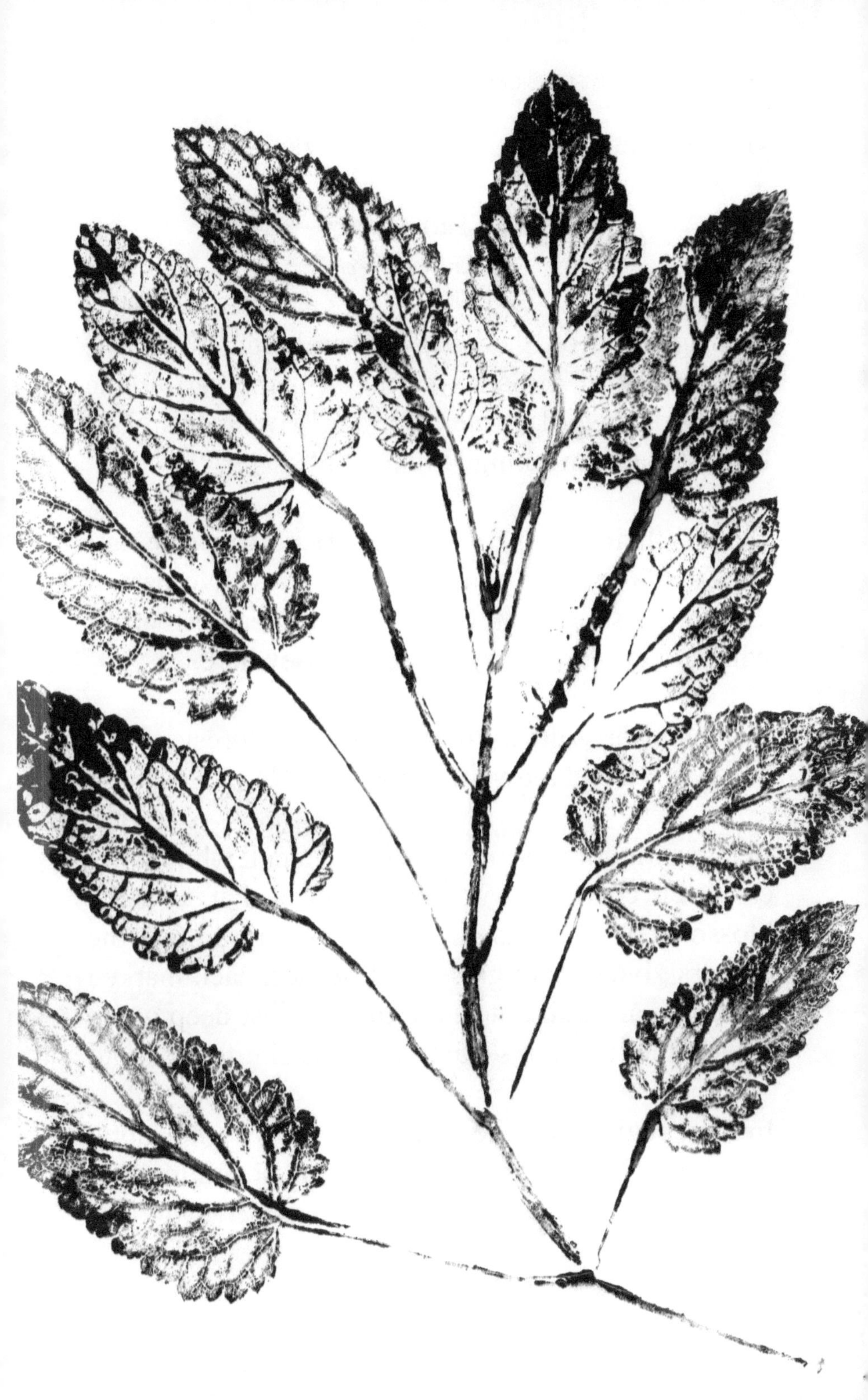

STREAMSIDE

Red Baneberry
Actaea rubra

Bright red on the path, beware! Sometimes the history of a plant's common name carries the history of a word inside it. "Bane" comes from Old English bana, meaning "killer," or "slayer."

Despite their beauty, the berries are poisonous if eaten. Even a few can cause serious illness. No part of the plant is safe to eat. Birds, however, eat the berries without harm and carry the seeds elsewhere.

Red baneberry grows in cool, shaded forests, often beneath firs and redwoods along the North Coast.

In late spring it lifts airy clusters of small white flowers, each crowded with fine stamens that give the blossoms a soft, brushlike look. By midsummer the flowers give way to glossy red berries, each marked with a small dark dot at the tip. Against deep green leaves, the fruit can seem to glow in dim forest light.

In some regions a white-fruited form grows, but along the North Coast the red berries are most common.

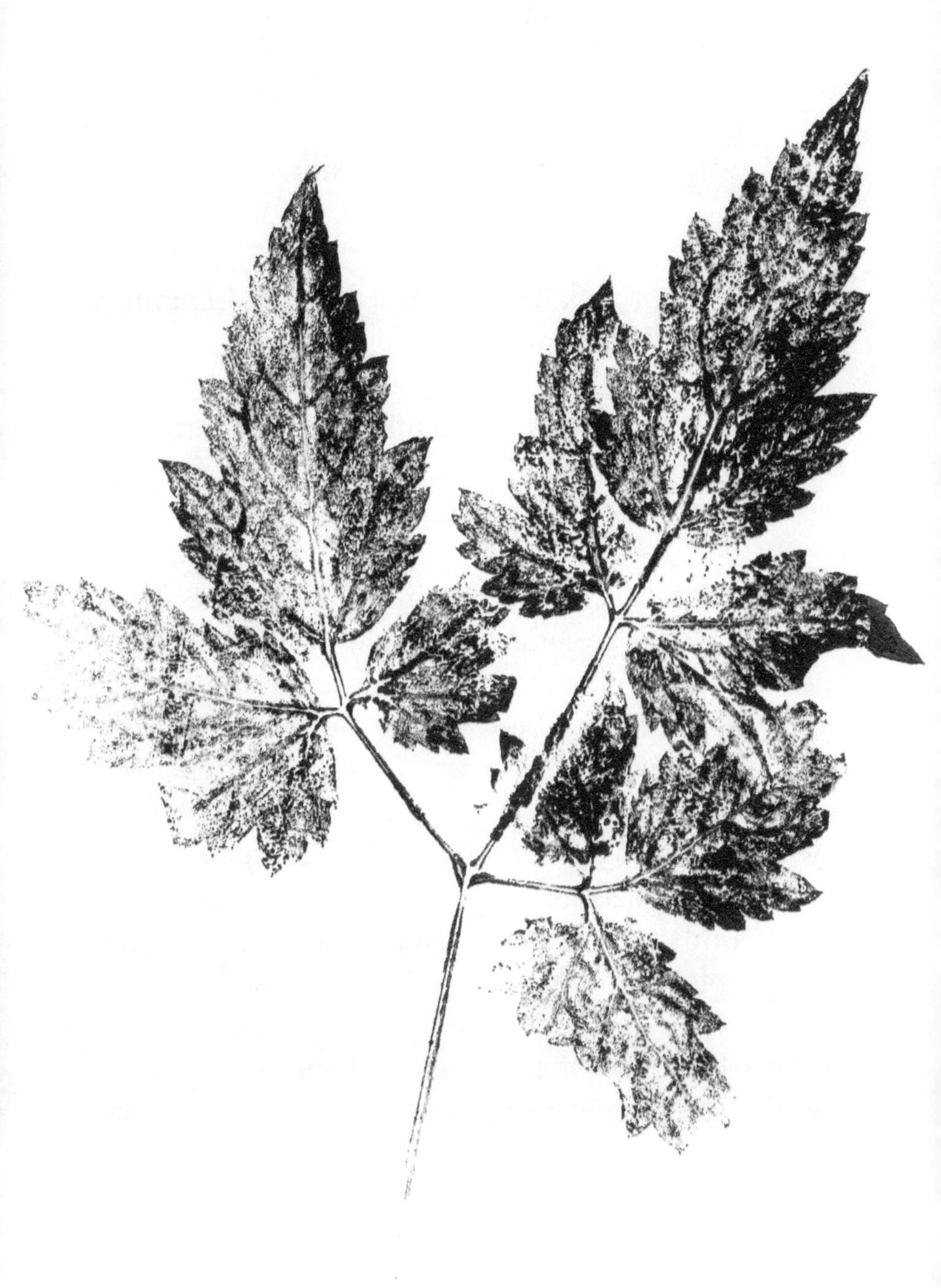

Pink-flowering Currant
Ribes sanguineum

A delight of pink flowers. And that odd, humming sound? A hummingbird…

Pink-flowering currant is one of the earliest shrubs to bloom along the North Coast, opening while the hills are still wet with winter rain.

Long, drooping clusters of pink to deep rose flowers hang from bare branches in late winter and early spring. Rich with nectar, the blossoms draw hummingbirds in. Native bees visit as well, especially on warm days between storms.

By summer, small blue-black berries replace the flowers. The berries are edible but not especially sweet; birds are far more enthusiastic about them than people.

At Sea Ranch it often appears along sunny forest margins and in sheltered swales protected from heavy salt spray.

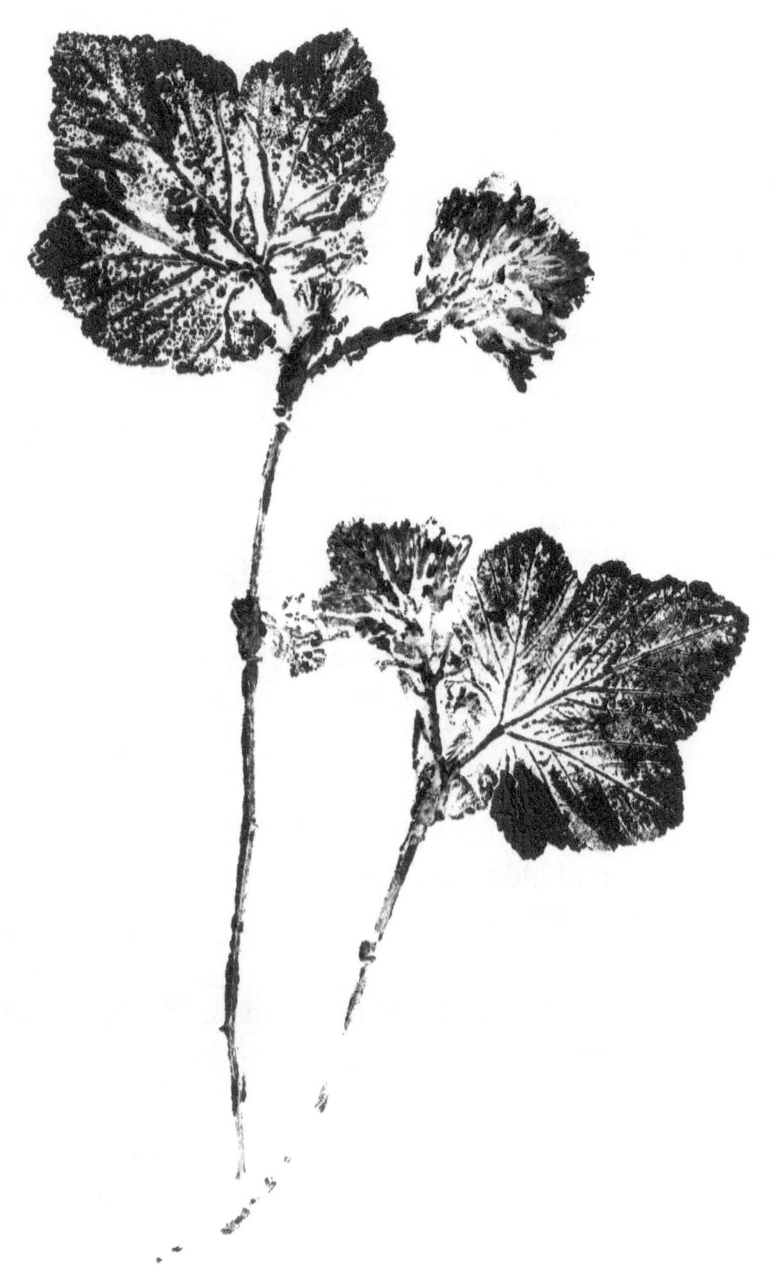

STREAMSIDE

Bigleaf Maple
Acer macrophyllum

As we walked along the gravel river, large yellow maple leaves dropped to the ground. Names often do not define us, or plants. Bigleaf? Sometimes. But also small…

In spring the tree leafs out with bright green, lobed leaves that cast a cool, dense shade. Long dangling clusters of yellow-green flowers soon appear, often before the leaves have fully expanded.

By late summer and fall, paired winged seeds — classic maple "helicopters" — spin to the ground in the wind.

At Sea Ranch it is most often found in sheltered ravines and along creeks, where fog and runoff provide steady moisture.

The tree can live for centuries and may reach over 100 feet tall in favorable conditions.

Indigenous peoples of the Pacific Northwest used the wood for tools and carved items, and the inner bark for rope and basketry.

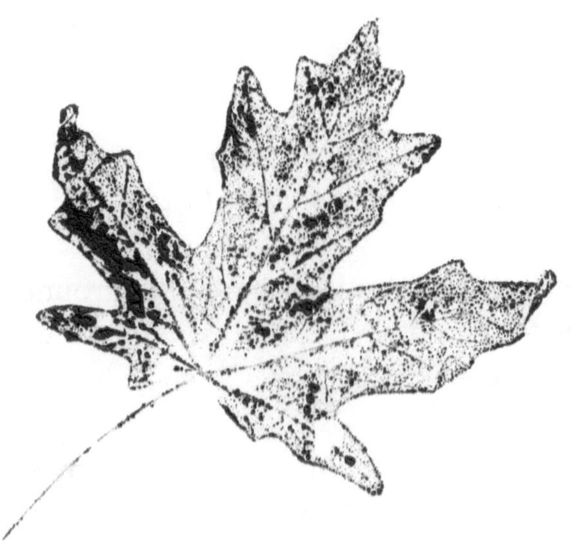

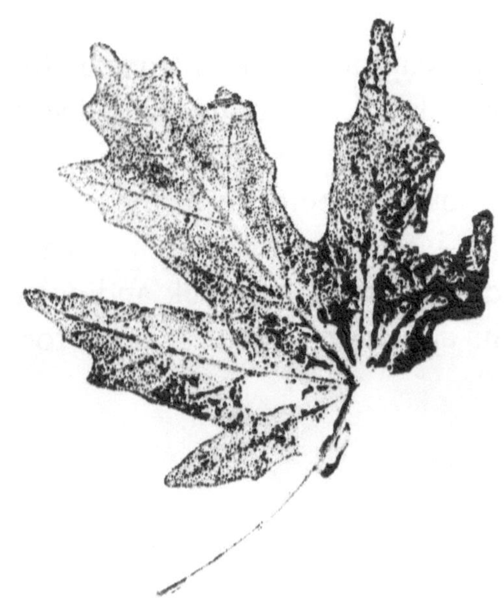

Water Parsley
Oenanthe sarmentosa

Water parsley grows where the ground stays wet — along seeps, creeks, and the edges of slow-moving water.

Clusters of tiny white, umbrella-like flowers rise above the leaves in flat-topped umbels during late spring and summer.

Crushed foliage has a mild, green scent, not strongly aromatic.

At Sea Ranch it often appears in drainage swales, wet meadows, and along shaded streambanks.

Though it belongs to the carrot family, water parsley is considered toxic. It is easily confused with the deadly water hemlock and poison hemlock. Despite its appetizing name, it is not for eating.

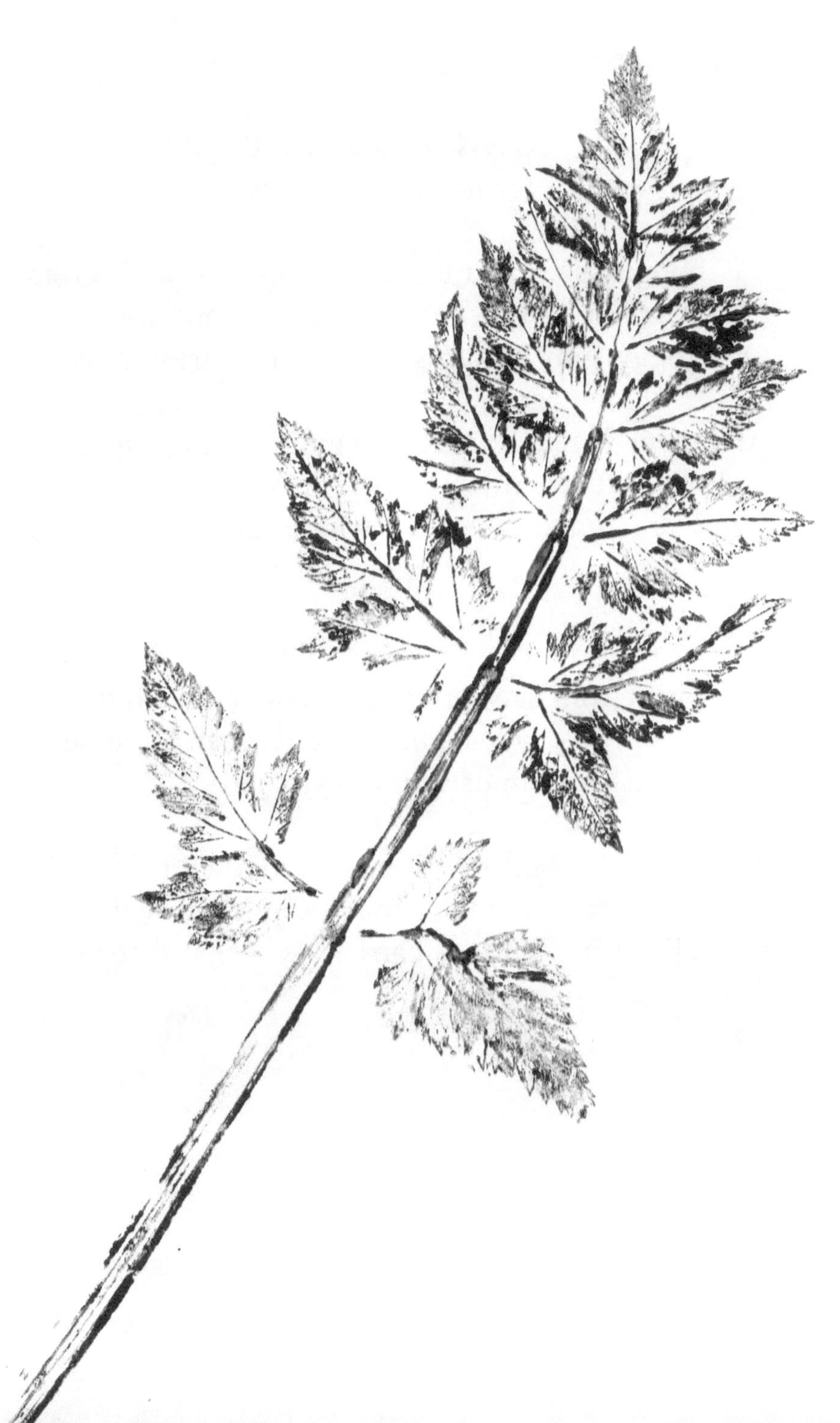

STREAMSIDE

American Speedwell
Veronica americana

Though small and easily overlooked, its flowers brighten the quiet edges of creeks and wetlands. On a foggy, gray day, this is a clear blue treat to see…

American speedwell grows along streams, springs, and wet ditches, often rooting in shallow water. Its stems creep and take hold where they touch damp soil, forming loose mats along muddy edges.

Small blue flowers with darker blue veins rise above the leaves from late spring into summer. Each flower has four petals, one slightly smaller than the others, giving the blossom its subtle asymmetry.

The name "speedwell" comes from Old English. Some say it referred to the plant's quick growth; others believe it was once carried as a charm for safe travel.

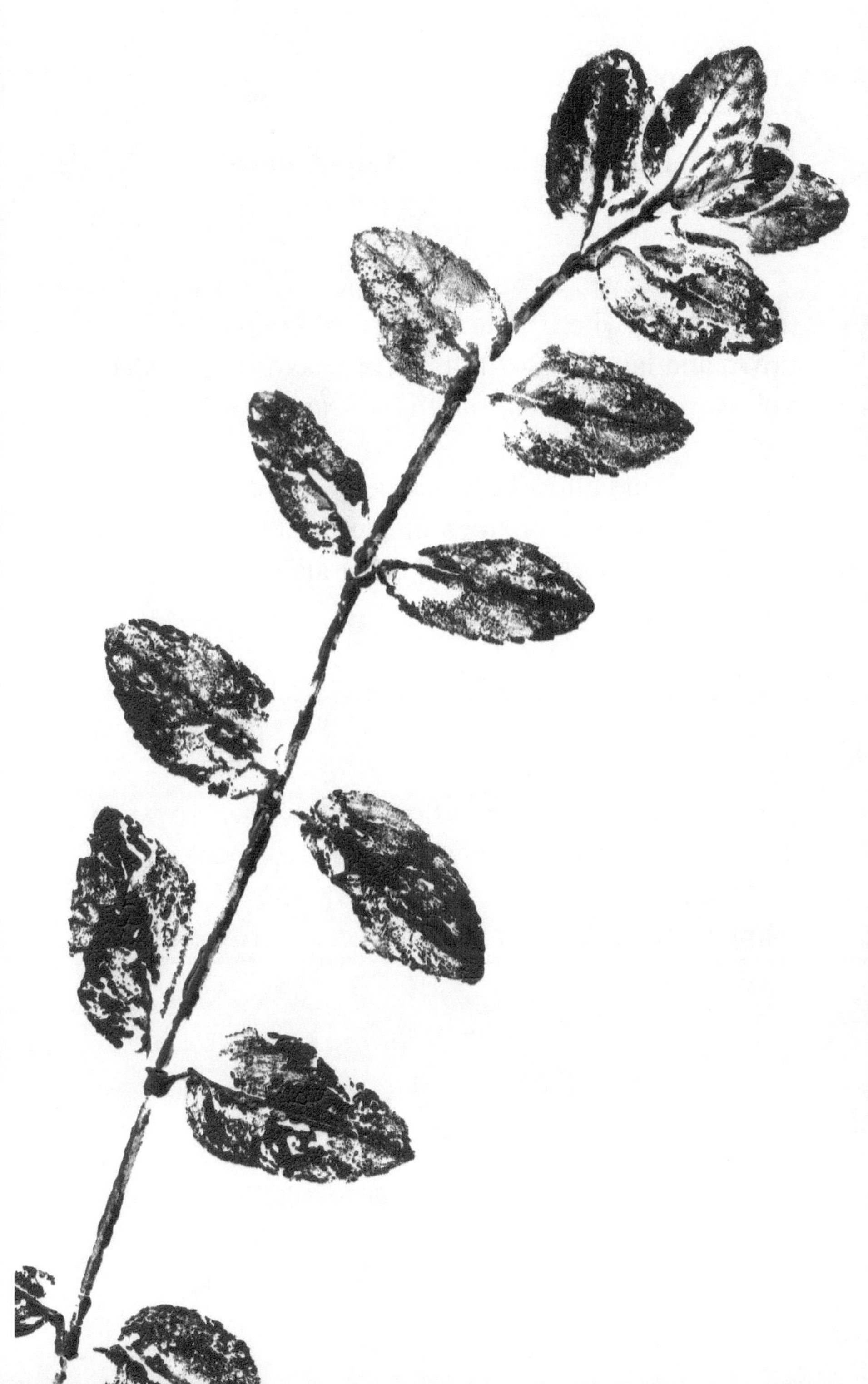

STREAMSIDE

Magnificent Seep Monkeyflower
Erythranthe grandis

Plump leaves cover the ground like a mat on the hillside, where water seeps through the soil. I sat down and laughed — in the droplets of fog, cheerful yellow monkey faces smiled back at me…

Large, bright yellow flowers open wide, often marked with reddish dots or lines inside the throat. Blooming begins in spring and can continue into summer if moisture remains steady.

The leaves are opposite, slightly sticky, and softly textured.

Magnificent seep monkeyflower grows where water slowly trickles from coastal bluffs and rocky slopes and the soil stays damp year-round. The "seep" in its name refers to the wet places where it grows.

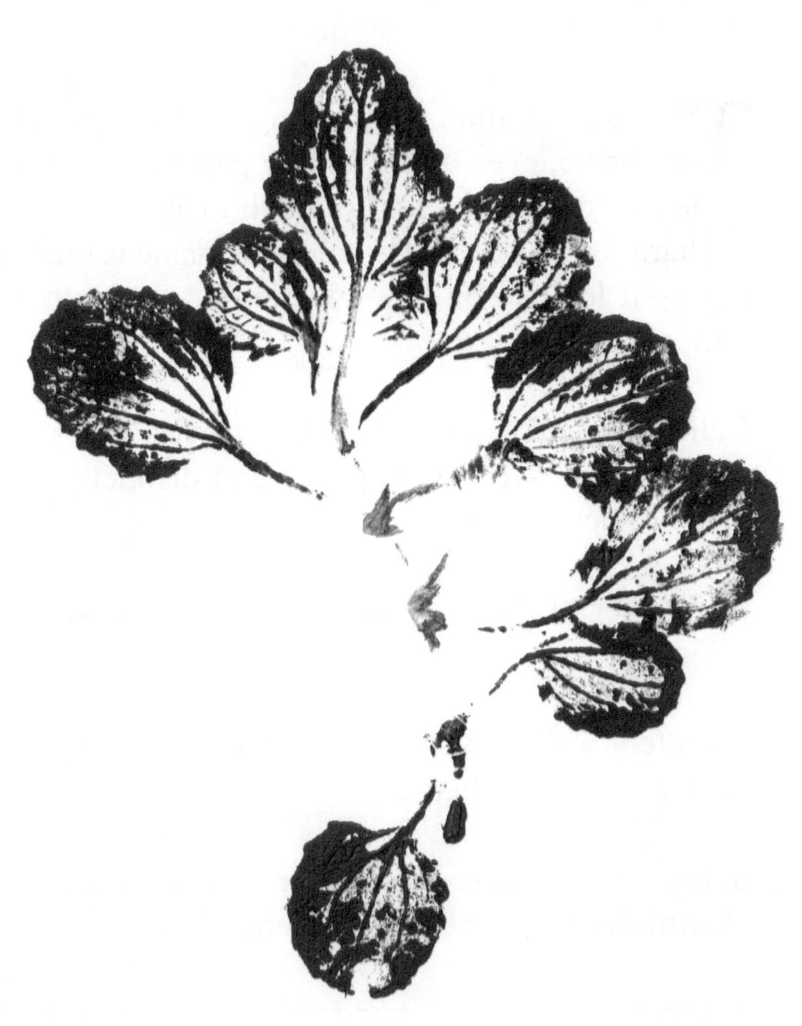

STREAMSIDE

California Hedgenettle
Stachys bullata

This is a common plant, though few people know its name, even after walking past it many times. Its leaves may feel slightly rough or hairy, but they are harmless to touch. The common name is misleading — it looks a bit like a nettle, but it won't sting you…

California hedge-nettle has soft leaves and square stems. The leaves are opposite and distinctly wrinkled or puckered.

A member of the mint family, it emits a mild scent when crushed.

It prefers well-drained soils and tolerates dry summers once established.

In late spring and early summer, whorls of rosy-purple flowers circle the upright stems.

It spreads slowly by underground stems, forming small colonies over time.

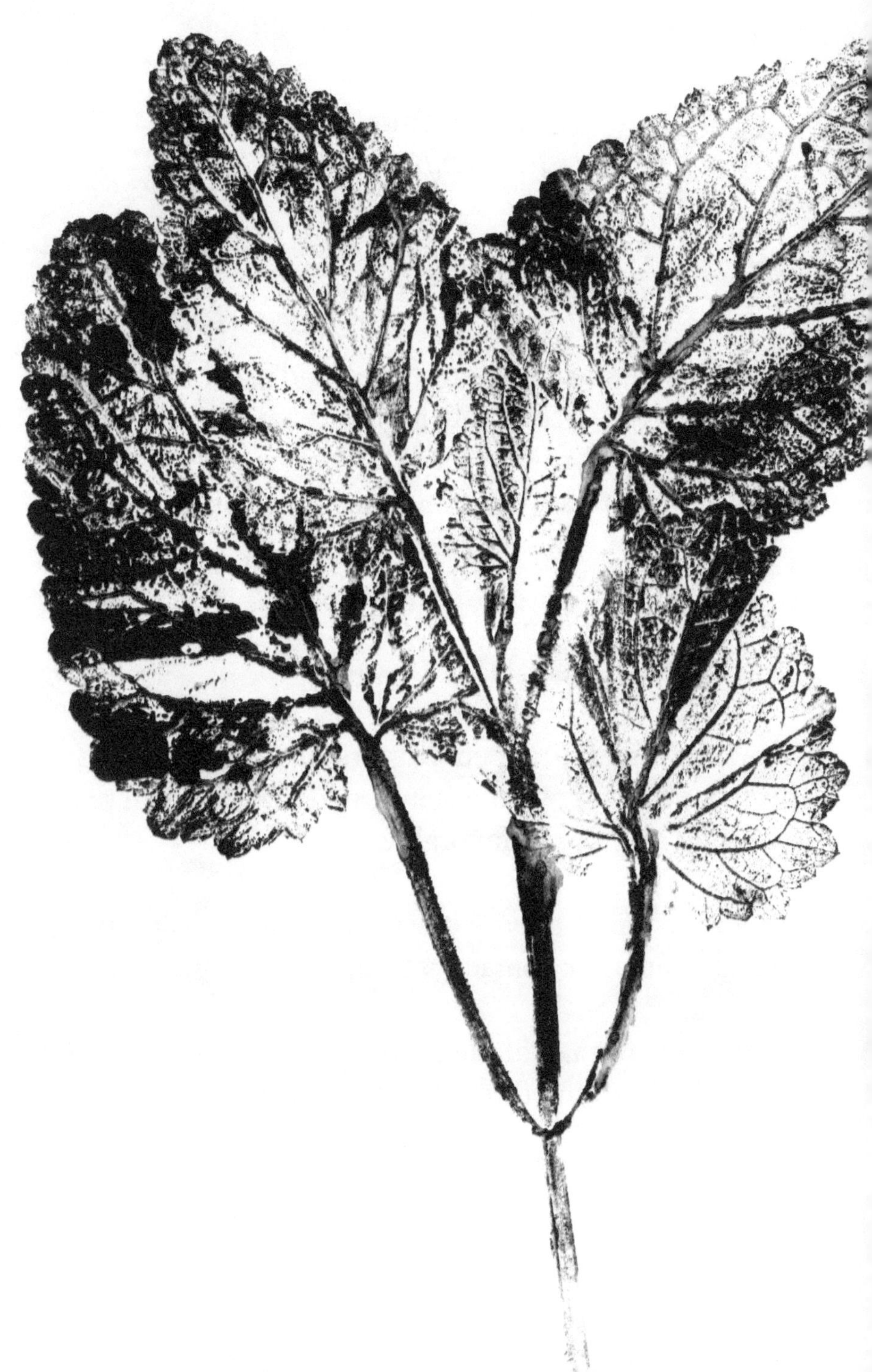

STREAMSIDE

Fennel
Foeniculum vulgare

Fennel's dense growth can displace native vegetation. A long-established invader…

Cultivated since ancient times and used by the Romans for flavoring and herbal remedies, fennel arrived in California in the late 18th or early 19th century — most likely with Spanish missionaries — and spread quickly along the coast.

It is easily recognized by its fine, feathery leaves and strong anise scent.

In summer, flat-topped clusters of tiny yellow flowers rise high above the stems, and the plant can reach six feet or more in favorable conditions.

Some people may experience skin sensitivity in bright sun after contact with the sap.

Fennel grows tall along roadsides, coastal bluffs, and disturbed ground throughout California.

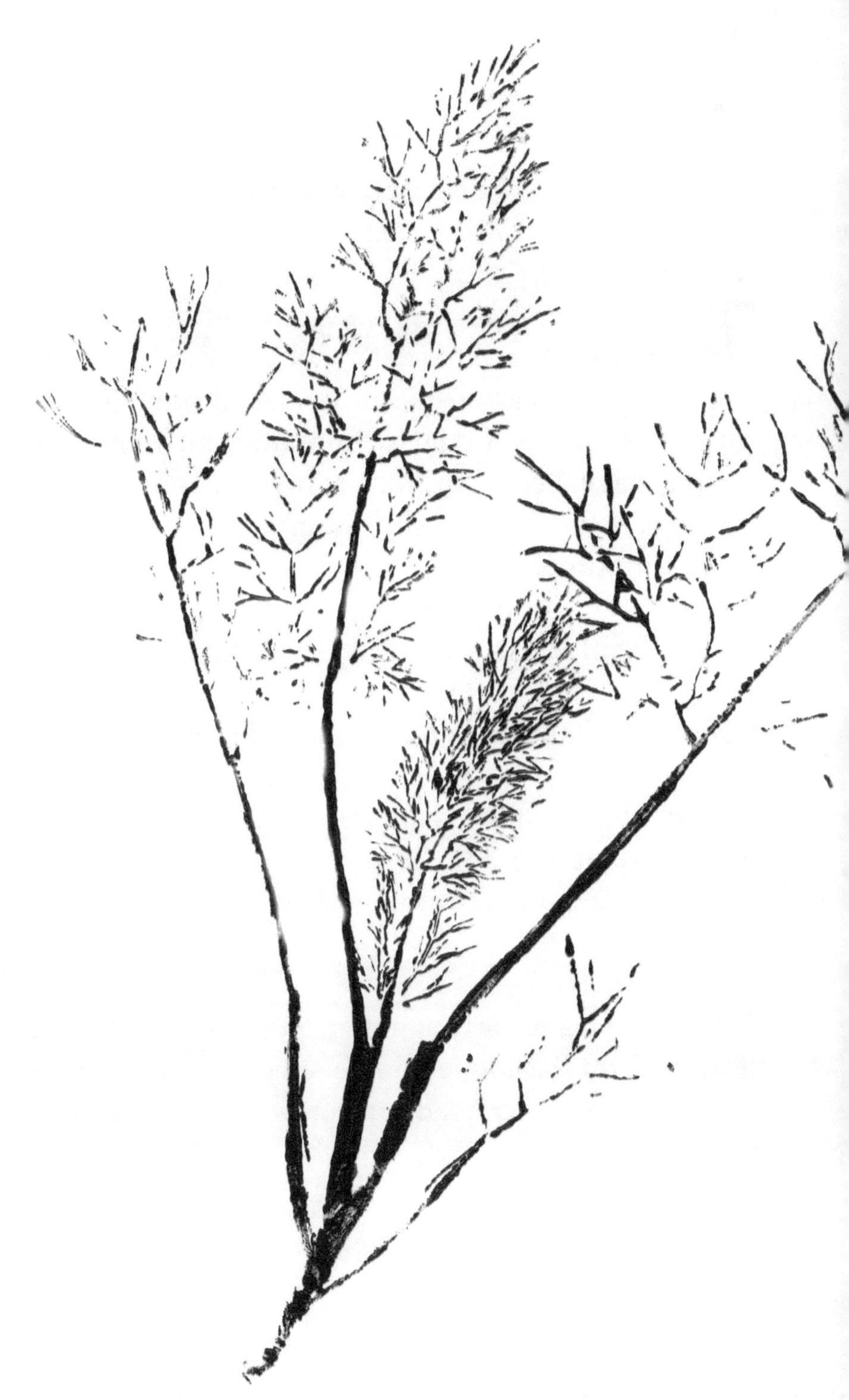

STREAMSIDE

Poison Hemlock
Conium maculatum

This invader from Europe grows throughout the U.S. Its stems have dark spots. It also has feathery leaves and carrot-like flowers. **All parts of the plant are highly toxic to humans and livestock.** People have been poisoned while clearing poison hemlock stands, especially when plant material becomes airborne.

Poison hemlock is a tall, invasive plant that grows along roadsides, creek banks, and disturbed ground throughout California. It can reach six to ten feet tall.

The smooth, hollow stems are often marked with distinctive purple blotches or streaks. Its leaves are finely divided and fern-like, bright green, and softly textured.

In late spring and early summer, clusters of tiny white flowers form flat-topped umbels typical of the carrot family. Each flower head can contain dozens of small blossoms.

Historically, poison hemlock was the plant used in the execution of Socrates in ancient Athens.

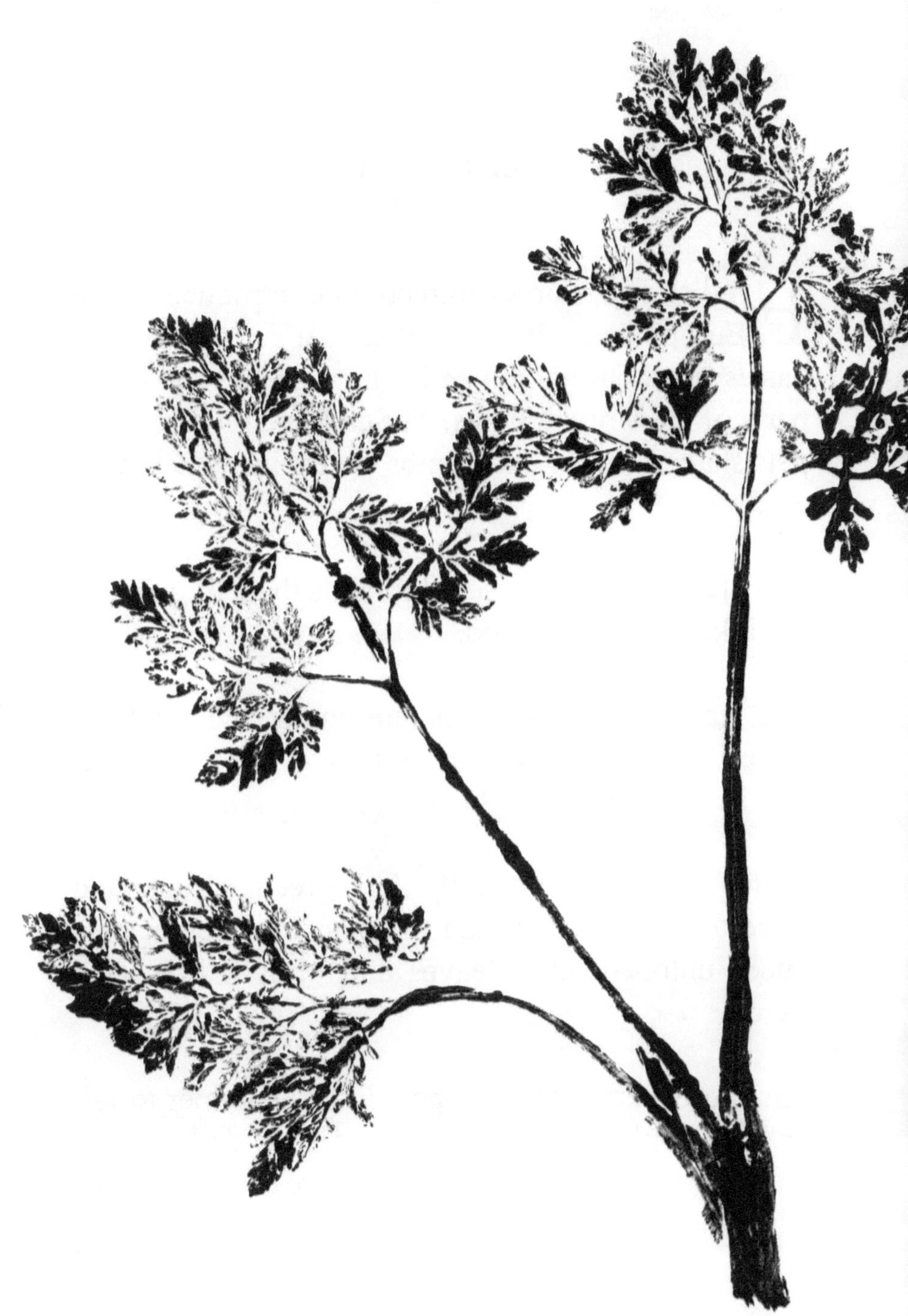

English Ivy
Hedera helix

English ivy is an evergreen vine introduced from Europe and widely planted as a groundcover. It has escaped cultivation and is now invasive in many parts of the United States. At Sea Ranch it often carpets shaded slopes and climbs trunks in sheltered areas.

The plant climbs with aerial rootlets that cling tightly to bark, stone, and wood.

The leaves and berries contain compounds that are toxic if ingested, and the sap may cause skin irritation in sensitive individuals.

Young leaves are typically dark green, glossy, and three to five lobed. When the plant matures, it produces unlobed adult leaves and upright flowering stems.

Small greenish flowers appear in late summer to fall on mature plants. By winter, clusters of dark blue to black berries develop. The berries are eaten by birds, which help spread the seeds.

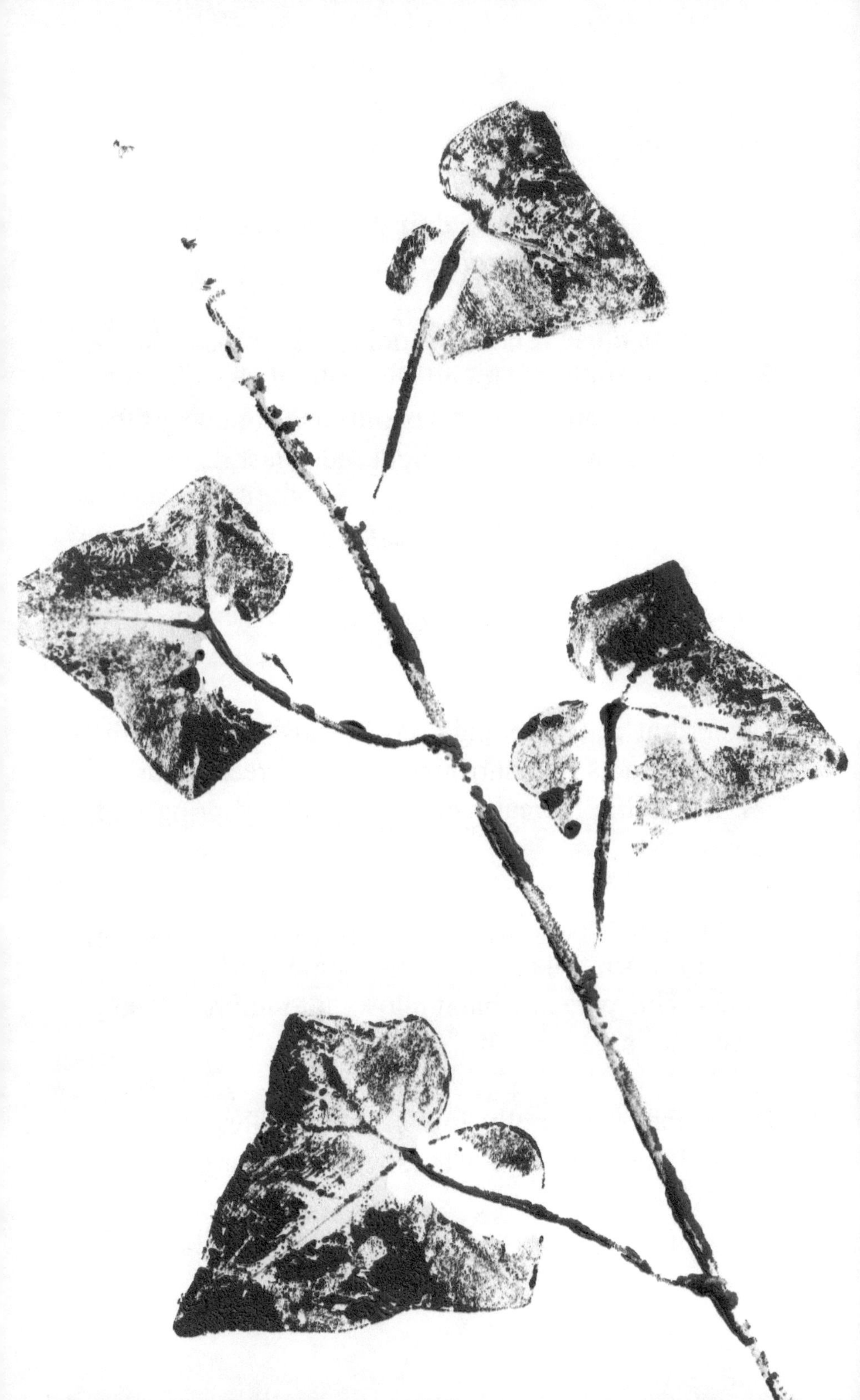

STREAMSIDE

Wight's Paintbrush
Castilleja wightii

Like its close relative, "Indian paintbrush" (Castilleja miniata), found throughout the northern Rocky Mountains, Wight's paintbrush announces the arrival of summer with a bright red splash…

Wight's paintbrush is a coastal wildflower found along the northern California coast. It grows on bluffs, coastal scrub, and grassy slopes exposed to wind and salt air.

The bright red to orange-red "petals" are actually colorful bracts that surround smaller greenish flowers. Blooming typically occurs from late spring into summer.

Wight's paintbrush is partially parasitic, attaching its roots to nearby plants to obtain some water and nutrients. This parasitic habit allows it to thrive in lean, coastal soils.

The plant is generally low-growing, often under a foot tall, though height varies with exposure.

At Sea Ranch, look for it along the Salal trail.

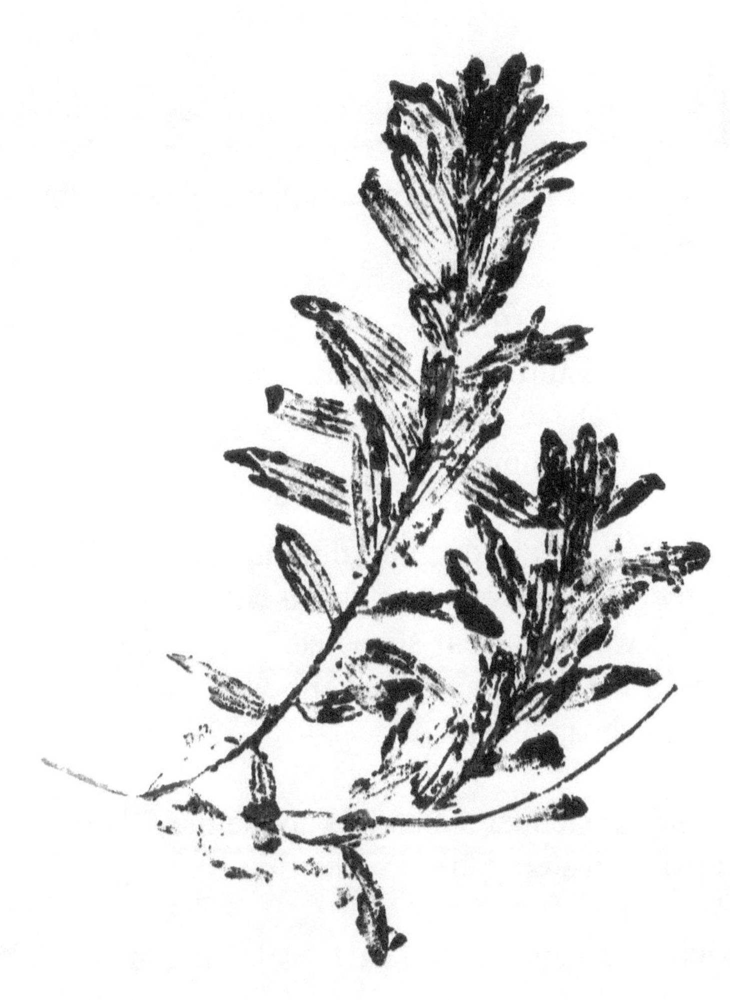

STREAMSIDE

Threeleaf Foamflower
Tiarella trifoliata

It blends and hides in the understory until delicate flowers rise on slender stems, never quite the same twice. The flowers remind me of ocean foam on windy days…

Threeleaf foamflower grows in cool, shaded forests where moisture lingers in the soil through spring. It prefers rich, well-drained soil and does not tolerate prolonged summer drought.

Its leaves are divided into three leaflets, often lightly toothed and sometimes flushed with reddish tones in cooler weather. Leaf shape can vary regionally, and some forms may appear shallowly lobed rather than clearly separate leaflets.

In spring, slender stems rise above the foliage, holding airy clusters of tiny white flowers.

Each small bloom has fine projecting stamens that give the flowers their soft, mist-like appearance.

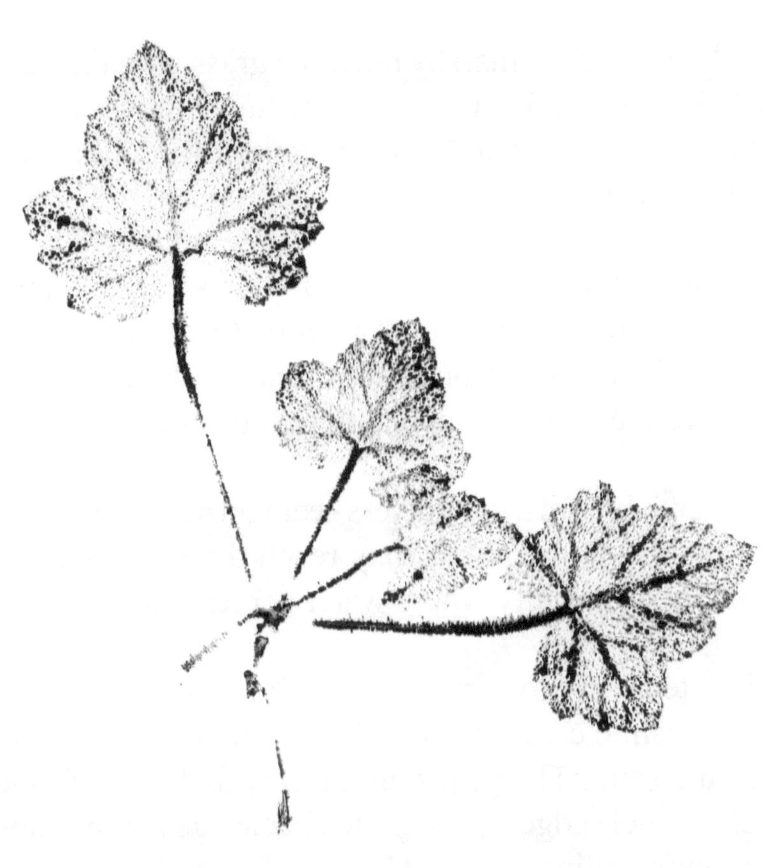

STREAMSIDE

Fringed False Hellebore
Veratrum fimbriatum

Across low, marshy meadow grass with the ocean beyond, this rare but unmistakable plant stands tall, its huge parallel-veined leaves lifting like fabric in the wind…

Fringed false hellebore is native to coastal northern California and southwestern Oregon. It grows in moist forests, along seeps, and in shaded ravines where the soil stays cool and rich through spring.

When it blooms, the flowers seem intricate and slightly wild. Mature plants may reach three to six feet in height, especially where water is plentiful.

In late spring to early summer, branching clusters of greenish to creamy white flowers appear near the top of the stem. The petals are narrow and often fringed along their edges, giving the species its name fimbriatum, meaning "fringed."

All parts of the plant are poisonous if consumed.

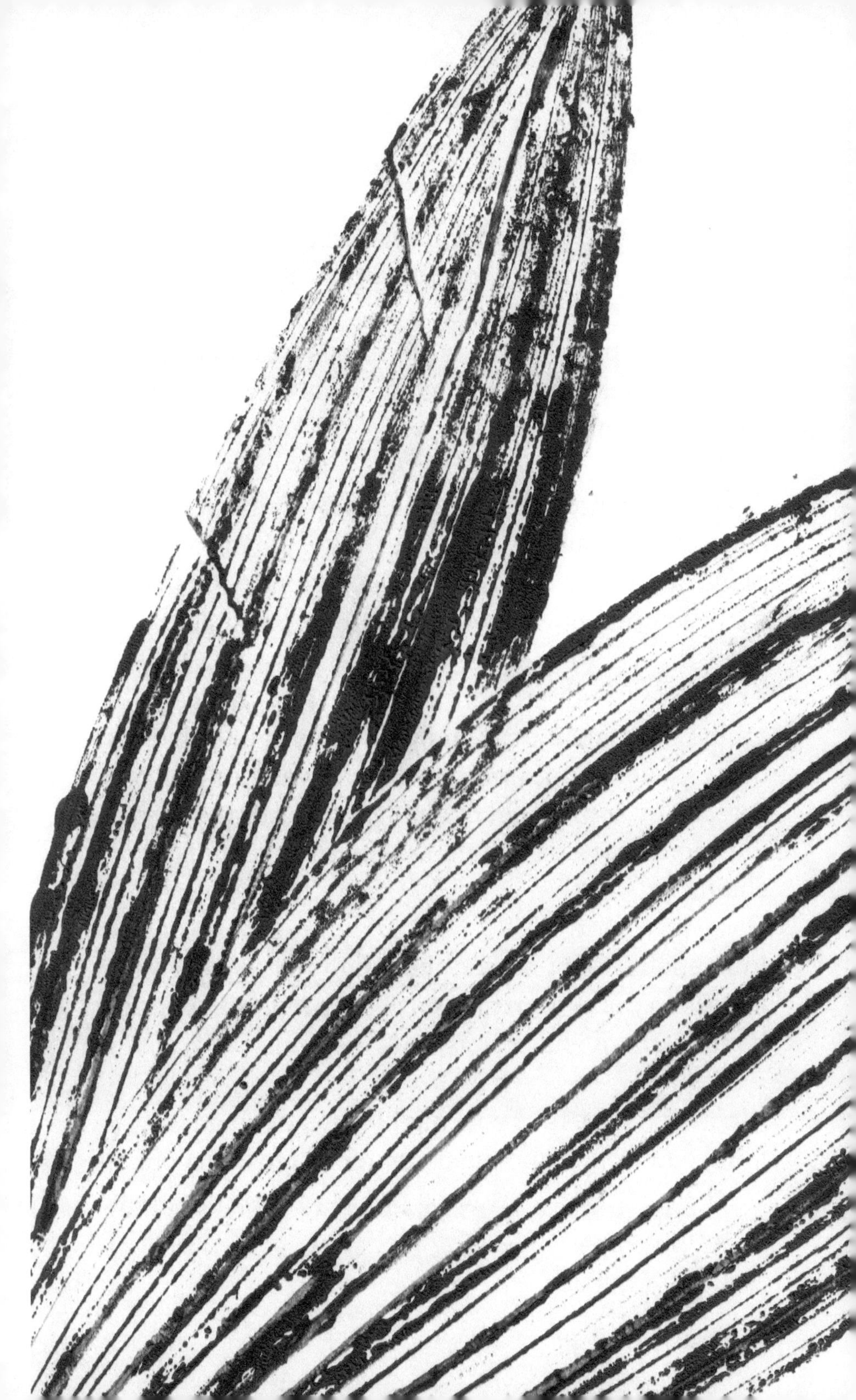

STREAMSIDE

Giant Chain Fern
Woodwardia fimbriata

As you pass by, the large fronds extend in all directions, impatient and wild, as if wanting to be everywhere at once…

One of the largest ferns on the North Coast, its fronds can stretch four to eight feet long where water is plentiful. At Sea Ranch, it is most often found in cool forested drainages where fog and runoff linger.

The broad fronds arch outward in heavy green curves, giving the plant a bold, almost fountain-like shape in deep shade. It does not produce flowers or seeds. It spreads by spores. On the underside of fertile fronds, the spore cases form long, linked rows that resemble chains.

Indigenous peoples used the tough fibers and fronds in basketry and sometimes as lining material in traditional earth ovens.

When sunlight filters through redwoods and strikes the broad fronds, the plant can feel almost ancient — another reminder that ferns predate flowering plants by millions of years.

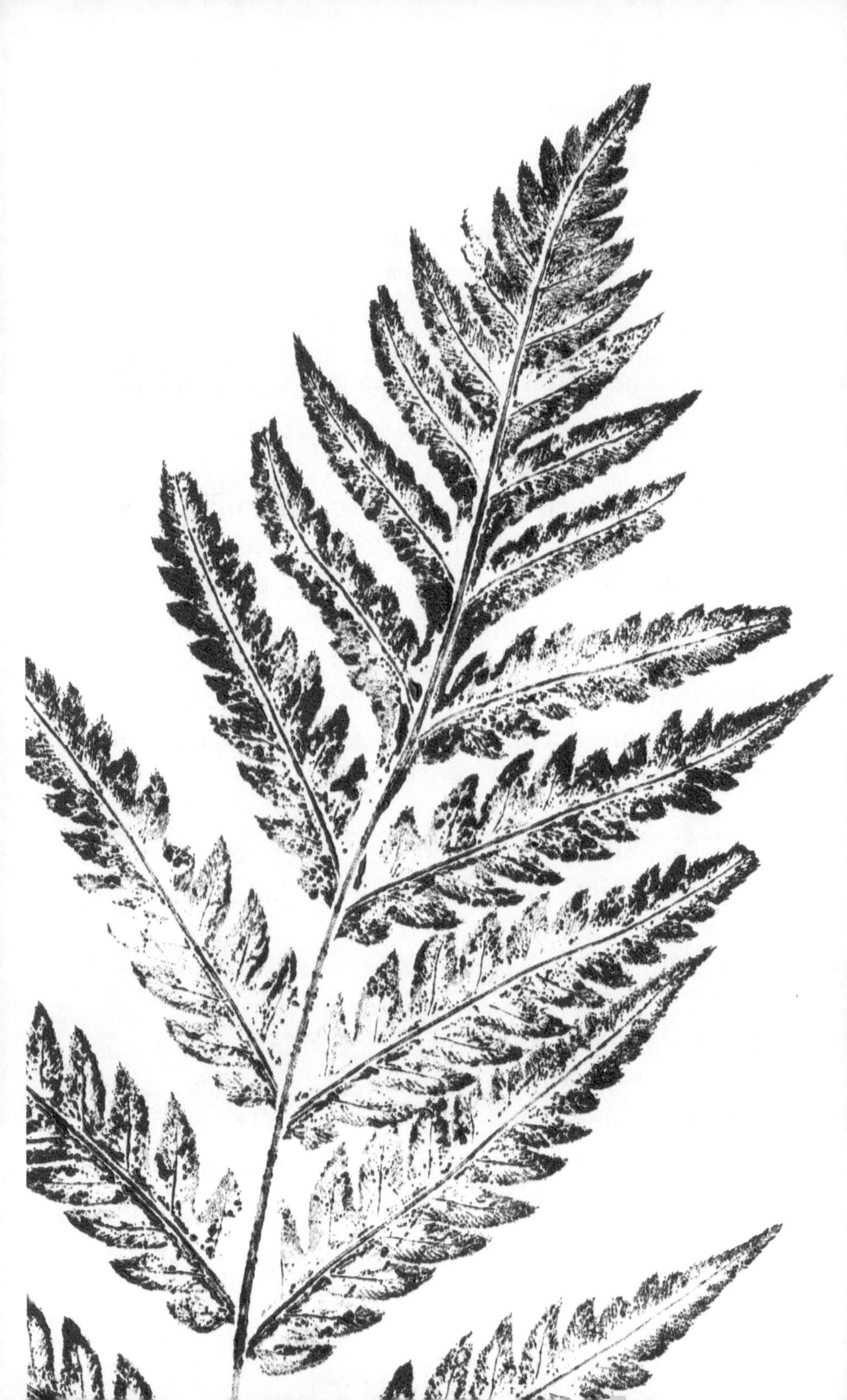

STREAMSIDE

Mexican Fleabane
Erigeron karvinskianus

Delicate, daisy-like flowers bloom above soft greenery along damp creek banks. It reminds me to slow down and look closely…

Native to Mexico and Central America, this historic plant has been present in California for well over 100 years, first in gardens and later along coastal settlements, becoming a familiar, soft-edged presence that blurs the line between cultivated and wild. At Sea Ranch, it often appears along paths, near buildings, and in sunny openings where soil is thin and well-drained.

The plant blooms for an unusually long season, often from spring into late fall in mild coastal climates. Its daisy-like flowers open white and gradually age to pink, so one plant may carry both colors at once.

The genus name *Erigeron* comes from Greek words meaning "early old man," referring to the plant's early blooming and fluffy seed heads. The common name "fleabane" comes from an old belief that dried plants of this group repelled fleas.

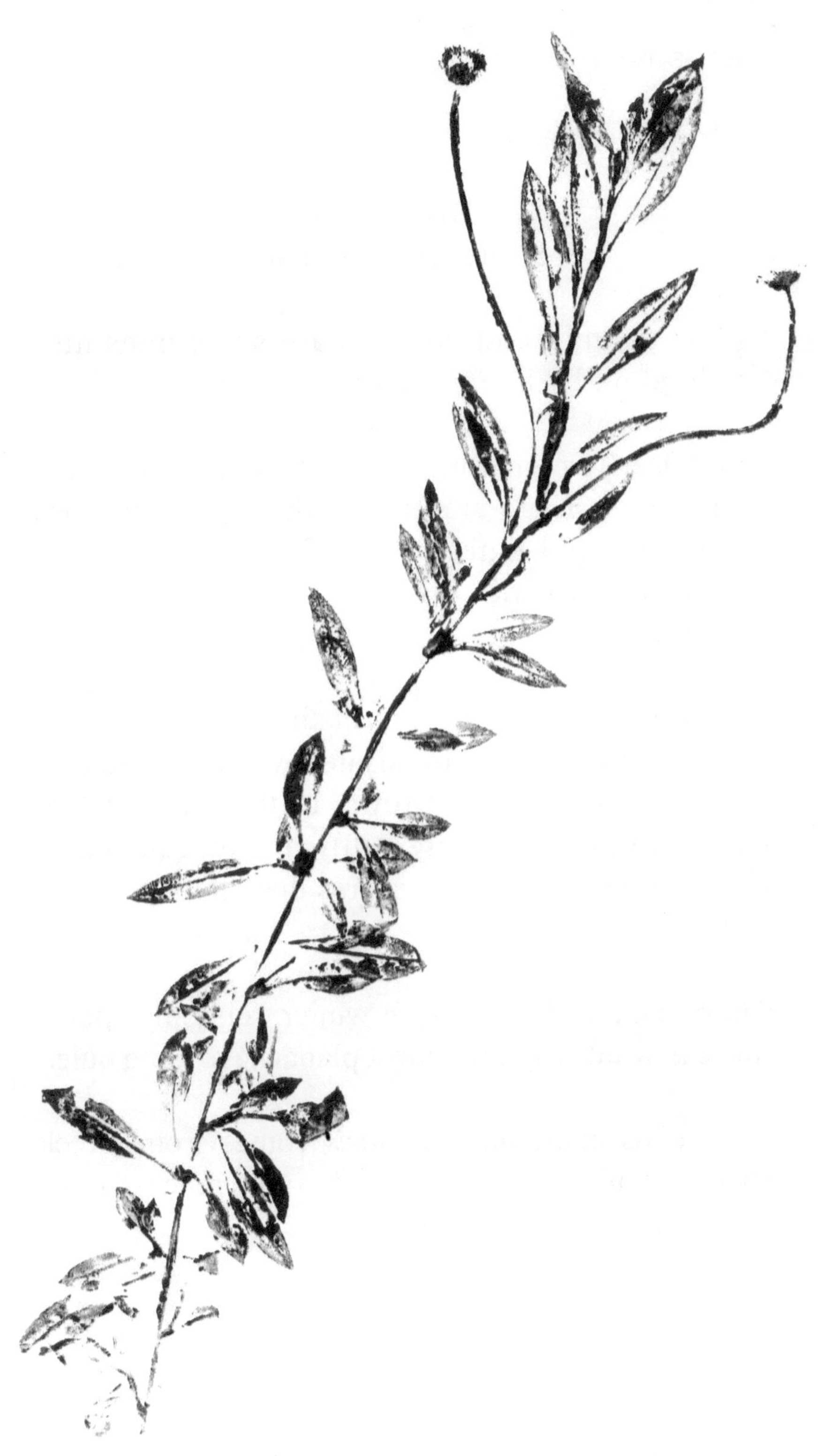

Deer Fern
Struthiopteris spicant

The young, tender leaves are sometimes nibbled on by hungry deer in winter…

I find deer fern growing in the redwood forests and near creeks. There are places where a patch looks almost arranged—green sterile fronds spread like a collar, with the darker "spikes" rising from the center like quiet signals.

Unlike many ferns, it has two distinct kinds of fronds. The dark green sterile fronds lie low and spread outward in neat, evergreen rows. In the center, taller, narrow fertile fronds rise stiffly and turn brown as they mature, carrying the spores that allow the plant to reproduce.

They stand upright through winter, releasing spores into the wind long after most plants have gone quiet.

The genus name *Struthiopteris* comes from Greek roots meaning "ostrich fern," a reference to the plume-like look of the fronds.

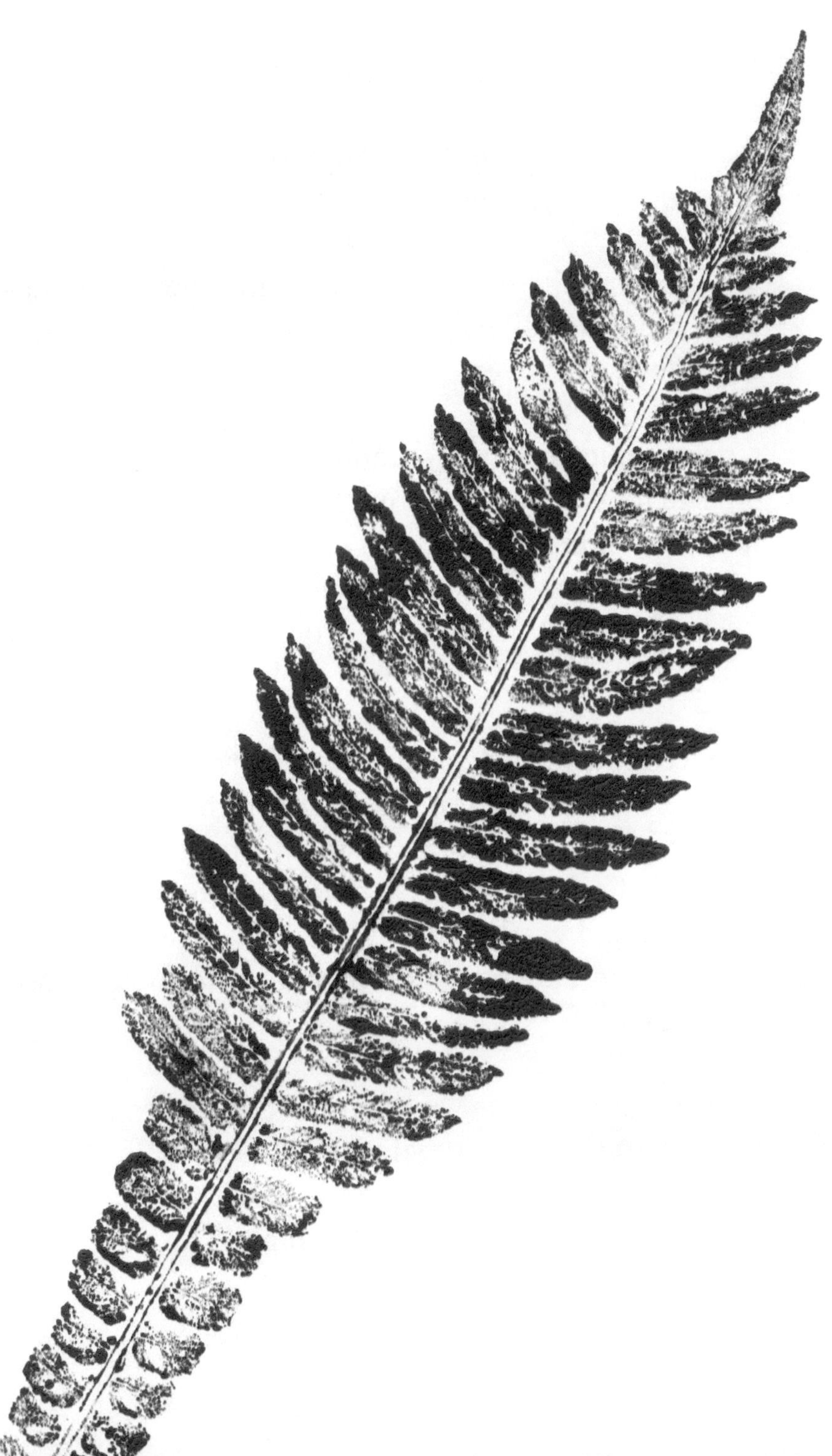

Coastal Mugwort
Artemisia suksdorfii

Crushing the leaves in your hand releases a pungent, sage-like fragrance. To me, it has a calming effect…

Coastal mugwort grows along the Pacific Coast, from Alaska down into northern California. At Sea Ranch, it appears streamside and in open coastal grasslands, especially along seasonal drainages where soil is sandy or disturbed. It holds its ground in wind and salt spray, where many neighboring plants struggle.

The leaves are divided and silvery beneath, giving the plant a soft, muted tone even on bright days. When flowering in late summer, narrow clusters of small, greenish flower heads rise above the foliage. Seeds are light and easily carried by wind. The plant also spreads by underground rhizomes, forming loose colonies.

The common name "mugwort" comes from older European Artemisia species once used to flavor ale; "mug" referred to the drinking vessel. Coastal mugwort carries some of that old, aromatic history.

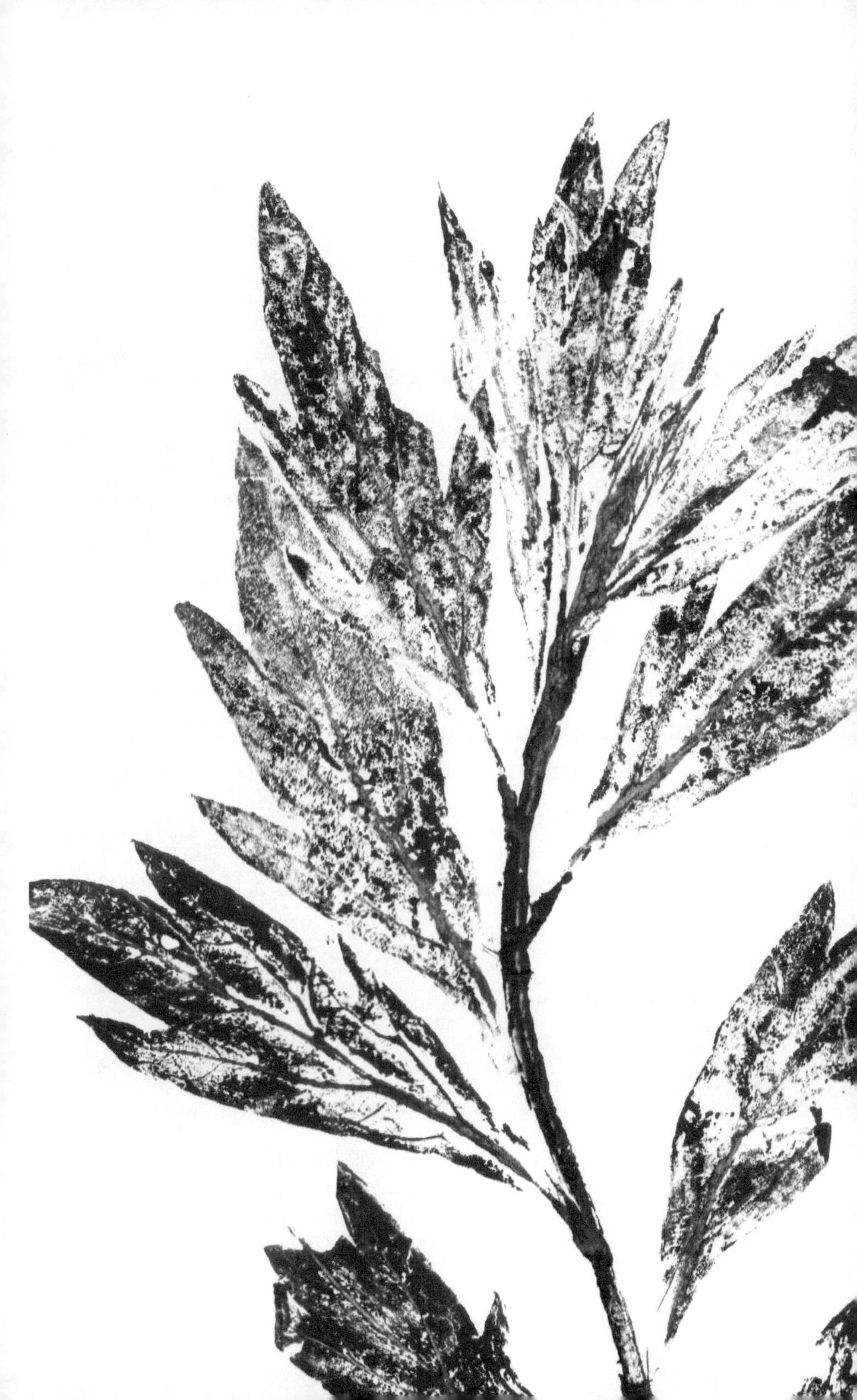

STREAMSIDE

Coast Angelica
Angelica hendersonii

With its many tiny flowers arranged in a large umbrella-like head, it stands tall…

At Sea Ranch, this native plant grows streamside as well as near the bluff trail and in open coastal grasslands. A sturdy perennial, it often reaches four to six feet in height.

In summer, large rounded clusters of small white to pale green flowers form broad umbels. They attract many insects, including native bees, flies, and small beetles. After flowering, flattened winged seeds develop and are carried by wind.

The common name "angelica" reflects a long herbal history. Angelica species were long valued in Europe for medicine and flavoring. Specific uses of this exact species are not well documented, though related angelicas were used as food and medicine in other regions.

Coast angelica, like many members of the carrot family, has sap that may cause skin irritation in sensitive individuals, especially when exposed to sunlight.

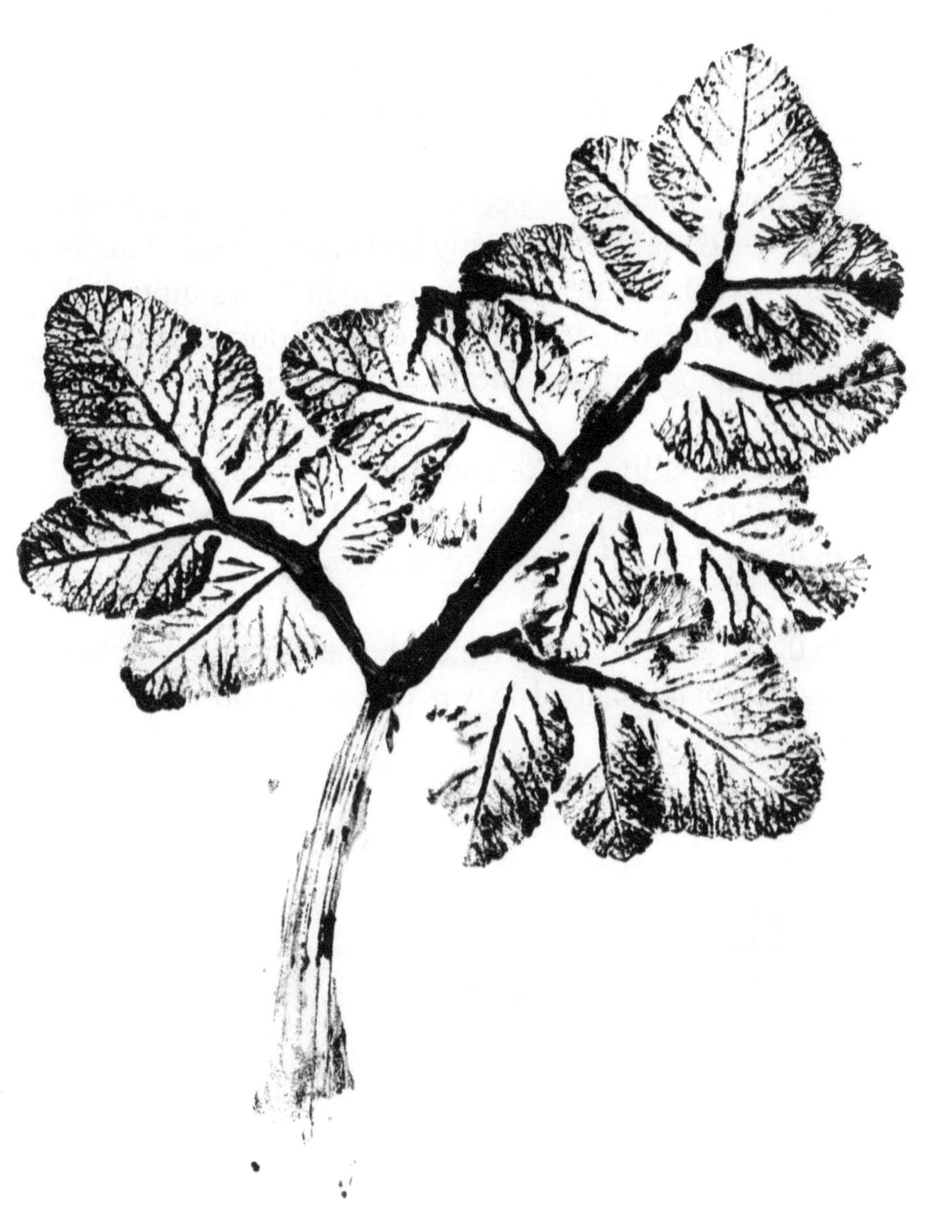

STREAMSIDE

Cow Parsnip (first-year)
Heracleum maximum

Cow parsnip is a perennial that may take several years before flowering and setting seed. This is a first-year rosette of leaves, which looks quite different, with rounded lobes instead of pointed tips. At first, I thought it was another plant entirely…

Large umbellifers like cow parsnip were sometimes associated with giants or powerful spirits because of their towering size and broad leaves.

In the second year (shown on the next page), it makes jagged, palm-shaped leaves and sends up its umbel of flowers.

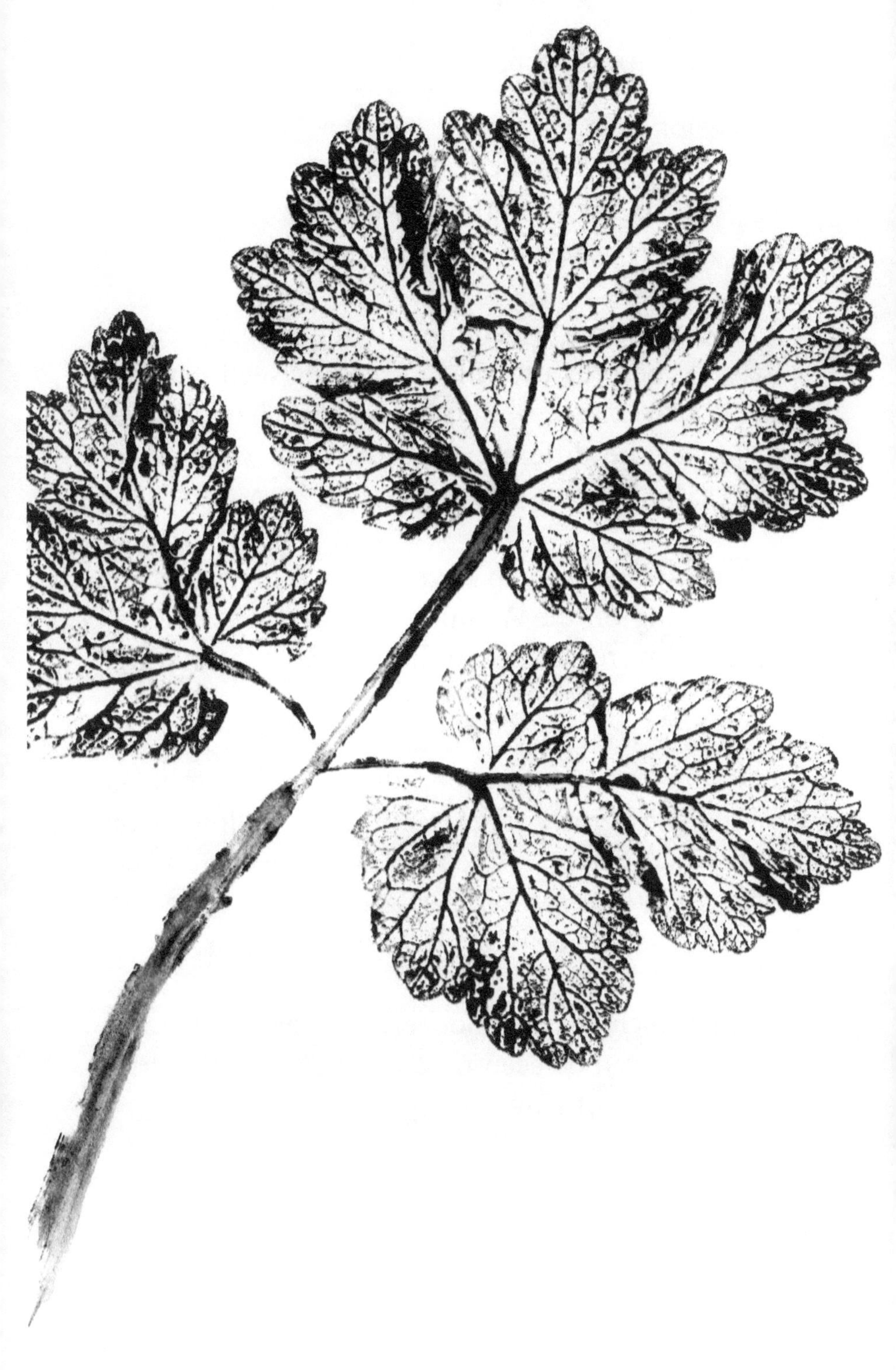

Cow Parsnip (second-year)
Heracleum maximum

Cow parsnip is a perennial that may take several years before flowering and setting seed. This is a second-year rosette, with jagged, palm-shaped leaves that look quite different from the rounded lobes of the first year (shown on the previous page).

The largest cow parsnip I ever saw was over five feet tall, growing on the Aleutian Islands alongside Angelica. We were careful on the rare days the sun was out, not to rub against the leaves…

Its sap can irritate skin, especially if sunlight follows. Cow parsnip grows large, with thick hollow stems and divided leaves that can span more than a foot across. In late spring and early summer, broad white flower clusters open outward in wide umbels.

At Sea Ranch, black phoebes, one of my favorite birds, can often be seen perched on top of the dried flat seed heads of cow parsnip.

The hollow stems were used by Indigenous peoples to make whistles or simple flutes for children.

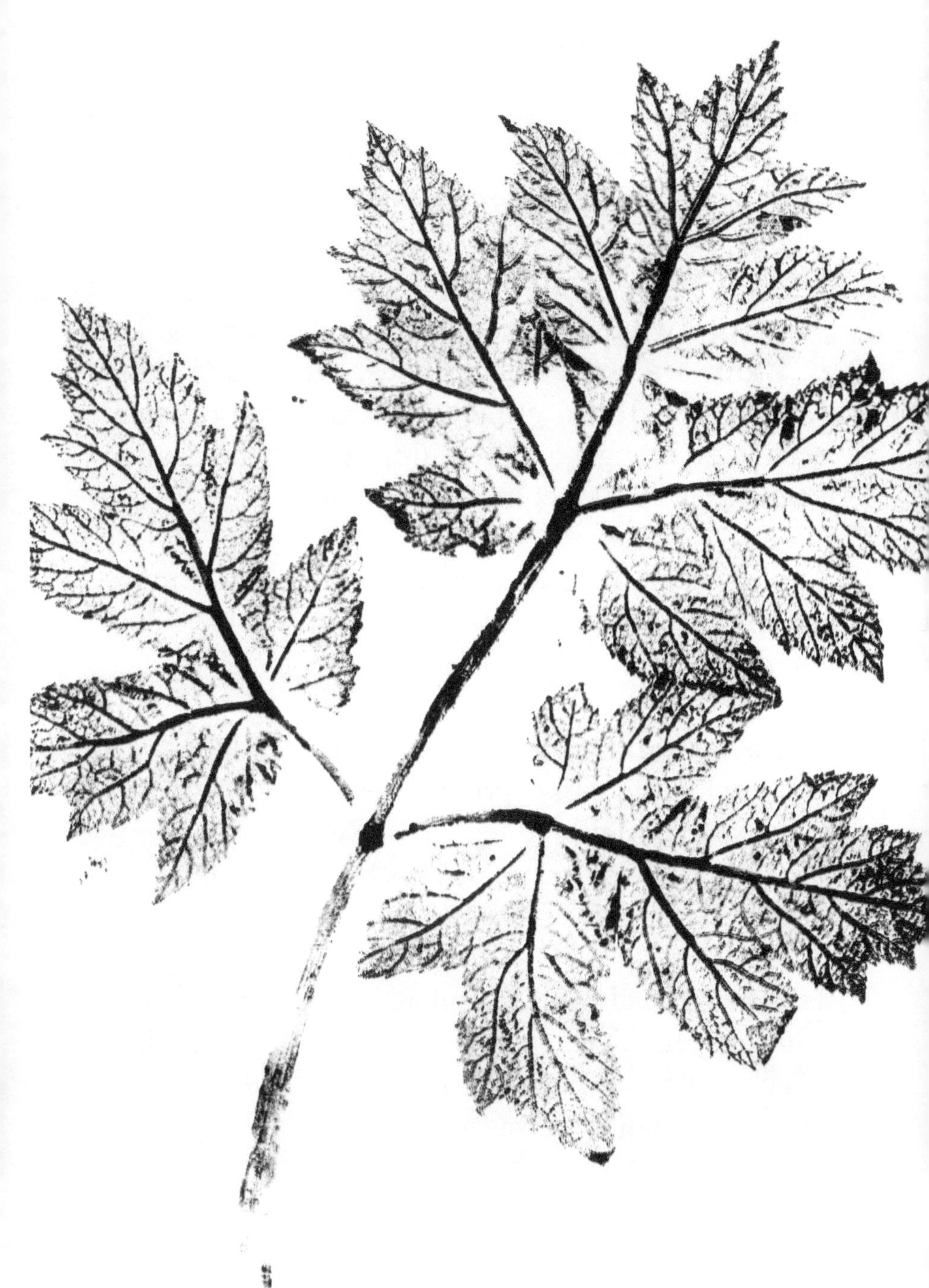

Arroyo Willow
Salix lasiolepis

Arroyo willow is a native California willow that grows along creeks, ponds, seeps, and other moist places. It can grow as a large shrub or small tree, with orange and red tipped branches, often reaching 15 to 30 feet in height.

The leaves are long and narrow, bright green above and paler beneath, sometimes softly hairy when young.

Like other willows, it produces soft, upright catkins in late winter to early spring, often before the leaves fully expand. Male and female flowers grow on separate plants. Male Arroyo catkins have 2 stamens and female catkins have glabrous (naked) ovaries.

Its roots spread widely and help stabilize streambanks, especially after heavy coastal rains. Broken branches that fall into damp soil can sometimes root and grow into new plants.

Indigenous peoples throughout California used willow branches for basketry, fish traps, cordage, and structural frames.

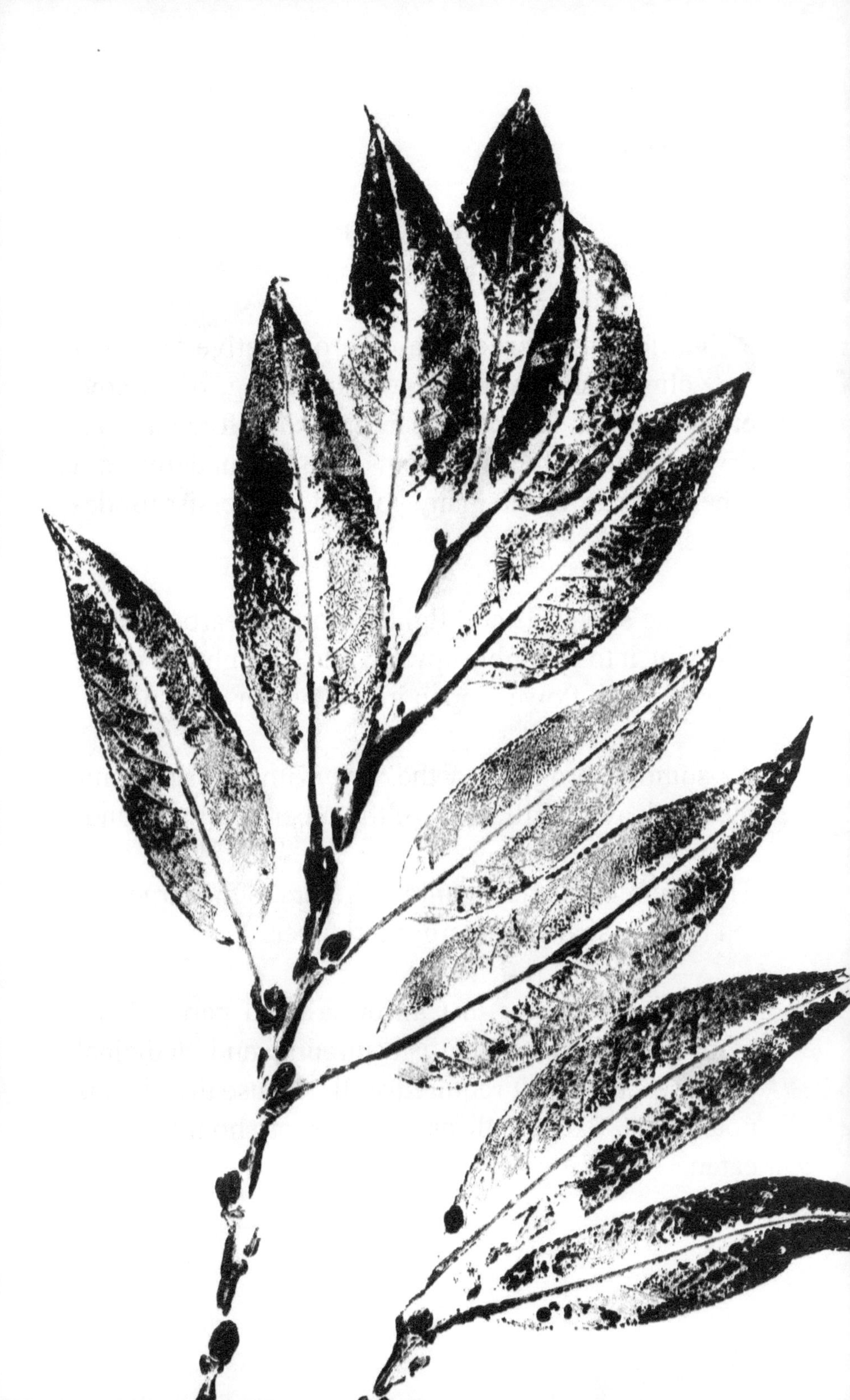

California Manroot
Marah fabacea

California manroot is a vigorous native vine that climbs shrubs and fences in spring, often covering hillsides in fresh green growth before summer dryness sets in. It grows from a massive underground tuber that can weigh many pounds and persist for decades.

The vine's tendrils coil tightly around nearby plants, allowing it to scramble upward into sunlight. Its white to pale green flowers open in late winter and spring.

As summer progresses, the vine withers back completely, leaving little sign of the tuber below ground.

The common name "manroot" refers to the large, often human-shaped underground tuber.

Indigenous peoples in California used parts of the plant carefully for soap, fish stunning, and medicinal purposes, though it required skill because the plant is potentially toxic. California manroot should not be eaten.

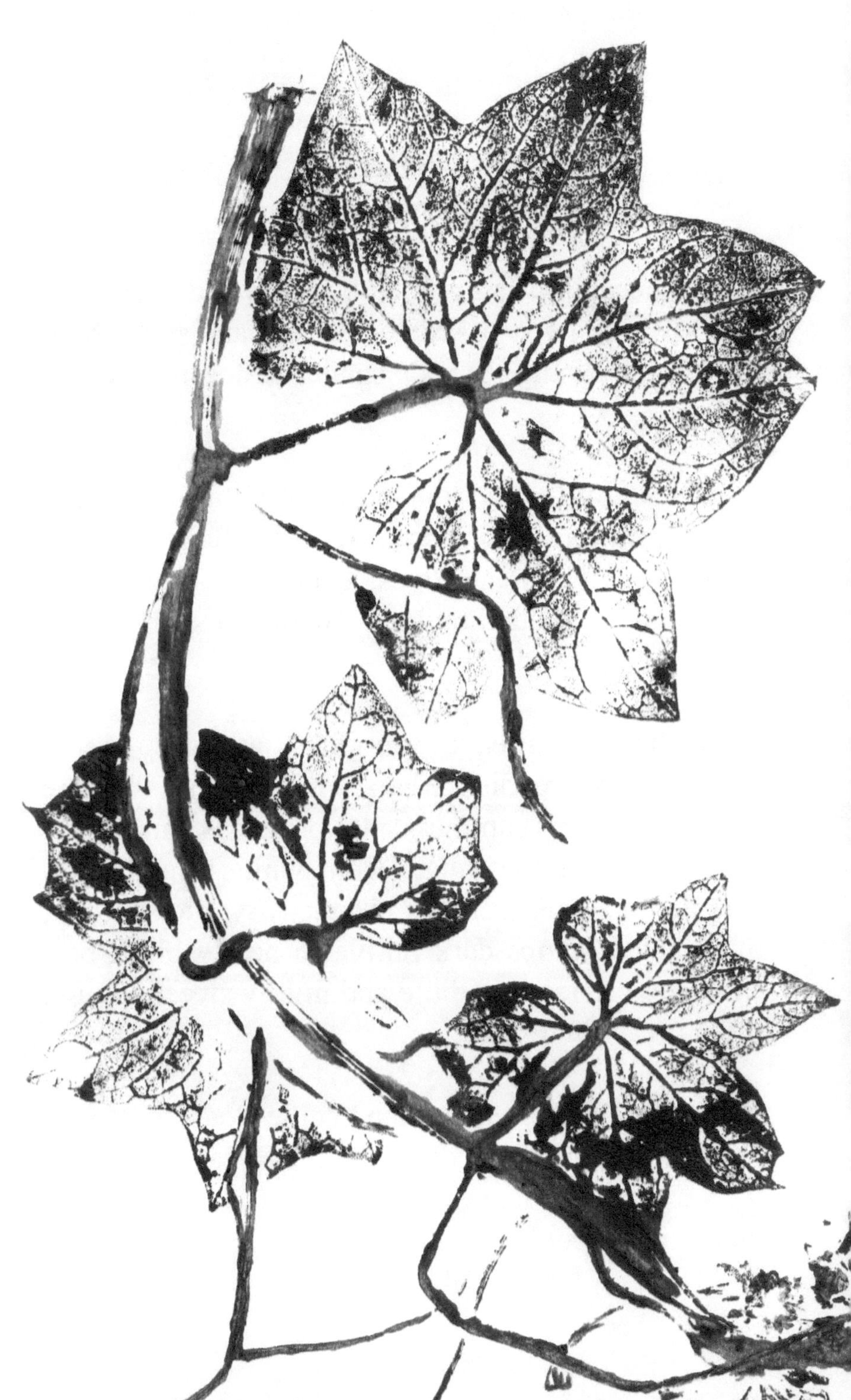

WOODLAND

Salal
Gaultheria shallon

On ocean bluffs buffeted by wind and in the forest, strong, wax-coated leaves and pink, bell-like flowers hang. Sun or shade, it doesn't care. It thrives…

Salal is a low, evergreen shrub native to the Pacific Coast from California north to Alaska. It forms dense thickets along forest edges, beneath coastal pines, and in moist, shaded ravines. There is a short trail at Sea Ranch named after it.

Its leathery, oval leaves are glossy and deep green, often turning reddish when winter comes. In late spring and early summer, salal produces small, urn-shaped flowers that range from white to soft pink. The flowers hang in short clusters. By late summer, the plant develops dark purple to nearly black berries. The berries are edible and mildly sweet, though often mealy in texture.

Indigenous peoples along the Pacific Coast harvested salal berries fresh and dried them into cakes for winter storage. The leaves were also used medicinally, including as poultices and teas.

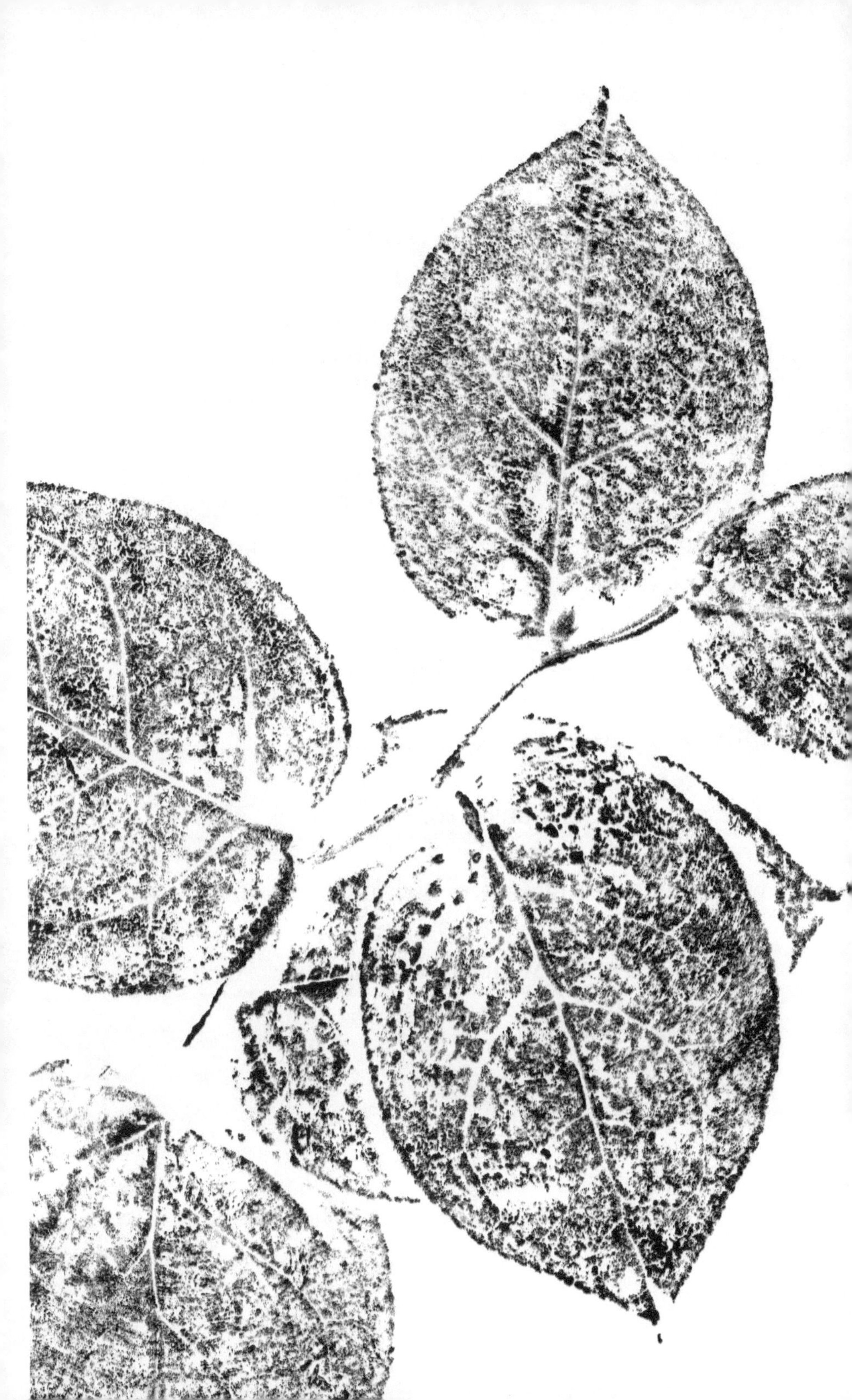

WOODLAND

Pacific Sanicle
Sanicula crassicaulis

After a morning walk, I have to remove a few prickly seeds from my socks…

It is found along the Pacific Coast from central California north into Oregon and Washington. At Sea Ranch, it grows in coastal grasslands, on open bluffs, and in lightly shaded forest edges.

Pacific Sanicle remains relatively low to the ground, usually under two feet tall. It blooms from late spring into early summer along the coast.

The plant forms a basal rosette of thick, glossy, dark green leaves. In spring, it sends up short stems topped with small yellow to greenish umbrella-shaped clusters. After flowering, the plant produces small, rounded fruits covered with hooked bristles. These bristly fruits cling to fur or clothing.

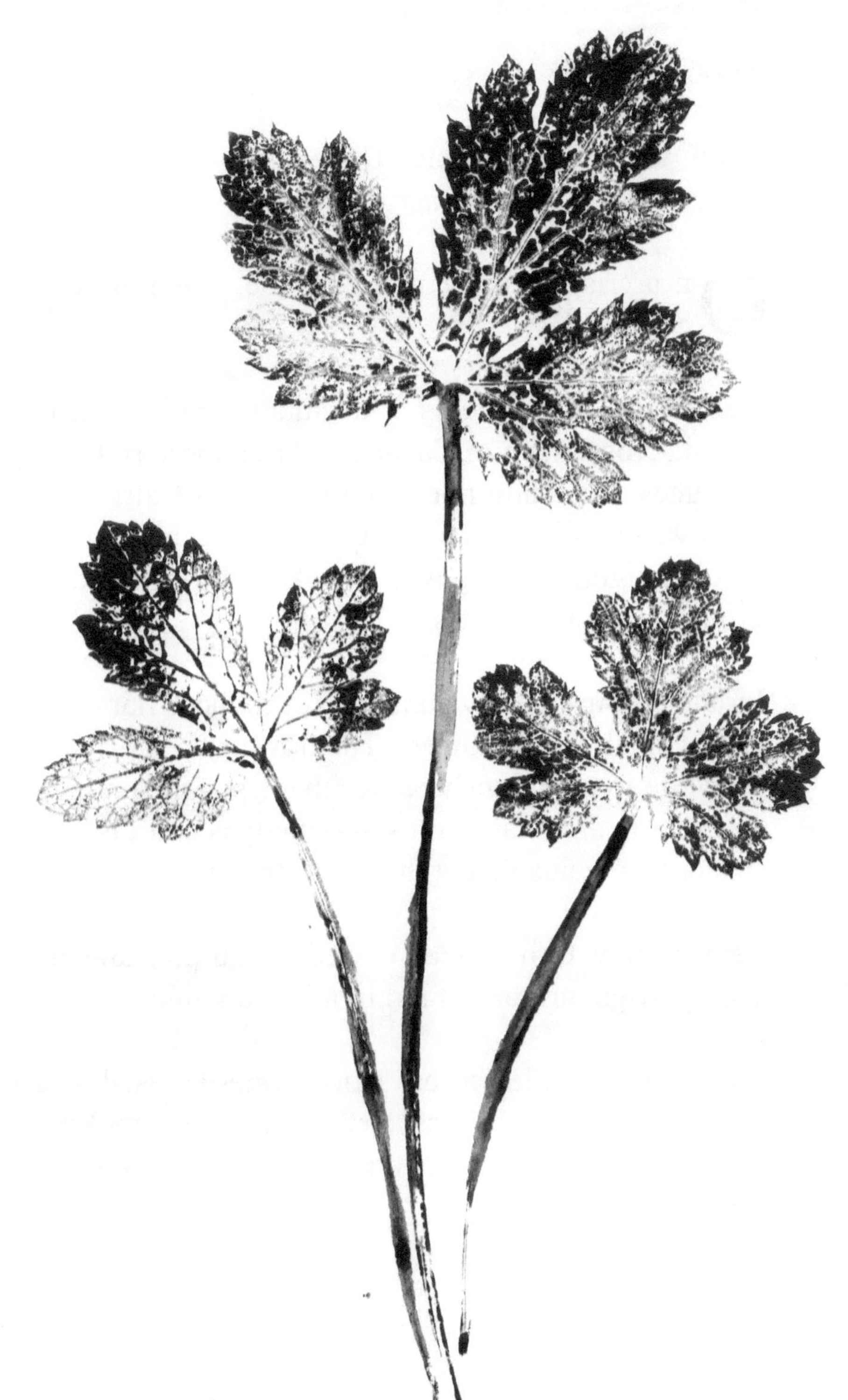

WOODLAND

Red Osier Dogwood
Cornus sericea

On a crisp October morning, the subtle autumn colors…

Red Osier Dogwood is a deciduous native shrub found across much of Canada and the northern United States, including northern and central California. It grows in moist habitats. It typically reaches 6 to 12 feet in height, forming dense thickets through underground spreading stems.

In late spring to early summer, it produces flat clusters of small white flowers. The flowers are followed by white to pale bluish berries that ripen in summer. The leaves are oval, with smooth edges and distinctive curved veins that arch toward the tip.

Leaves may turn shades of red or purple, and its young twigs turn bright red in fall and winter.

Indigenous peoples across North America used Red Osier Dogwood for basketry, tools, and smoking mixtures; the inner bark was sometimes included in traditional blends.

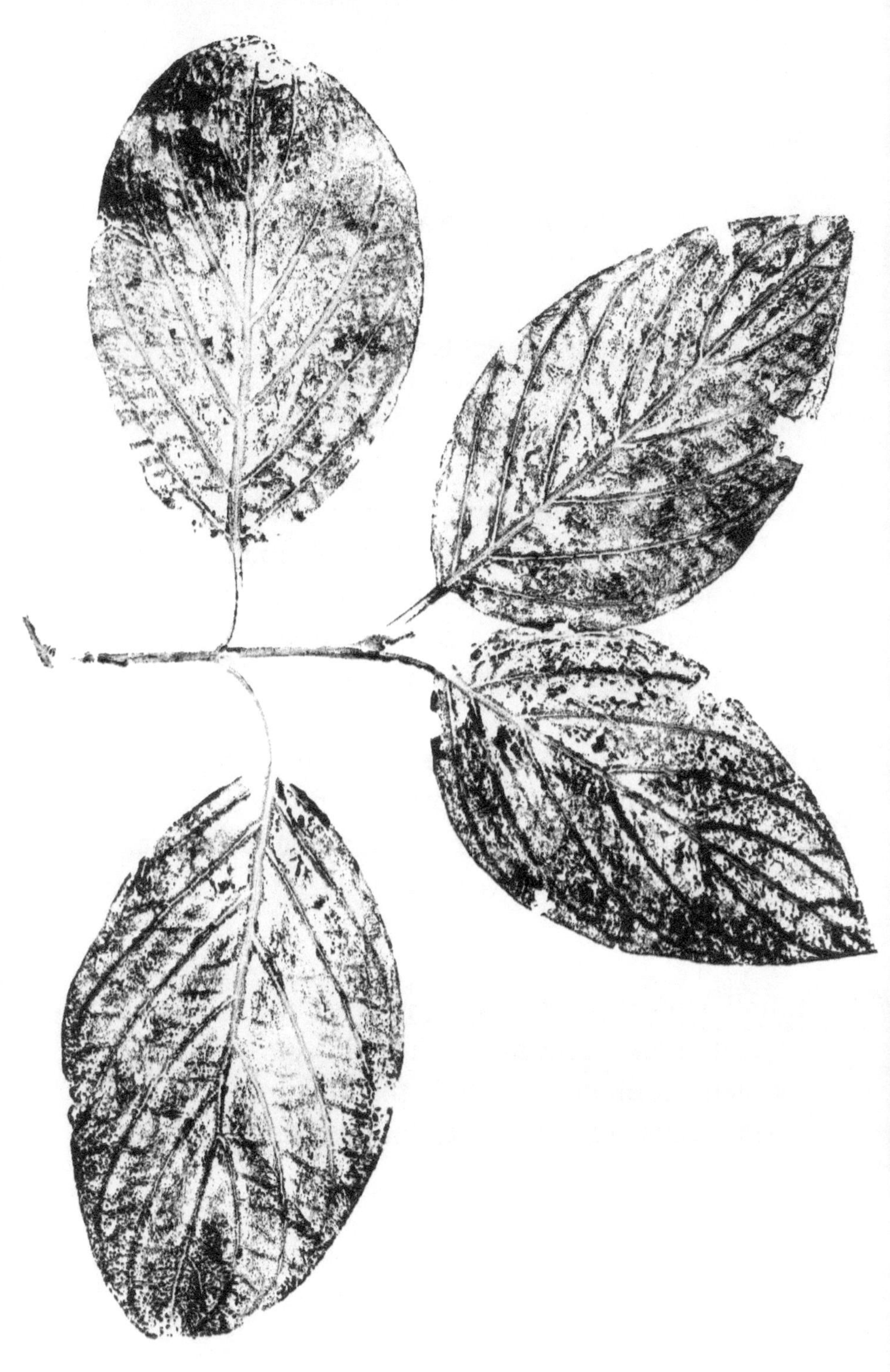

WOODLAND

Mountain Sweet Cicely
Osmorhiza berteroi

In January, these sweet leaves come up, a welcome bit of fresh green. Be patient, and soon small white flowers will appear along the trail…

Mountain sweet cicely is a native woodland perennial found in moist forests and shaded mountain slopes of western North America. In California, it grows in cool, damp places, especially in mixed conifer forests and along shaded streambanks.

The plant sends up delicate stems in spring, usually one to three feet tall. Its leaves are finely divided and fern-like, giving the plant a soft, airy appearance. When crushed, the leaves and roots have a sweet, anise-like scent.

Small white flowers bloom in loose clusters in spring, typical of the carrot family. The flowers are followed by slender, elongated seeds that taper at both ends. These seeds cling lightly to fur or clothing.

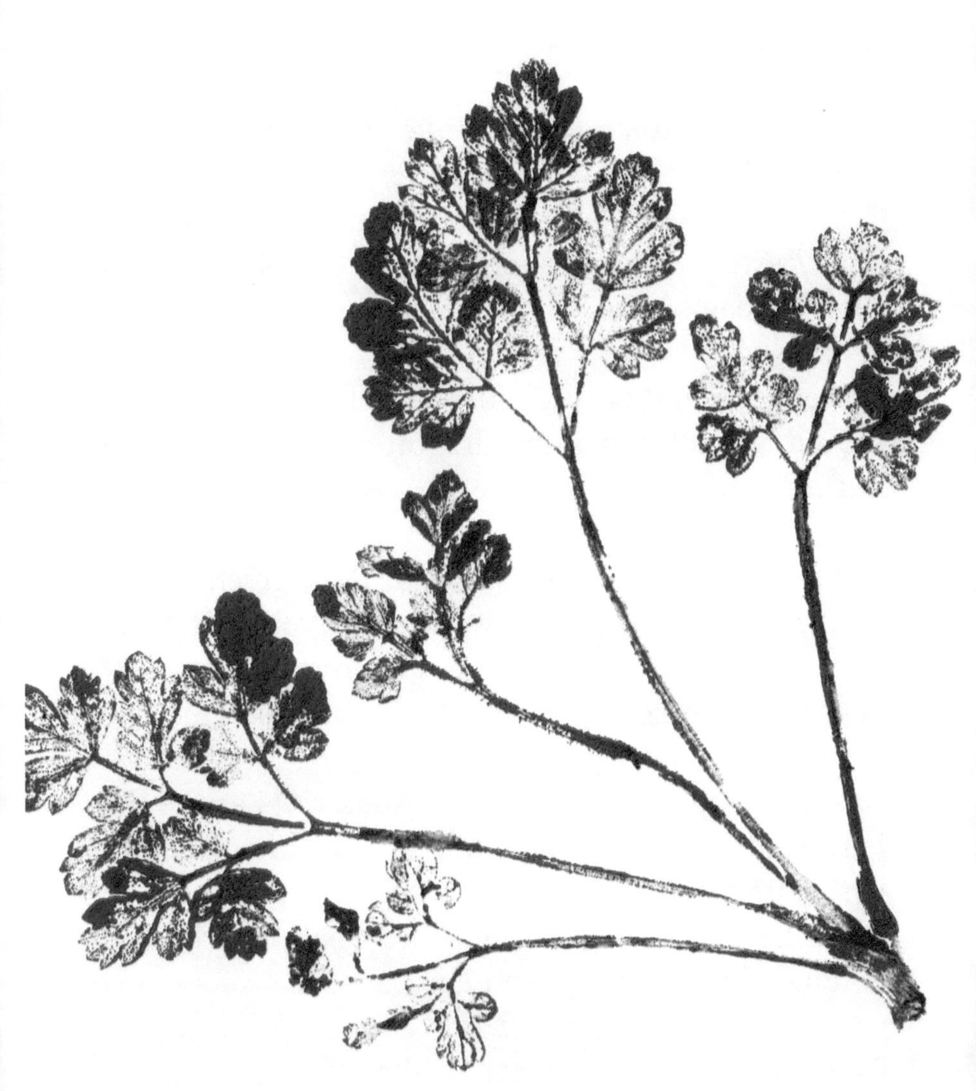

WOODLAND

Western Rattlesnake Plantain
Goodyera oblongifolia

Western Rattlesnake Plantain is a small evergreen orchid native to western North America.

At Sea Ranch, it grows in the quiet forest understory, tucked beneath pines and firs, often partly hidden in duff.

The plant forms a low rosette of dark green leaves marked with a pale, net-like pattern of veins. The leaf markings are present year-round and make the plant easy to recognize even when not in bloom.

In summer, a slender flowering stalk rises above the leaves, often 6 to 18 inches tall. Small white to greenish-white flowers spiral along the upper part of the stem. Each flower is delicate and easily overlooked among surrounding forest plants.

The common name "rattlesnake plantain" comes from the mottled leaf pattern, which resembles the skin of a rattlesnake. "Plantain" refers only to the leaf shape, not to the edible plantain herb.

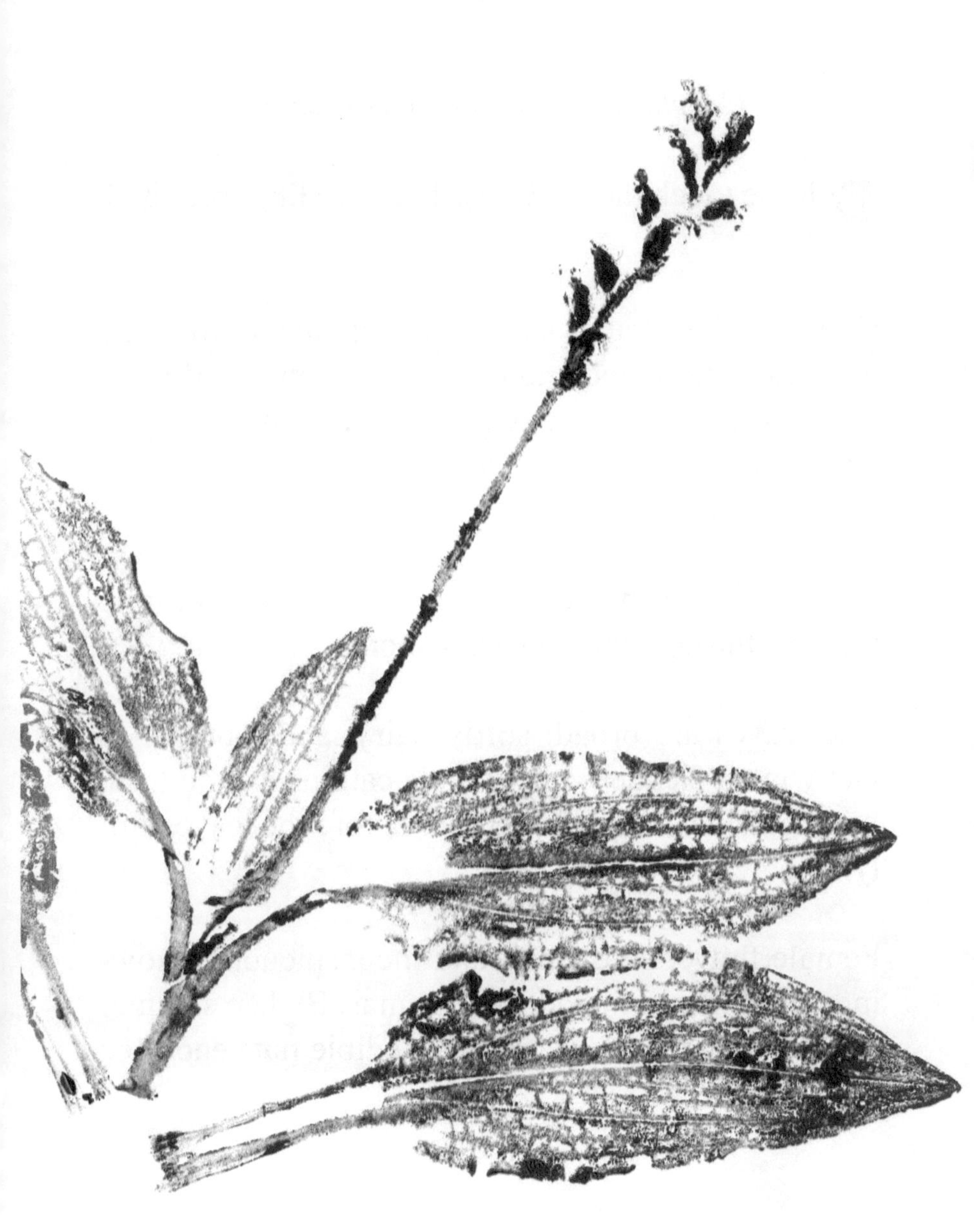

WOODLAND

Hazelnut
Corylus cornuta subsp. *californica*

P lease touch these leaves. They are like soft, thick velvet…

California hazelnut is a native deciduous shrub found in forests and woodland edges across much of California. It often grows along streams, on moist slopes, and in openings within mixed evergreen and oak woodlands.

It typically reaches 6 to 12 feet in height, forming thickets through underground shoots.

The leaves are broad, softly hairy, and toothed. In late winter, slender yellow male catkins dangle from bare branches, releasing pollen before the leaves fully emerge.

Female flowers are small and inconspicuous, showing only tiny red thread-like stigmas. By late summer to early fall, the plant produces edible nuts enclosed in a long, beaked husk.

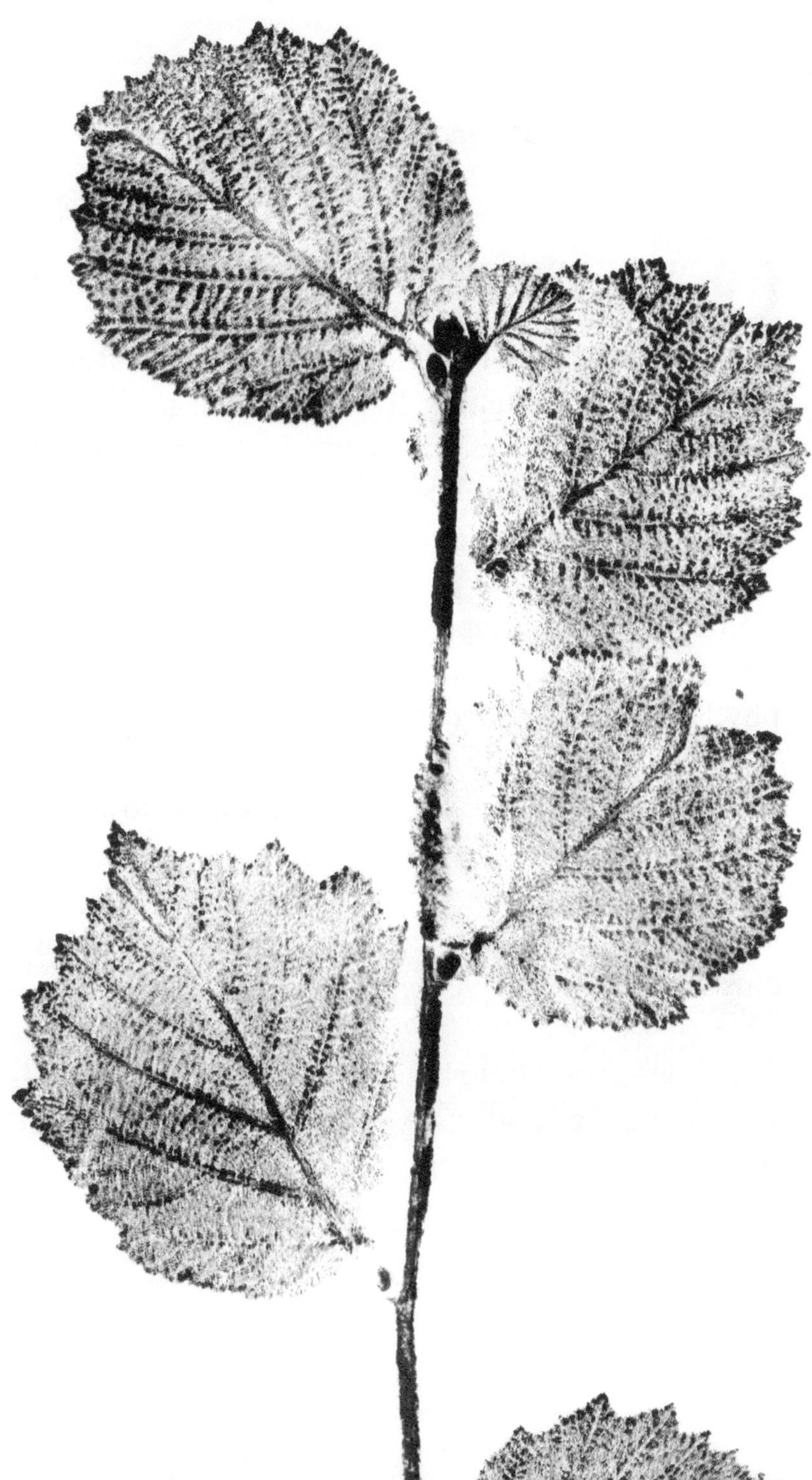

WOODLAND

California Wild Grape
Vitis californica

California wild grape is a native deciduous vine found along streams, riverbanks, and moist woodland edges in much of California. The fruit can be sharply tart, staining fingers purple. It climbs by means of slender, curling tendrils that wrap around shrubs, trees, and fences. The vine can stretch for many yards, spilling over trees along the creeks.

California wild grape and other North American grape species contributed to the development of phylloxera-resistant rootstocks.

Its leaves are broad and heart-shaped, with toothed edges and a soft texture when young. In spring, small greenish flowers appear in loose clusters. By late summer to early fall, the plant produces dangling clusters of dark purple to nearly black grapes.

The grapes are edible but often tart and full of seeds. In autumn, the leaves may turn shades of yellow, red, or bronze before dropping to the ground.

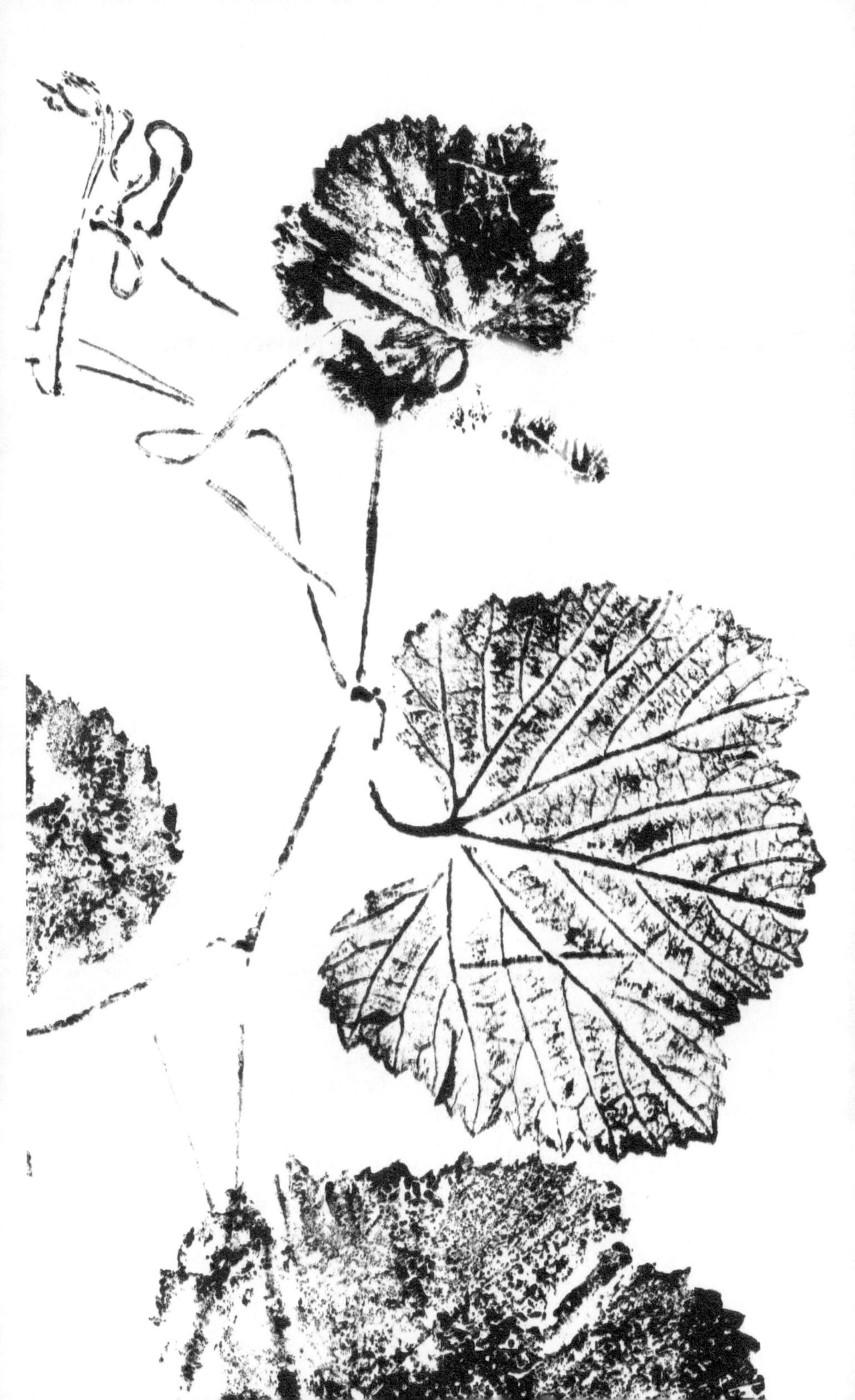

WOODLAND

Huckleberry
Vaccinium ovatum

Huckleberry almost asks us to pause, gather, and share…

At Sea Ranch, huckleberry thrives beneath coastal pines and firs, often forming dense understory patches along forest trails. The name "huckleberry" is used for several related species; along the coast, this one is commonly called evergreen huckleberry.

It is an evergreen shrub, typically 3 to 6 feet tall, though it can grow taller in sheltered sites. The leaves are small, glossy, and oval, with fine serrations along the edges.

New growth often emerges with reddish or bronze tones before turning deep green. In spring, small urn-shaped flowers—white to pink—hang in short clusters.

By late summer, dark purple to nearly black berries ripen among the leaves. They are edible and sweet to mildly tart, often richer in flavor than many cultivated blueberries. Some years the berries are abundant, and some years there are almost none.

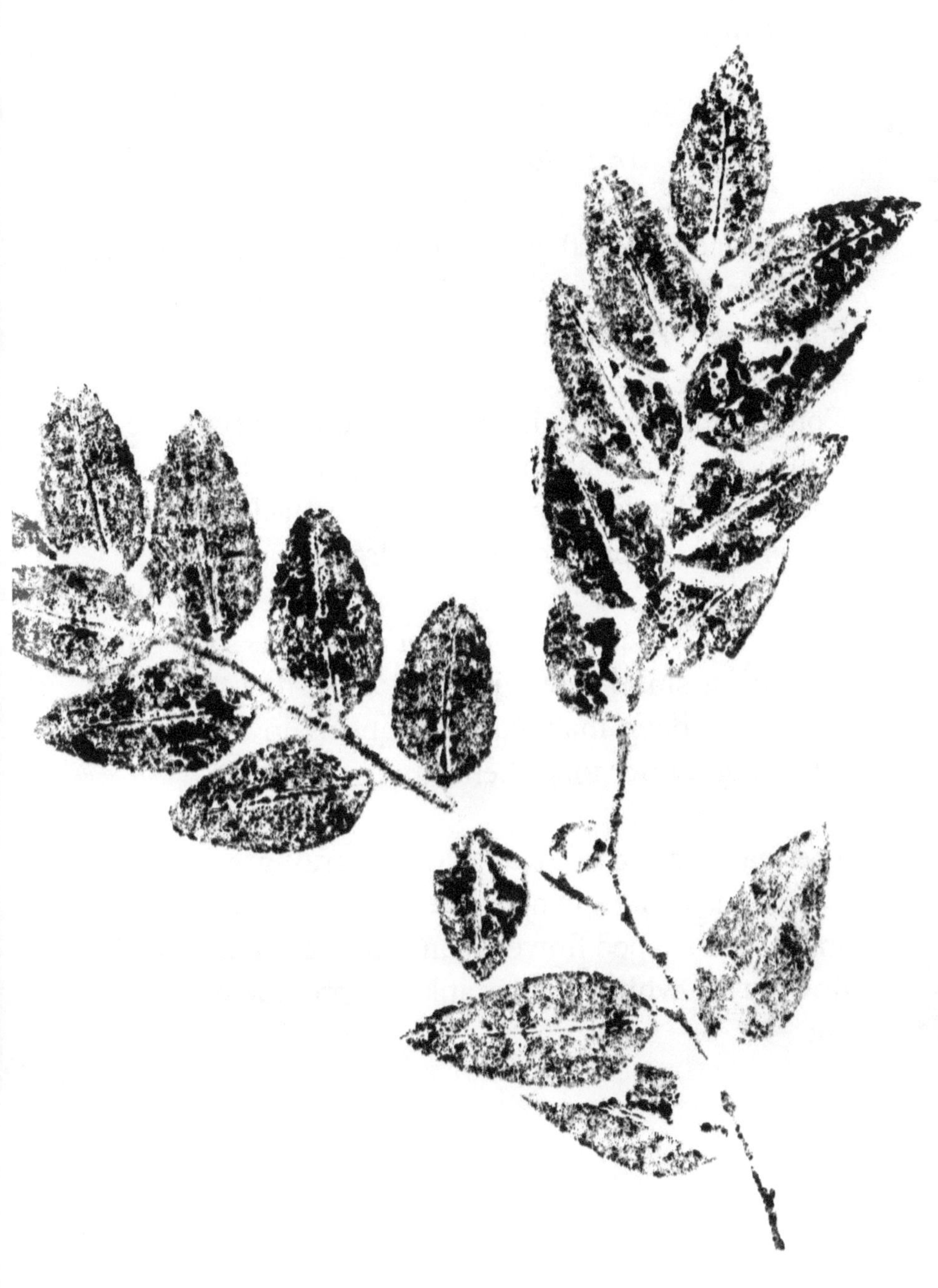

WOODLAND

Manzanita
Arctostaphylos manzanita

I have collected these beautiful dark red branches to make magic wands and garden features, where migrating birds often perch and rest...

Common manzanita is an evergreen shrub native to California, especially in chaparral, coastal scrub, and open woodlands. It grows on dry, well-drained soils and is well adapted to summer drought.

It typically reaches 6 to 15 feet in height, sometimes forming a small tree with age. The smooth bark is reddish to deep mahogany and peels in thin layers, revealing lighter tones beneath.

The leaves are oval, leathery, and gray-green to bluish-green. In late winter to early spring, clusters of small, urn-shaped flowers hang from branch tips. The flowers are white to pale pink and provide early nectar.

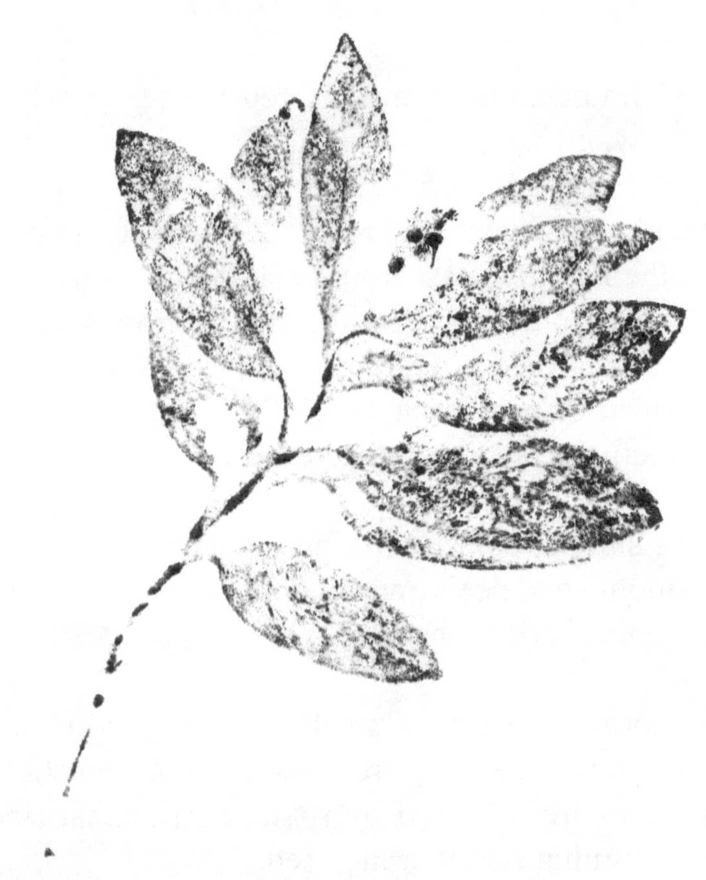

WOODLAND

Madrone
Arbutus menziesii

The hanging clumps of red berries attract cedar waxwings, one of my favorite birds…

Pacific madrone is a broadleaf evergreen tree native to the Pacific Coast from central California north to British Columbia. In California, it grows in coastal forests, mixed evergreen woodlands, and on well-drained slopes. It can reach 30 to 80 feet in height, sometimes taller in protected sites.

The smooth bark is striking—reddish-orange to cinnamon—and peels away in thin sheets to reveal fresh greenish bark beneath.

In spring, clusters of small white to pale pink, urn-shaped flowers hang from the ends of branches. The flowers are followed by round berries that ripen in fall, turning bright orange-red.

Madrone wood is dense and hard, burning hot and long in a winter stove.

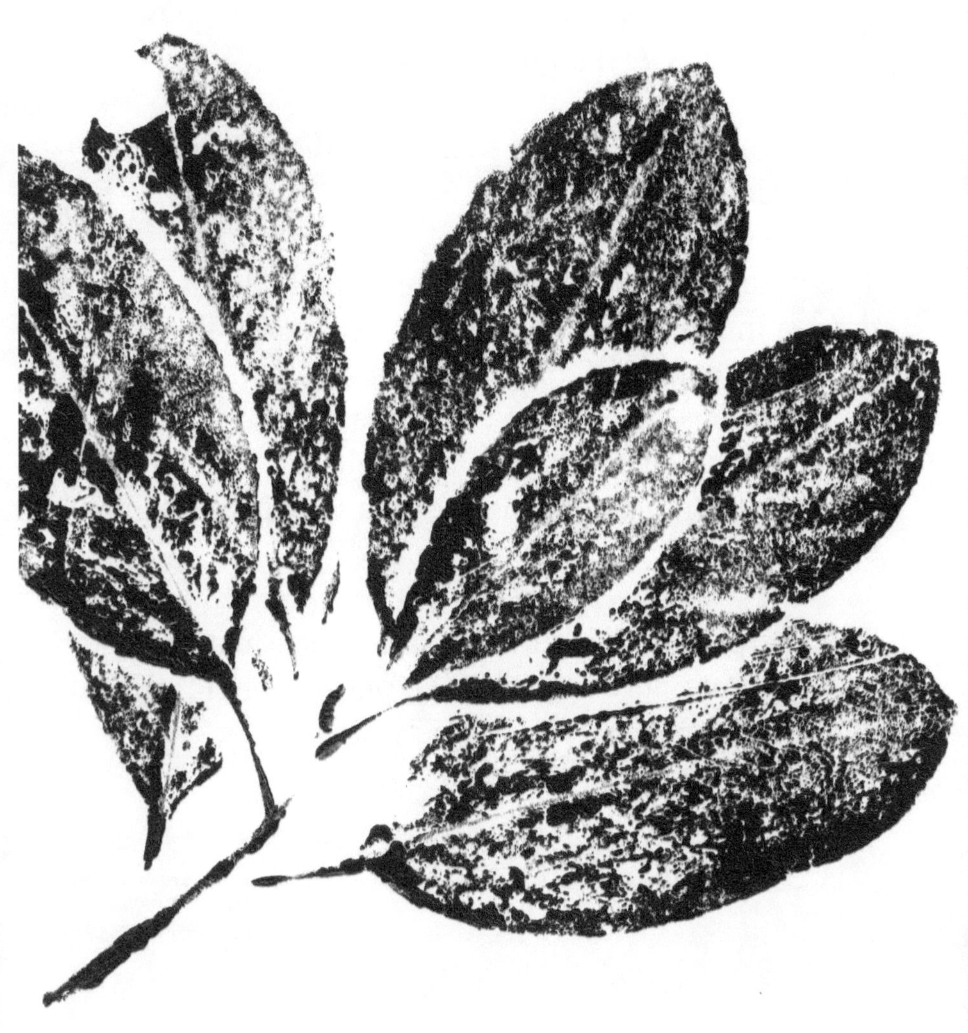

WOODLAND

Giant Chinquapin
Chrysolepis chrysophylla

Turn a leaf over and you'll see the rust-colored underside…

This small tree grows among manzanita and Labrador tea in the forest. It can grow as a dense shrub or as a tree reaching 30 to 100 feet in height, depending on conditions. The leaves are leathery and dark green above, with a distinctive golden, felt-like underside. In late spring to early summer, small yellowish flowers rise in upright clusters.

The sharp, spikey burs split open when mature, revealing glossy brown nuts. The nuts resemble small chestnuts and are edible when roasted.

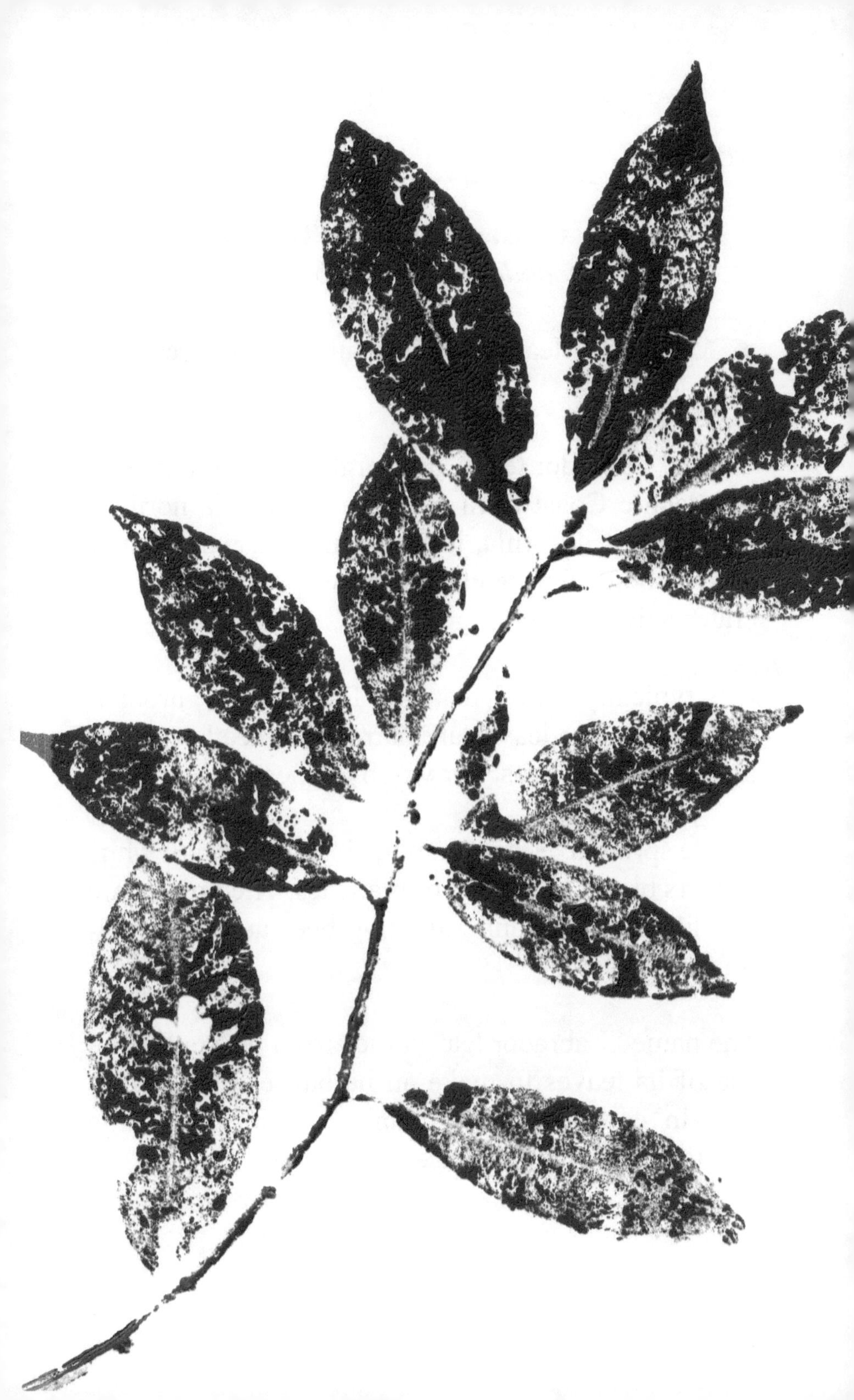

WOODLAND

Coastal Labrador Tea
Rhododendron columbianum

C rush the leaves and breathe in the resinous scent...

Coastal Labrador tea is an evergreen shrub native to the Pacific Coast from northern California north to Alaska. In California, it grows in cool, wet habitats such as bogs, fens, and forested seeps. The plant tolerates acidic, waterlogged soils.

It is typically 2 to 5 feet tall, forming low, aromatic thickets. The leaves are narrow and leathery, dark green above and rusty or woolly beneath.

In late spring to early summer, clusters of small white flowers bloom at the tips of branches. The flowers are star-like and fragrant, attracting bees and other pollinators.

The name "Labrador tea" comes from the traditional use of its leaves to make an herbal tea. The leaves contain compounds that can be harmful in large amounts and should be used with care.

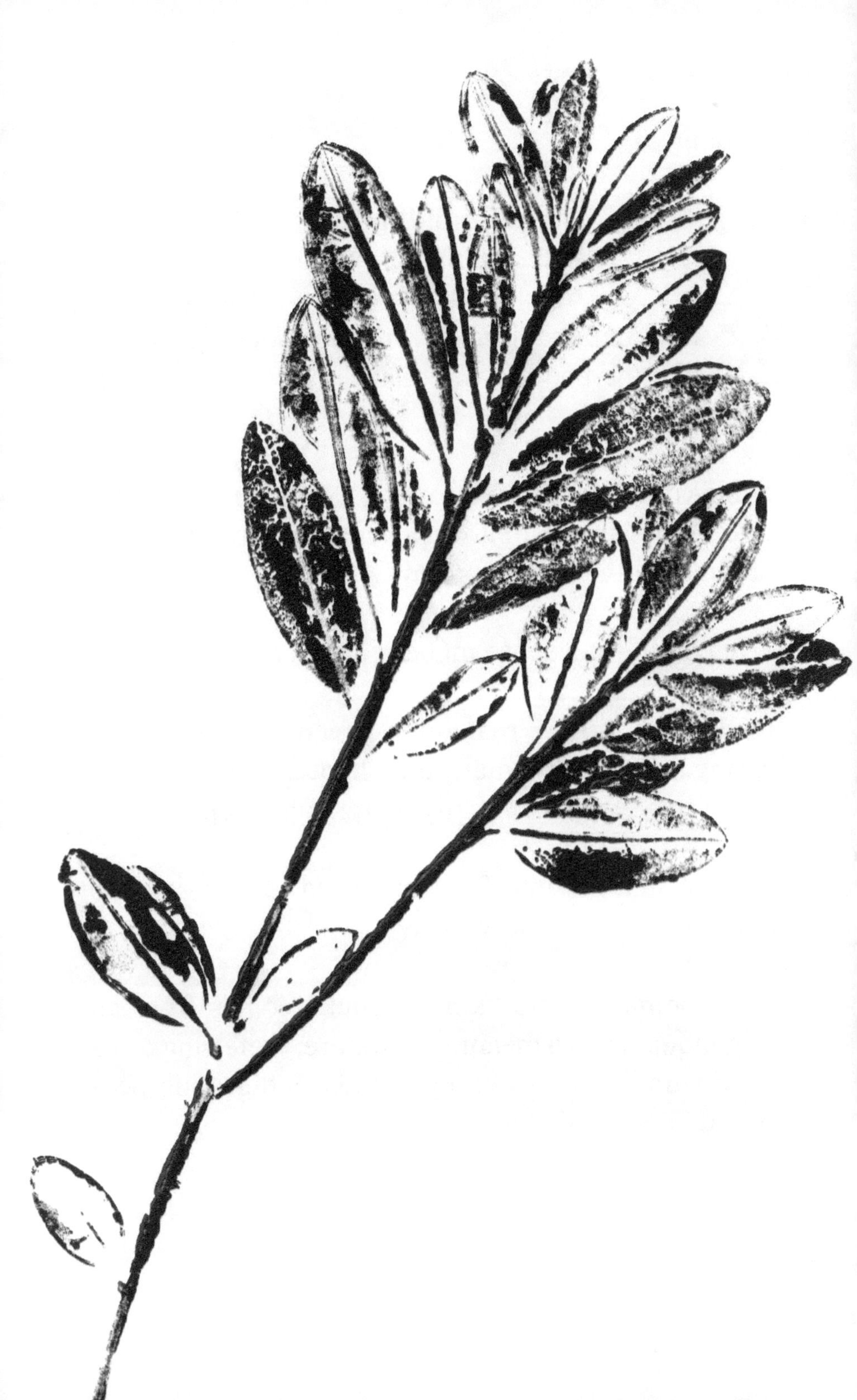

WOODLAND

Kinnikinnik
Arctostaphylos uva-ursi

Kinnikinnick tolerates wind and salt spray, much like the people who visit the northern California coast…

Kinnikinnick is a low-growing evergreen shrub native across much of the Northern Hemisphere, including northern and coastal California.

The plant forms dense mats through creeping woody stems that root as they spread. Its leaves are small, thick, and glossy, remaining green year-round. In spring, clusters of small, urn-shaped flowers bloom at the tips of stems, usually white to pale pink.

By late summer into fall, bright red berries develop and often persist into winter.

The common name "kinnikinnick" comes from an Algonquian word meaning "mixture," referring to its use in traditional smoking blends. Indigenous peoples across North America used dried leaves in ceremonial and social settings.

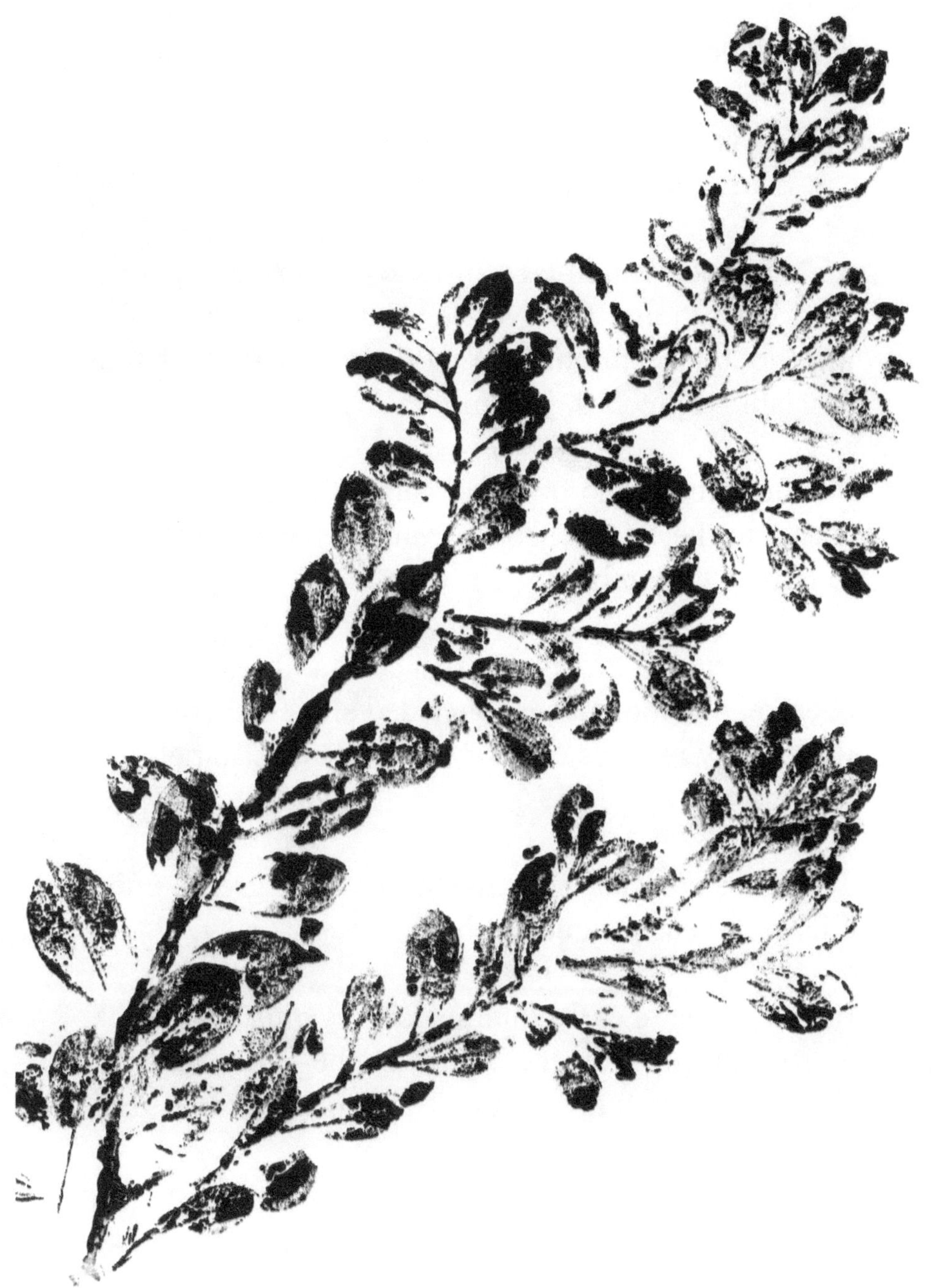

WOODLAND

Pacific Rhododendron
Rhododendron macrophyllum

Gardeners might try to mimic the perfectly placed landscaping that Mother Nature does by planting rhododendron, but the wild ones, with their free and lanky branches, just smile…

Pacific Rhododendron is a broadleaf evergreen shrub native to the Pacific Coast from northern California to British Columbia.

In California, it grows in moist coastal forests, mixed evergreen woodlands, and shaded slopes.
It typically reaches 6 to 15 feet in height, sometimes taller in protected sites.

The leaves are large, leathery, and dark green, often clustered near the ends of branches.

In late spring to early summer, showy clusters of pink to rose-purple flowers bloom at the tips of stems. Each flower is funnel-shaped and often marked with darker spots inside.

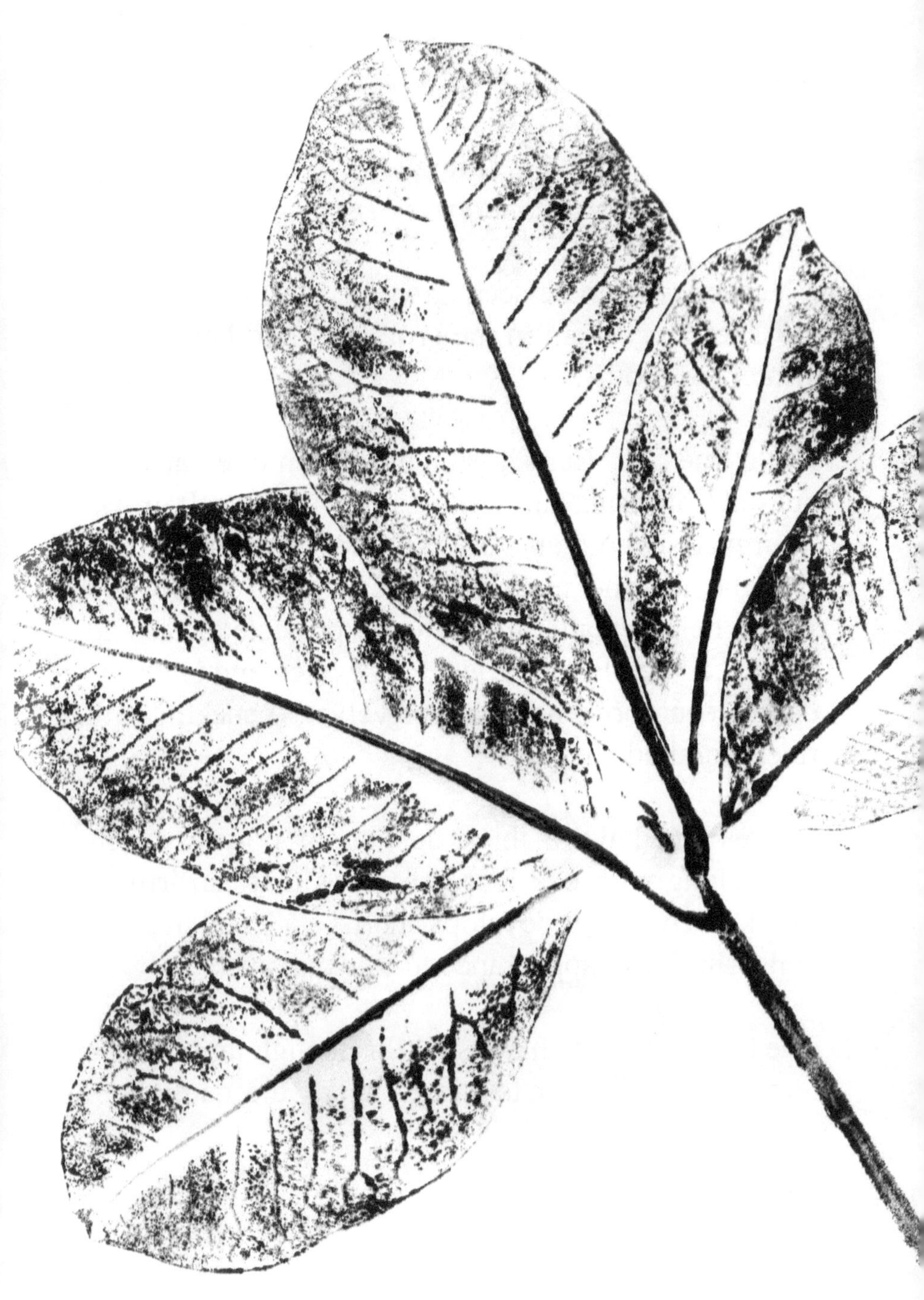

WOODLAND

Tanoak
Notholithocarpus densiflorus

Scrub jays can be seen carrying acorns in the fall. They bury them in the ground to find later in the winter for food…

Not a true oak, Tanoak is an evergreen tree native to coastal California and southwestern Oregon. It grows in mixed evergreen forests, often with redwood, Douglas-fir, and madrone. It can reach 40 to 100 feet in height, sometimes taller in protected sites and where fog persists. The leaves are thick and leathery, dark green above and pale or velvety beneath, with finely toothed edges.

Leaves can have a thick dusting of powdery mildew, along with oak leaf itch mites that can irritate the skin. By fall, it develops acorns enclosed in scaly cups, similar in appearance to true oaks.

The bark was once harvested for its high tannin content, used in leather tanning—hence the name "tanoak."

Tanoak forests have been heavily affected by sudden oak death in recent decades.

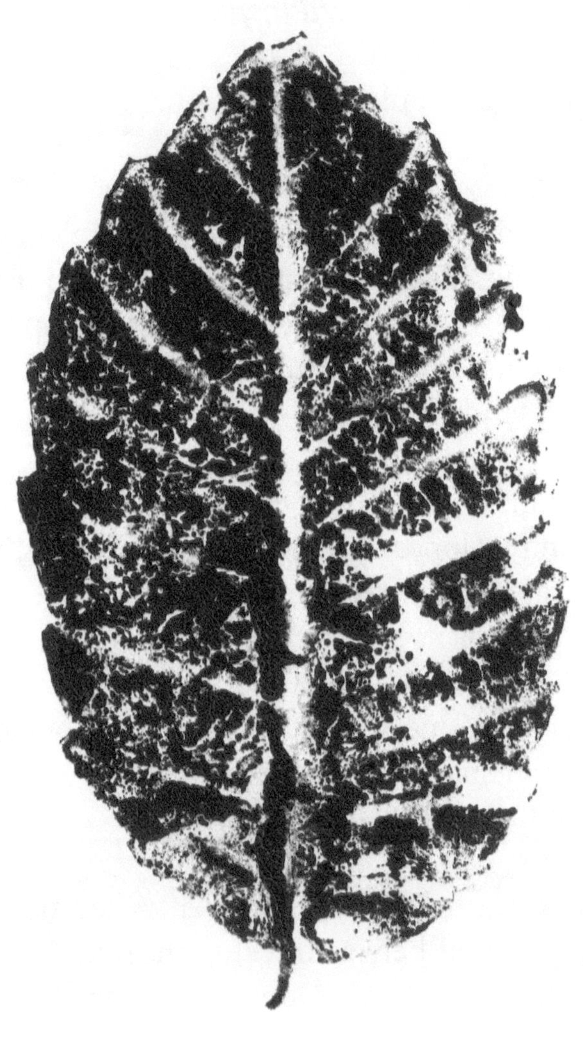

WOODLAND

California Honeysuckle
Lonicera hispidula

A hummingbird pleaser...

California honeysuckle is a twining native vine found in woodlands, chaparral, and coastal scrub through-out much of California. It climbs by wrapping its flexible stems around shrubs and small trees rather than using tendrils.

At Sea Ranch, it weaves through forest edges and along sunny slopes, often threading itself through coyote brush and young trees.

The leaves are oval and paired along the stem, often softly hairy. In late winter and spring, tubular flowers bloom in shades of pale pink, rose, or sometimes yellowish tones.

The flowers are long and slender. After flowering, clusters of round berries develop, turning bright red when mature. The berries are mildly toxic to humans and should not be eaten.

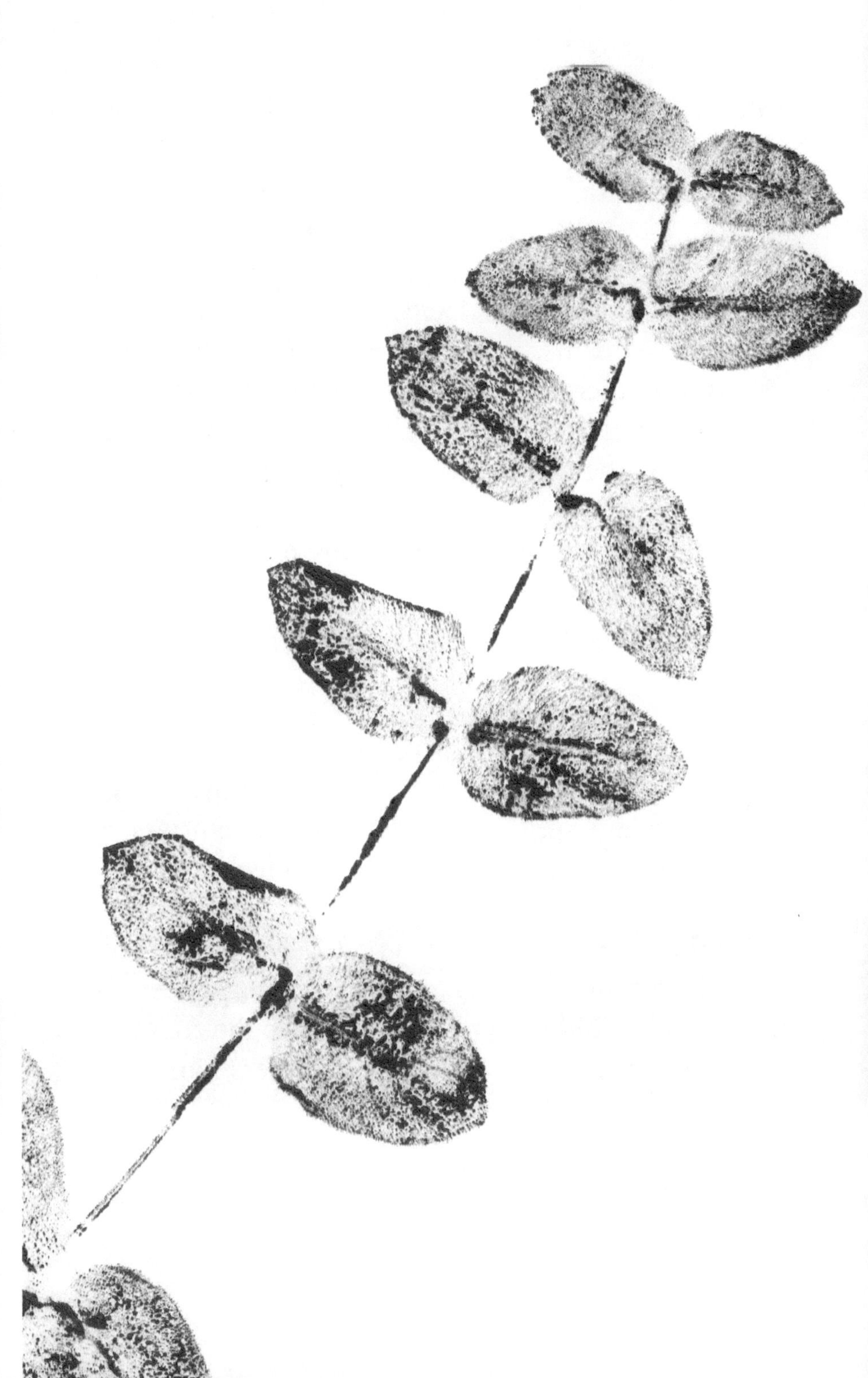

WOODLAND

Pacific Ninebark
Physocarpus capitatus

Pacific ninebark is a deciduous native shrub found along streams, wetlands, and moist forest edges from northern California to Alaska. In Montana, I have seen entire mountainsides turn red with ninebark during the first crisp-cold days of autumn…

In California, it grows mainly along the North Coast in riparian corridors and shaded drainages. It typically reaches 6 to 12 feet in height, creating arching thickets.

The leaves are three- to five-lobed, somewhat maple-like in shape, and turn yellow or yellow-orange in fall. In late spring to early summer, clusters of small white flowers bloom in rounded heads.

After flowering, inflated seed pods develop and turn reddish to brown as they mature. The bark peels in thin layers on older stems, giving rise to the common name "ninebark." The number nine refers loosely to the many layers of peeling bark.

Some stems grow so straight they were once used by Indigenous peoples for arrow shafts.

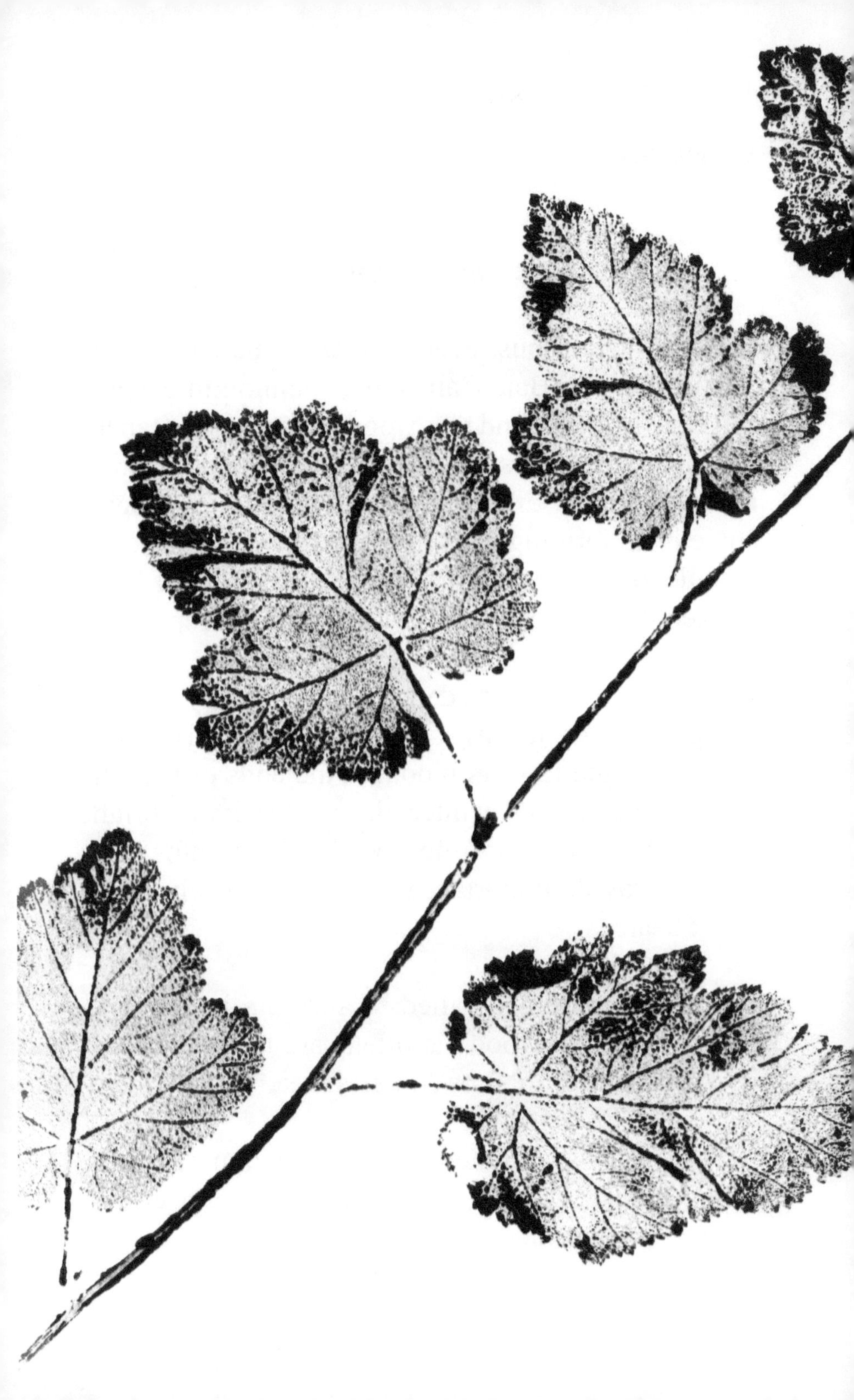

WOODLAND

Toyon
Heteromeles arbutifolia

Toyon is a robust evergreen shrub native to California and Baja California, common in chaparral, coastal scrub, and oak woodlands. At Sea Ranch, toyon appears on sunny hillsides and along forest margins. Plants often reach 6 to 15 feet in height, sometimes forming a small tree with age. It took me a while to find this plant. Then a friend asked if I had walked the "Toyon Trail" at Mill Bend Preserve…

The leaves are leathery, dark green, and finely toothed along the edges. In early summer, flat-topped clusters of small white flowers bloom at the ends of branches. By late fall and winter, dense clusters of bright red berries ripen and often persist for months. The berries provide important winter food for birds and black bears.

Toyon is sometimes called "California holly," and the name "Hollywood" is often said to derive from its abundance in the Los Angeles area.

Raw berries are somewhat bitter and may cause stomach upset if eaten; cooked berries have been traditionally consumed in moderation.

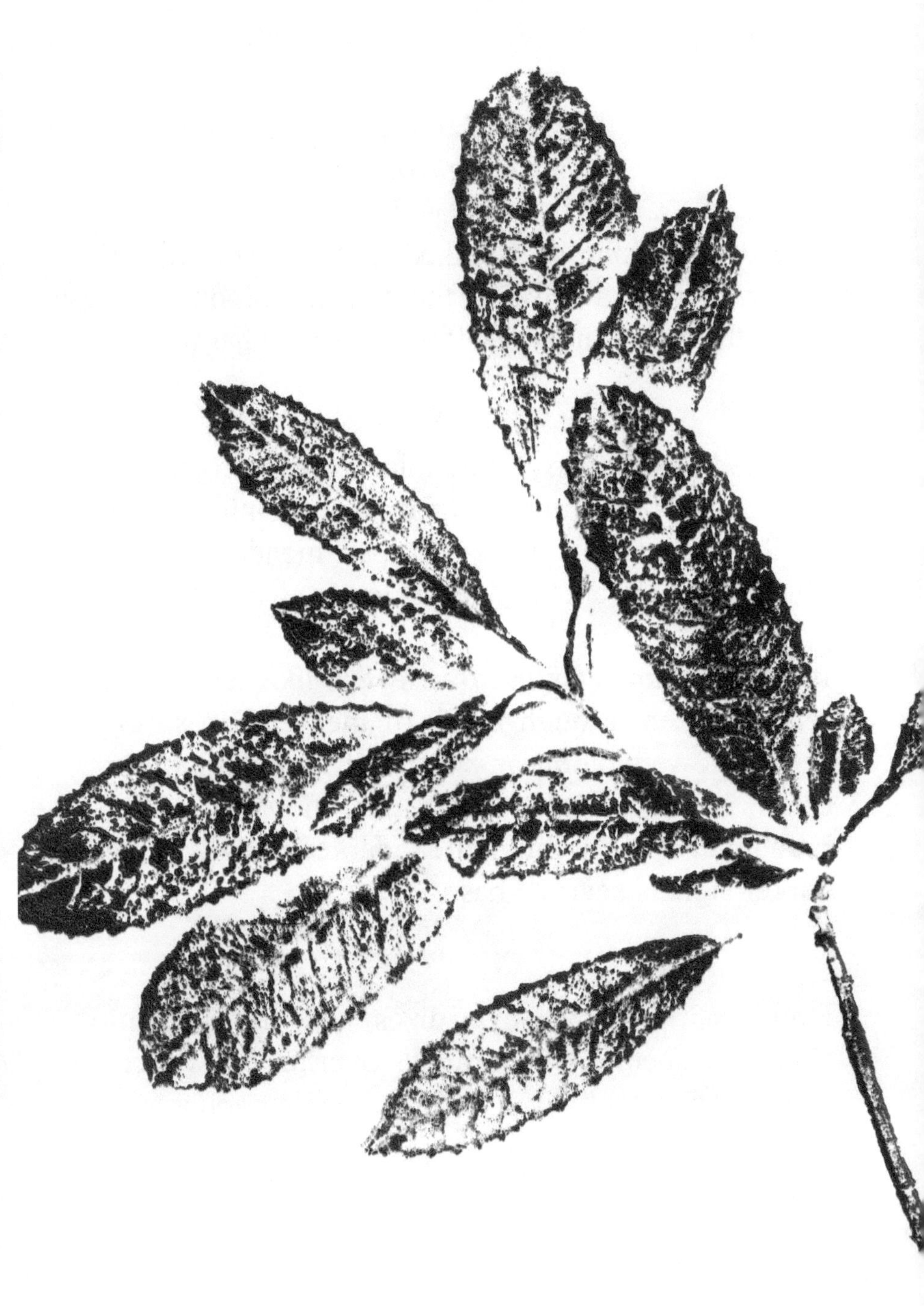

WOODLAND

Douglas Iris
Iris douglasiana

I rises have long been linked to the Greek messenger goddess Iris. When these spring blooms open along the trail, I find myself wondering what will follow…

Douglas iris is a native perennial found along the Pacific Coast from central California north into Oregon. At Sea Ranch, it appears in open meadows, along bluff trails, and at the edges of forest clearings.

It forms clumps of narrow, sword-like leaves that remain green through much of the year. In spring, showy flowers bloom in shades of purple, blue, lavender, or occasionally white. Each flower has three broad outer petals (falls) often marked with lighter or darker signals near the base.

Douglas iris readily hybridizes with other Pacific Coast iris species where ranges overlap. Flower color can vary widely even within a single population.

All parts of the plant can cause stomach upset if ingested; the sap may irritate sensitive skin.

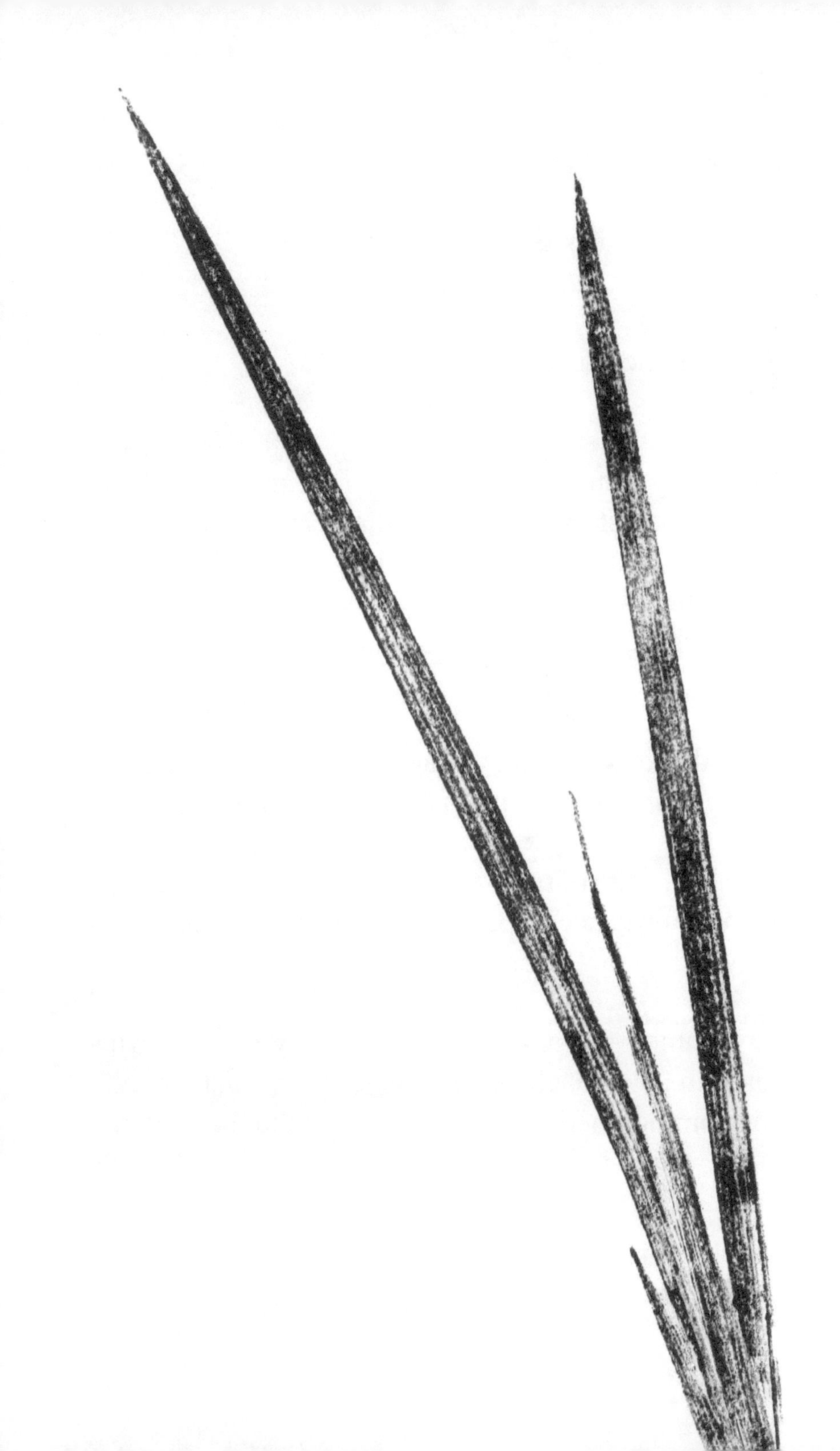

WOODLAND

Twinberry Honeysuckle
Lonicera involucrata

L eave these berries for the birds…

Twinberry honeysuckle is a deciduous native shrub found along streams, wetlands, and moist forest edges from California north to Alaska. In California, it grows mainly in the North Coast and mountain regions where soils remain cool and damp.

It typically reaches 3 to 10 feet in height, forming loose thickets. The leaves are oval and soft-textured, arranged in opposite pairs along the stems.

In spring, pairs of tubular yellow flowers bloom. Each flower pair is accompanied by a pair of conspicuous leafy bracts that later turn reddish.

By summer, the plant produces glossy black berries borne in pairs, each sitting above the reddish bracts. The common name "twinberry" refers to these paired fruits, which are considered mildly toxic to humans and should not be eaten.

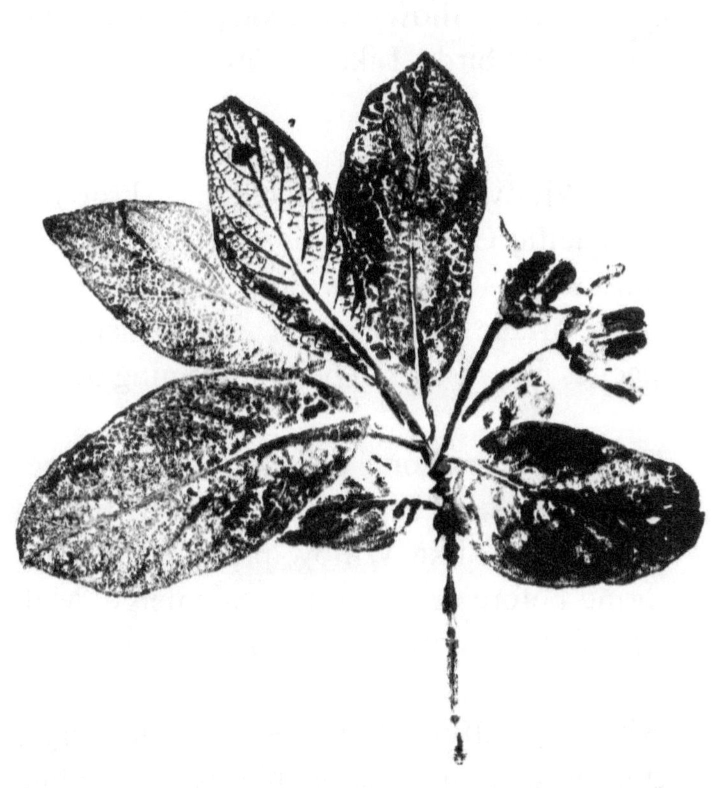

WOODLAND

Sitka Willow
Salix sitchensis

S tands of willows are good places to watch for migratory birds. Like me, many birds are drawn to willows…

Sitka Willow is a native deciduous shrub found along the Pacific Coast from northern California north to Alaska. This riparian willow, with its gray bark, fills many of the drainages at Sea Ranch. It typically reaches 6 to 15 feet in height, forming dense thickets.

The leaves are long and narrow, dark green above and rust-colored beneath, often softly hairy. Like other willows, Sitka Willow produces catkins in early spring before or as the leaves emerge. Male and female flowers grow on separate plants.

With a magnifying loupe, Sitka Willow can be distinguished by male catkins that have only one stamen. Female catkins have silky villous (hairy) ovaries. Sitka Willow spreads readily from seed and can also root from broken stems lodged in damp soil.

Its flexible branches have been used traditionally for basketry and weaving.

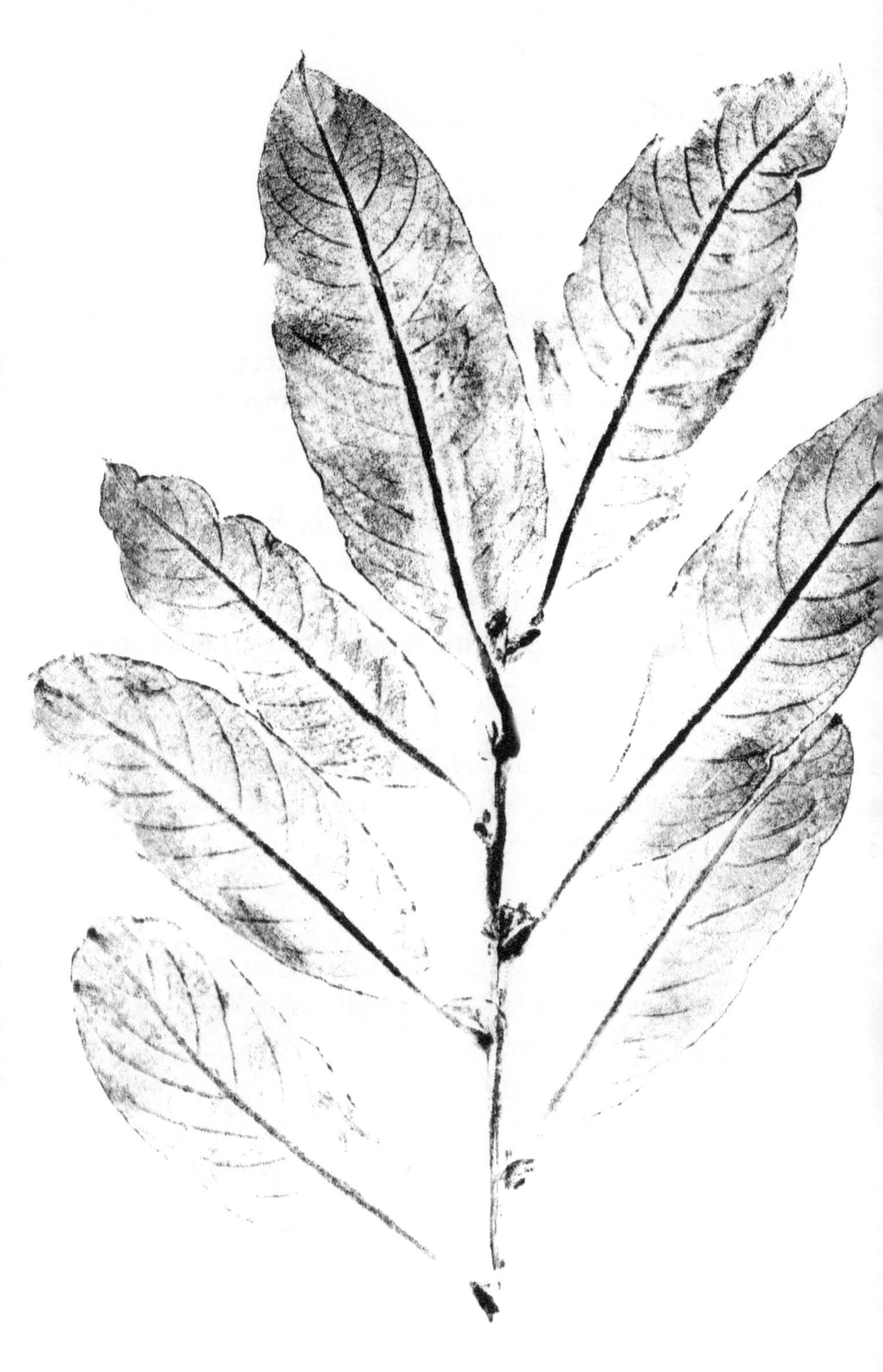

WOODLAND

Wax Myrtle
Myrica californica

Common at Sea Ranch, it grows in meadows and along drainages leading to the ocean. On a fall day, I saw a small flock of yellow-rumped warblers feeding in a wax myrtle…

Also known as Pacific Wax Myrtle, Wax Myrtle is an evergreen shrub native to coastal California and southern Oregon. It typically reaches 6 to 20 feet in height, sometimes forming a small tree in protected sites.

The leaves are narrow, leathery, and aromatic when crushed, with finely toothed edges near the tip. In spring, small inconspicuous flowers bloom along the stems.

Male and female flowers grow on separate plants. By late summer and fall, female plants produce small, waxy gray-purple berries.

The name "wax myrtle" refers to the waxy coating on the berries; related species were historically used to make bayberry candles.

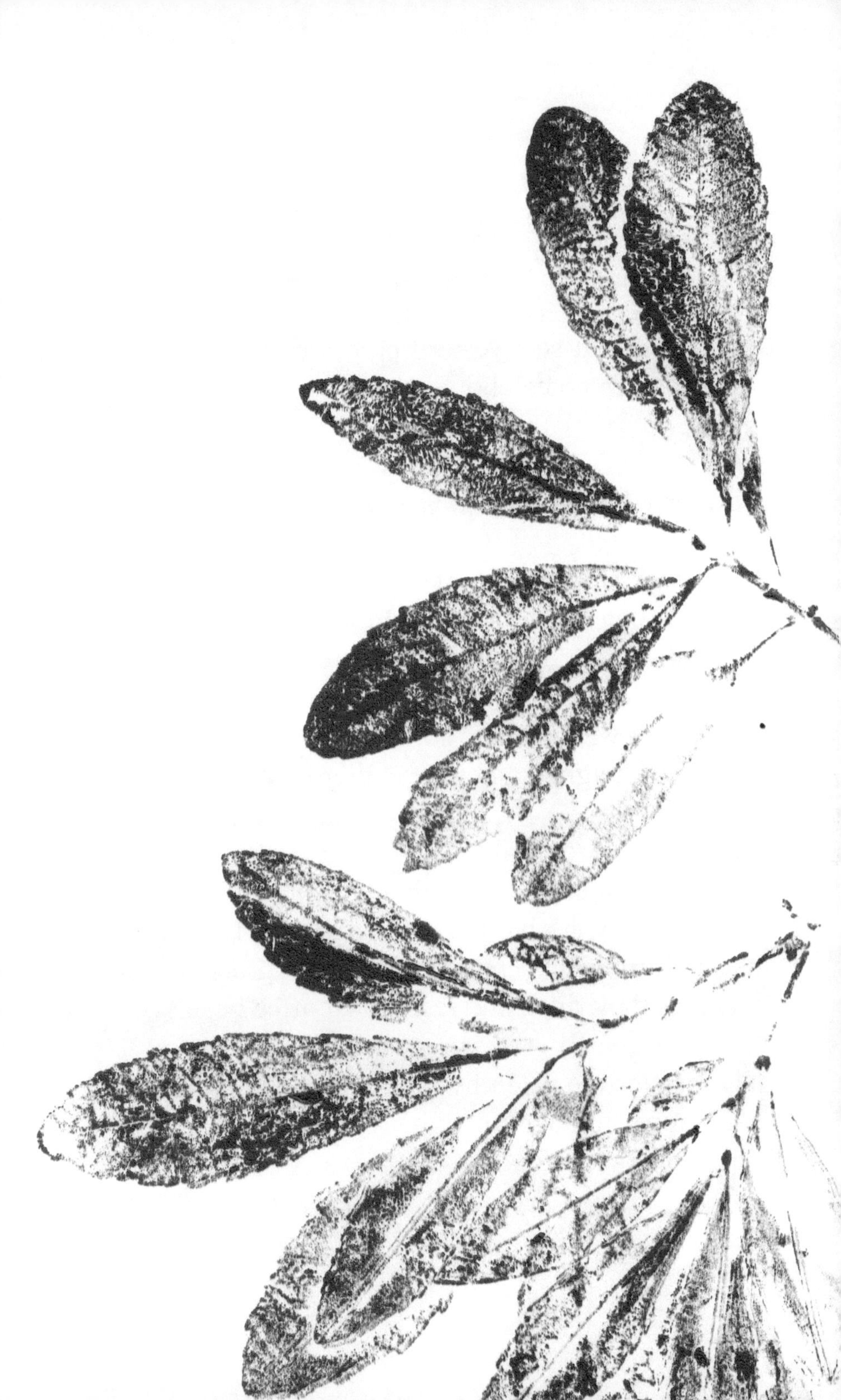

WOODLAND

Coffeeberry
Frangula californica

You might see western bluebirds with their new feather coats showing off while visiting these trees…

Formerly known as *Rhamnus californica.*

Coffeeberry is an evergreen shrub native to California and Baja California, common in chaparral, coastal scrub, and open woodlands. In California, it grows on dry slopes, canyon edges, and forest margins, thriving in well-drained soils. It typically reaches 3 to 10 feet in height, sometimes taller in sheltered sites.

The leaves are oval, glossy, and dark green, with pale undersides and smooth edges. In spring, modest greenish flowers bloom in clusters. By late summer and fall, the fruits change color from green to red to black as they ripen and resemble coffee beans.

The berries are eaten by birds and other wildlife but can cause stomach upset if eaten. They are not recommended as a food.

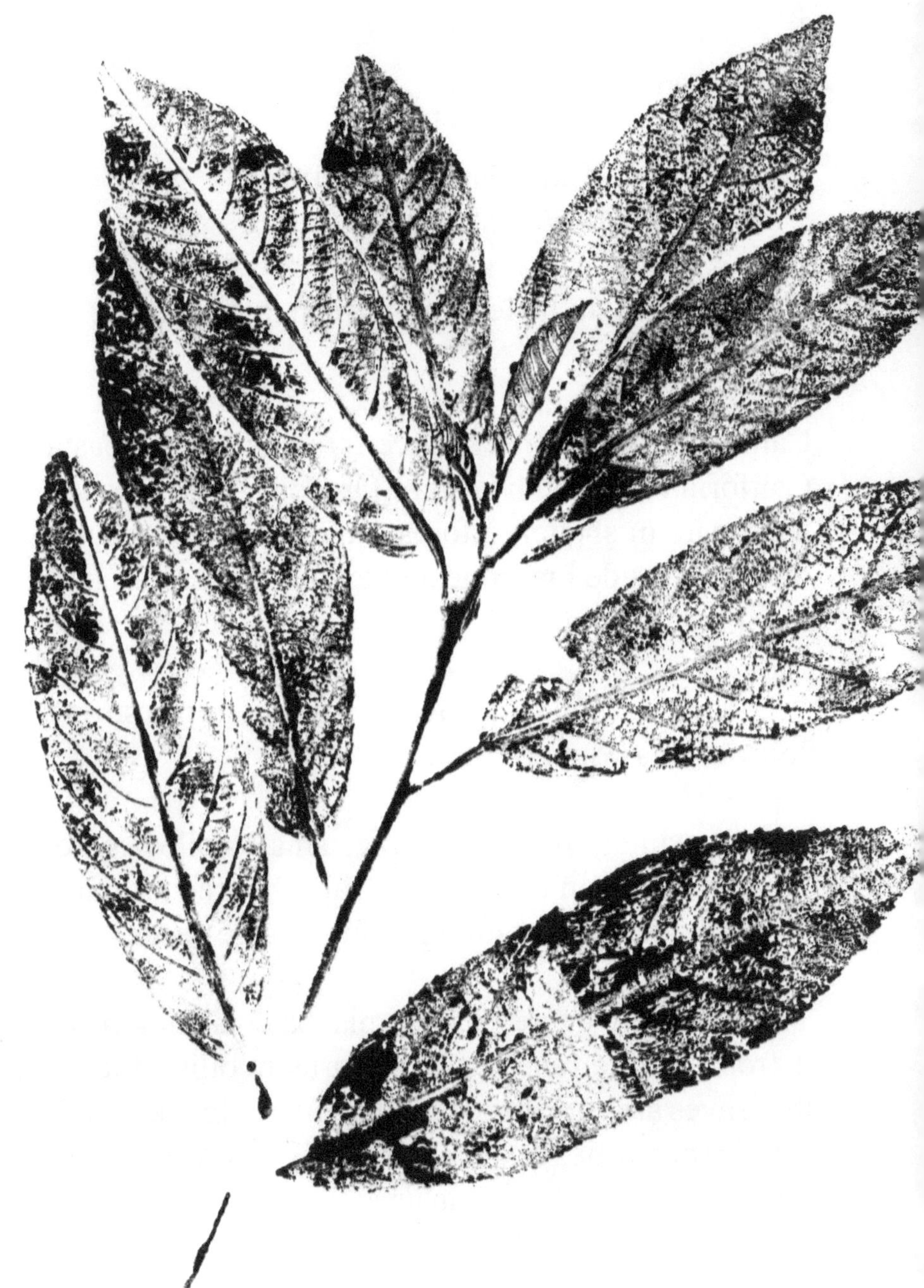

WOODLAND

California Bay Laurel
Umbellularia californica

I love to crush the leaves between my fingers…

California bay is an evergreen tree native to coastal California and southwestern Oregon. At Sea Ranch, it appears in sheltered forests and shaded drainages, often alongside madrone and tanoak. It can reach 30 to 80 feet in height.

The leaves are long, narrow, and glossy, with a strong, spicy aroma when crushed.

In late winter to early spring, small yellow-green flowers bloom in clusters. By fall, the tree produces olive-like fruits containing a single large seed.

The common name "California bay" distinguishes it from Mediterranean bay (Laurus nobilis), though the leaves are sometimes used similarly in cooking in smaller quantities due to their stronger flavor. Indigenous peoples in California used the leaves, seeds, and wood for food, medicine, and tools. The hard wood has been used for carving and specialty woodworking.

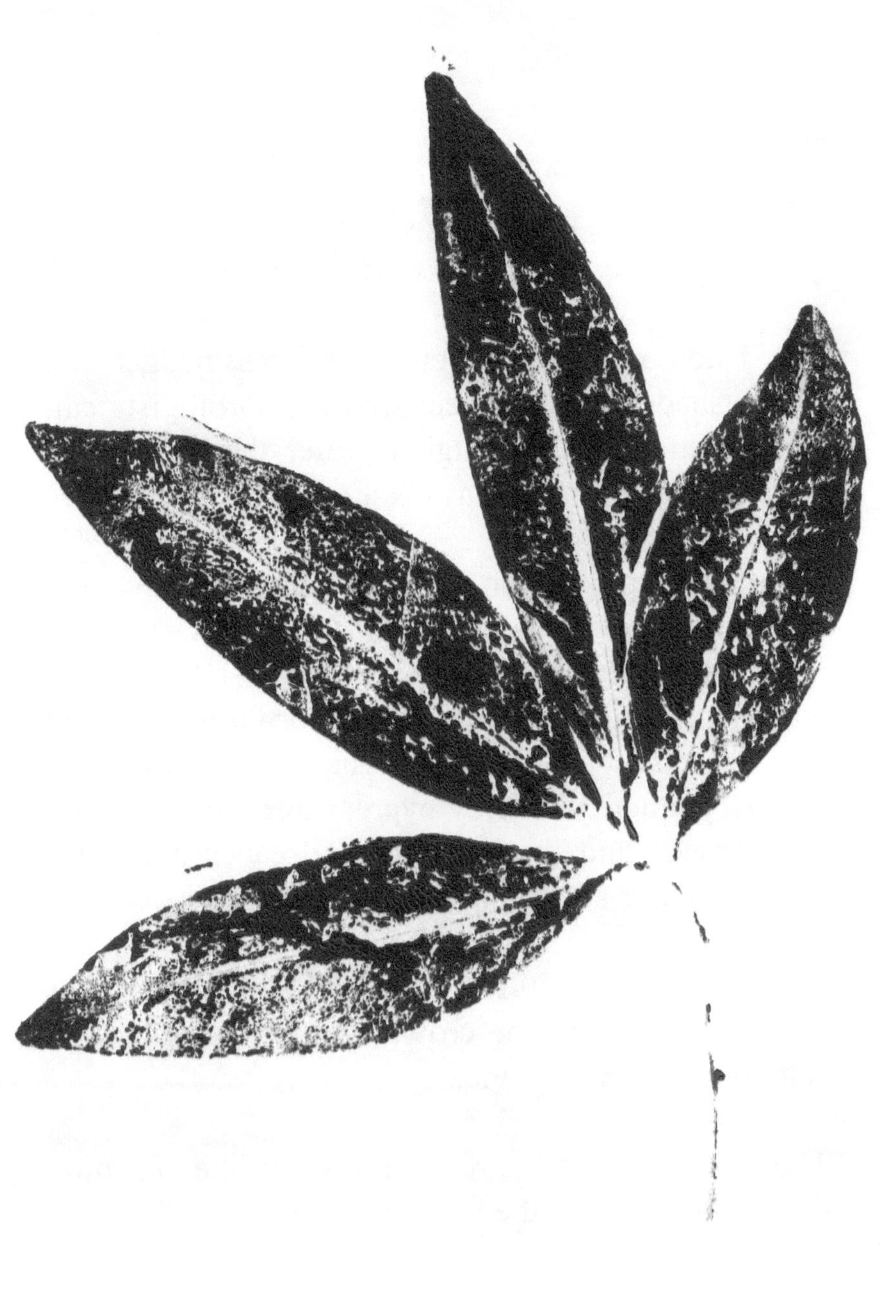

MEADOW

Monterey Cypress
Hesperocyparis macrocarpa

When ocean fog covers tall cypress hedgerows, shadows can appear that meteorologists call "crepuscular rays," though I prefer the term "God rays." A walk on such days is dreamlike…

Monterey cypress is an evergreen conifer native to a small stretch of the central California coast. It occurs naturally only near Monterey and Carmel. It has been widely planted elsewhere in California and around the world as a windbreak and ornamental tree. At Sea Ranch, planted Monterey cypress trees are common along roads and in sheltered landscapes and form majestic wind-sheltering hedgerows.

It can reach 40 to 70 feet in height, sometimes taller in protected sites. The crown is often irregular and sculpted by coastal winds.

The foliage is dark green and scale-like, forming dense sprays along the branches.

The cones are round and woody, with thick scales, and may remain closed on the tree for years. The cones also open and disperse seeds during forest fires.

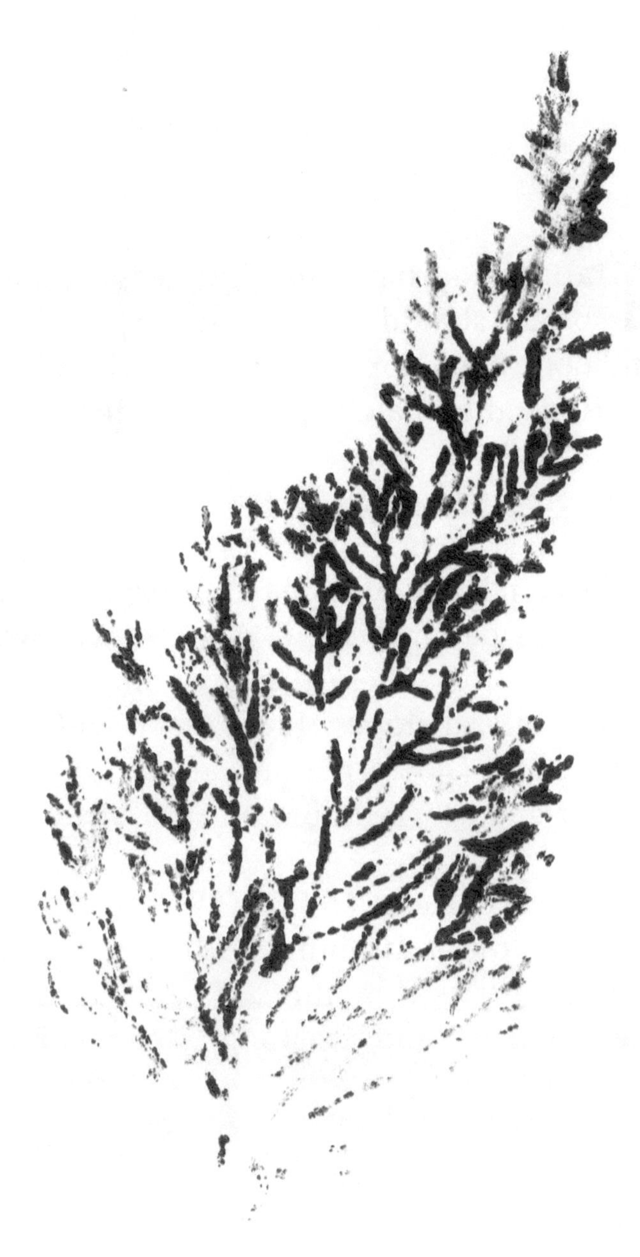

MEADOW

Monterey Pine
Pinus radiata

Tall and prominent, Monterey pine carries broad shoulders of long gray-green needles and cones that appear almost stuck to its branches. Red-tailed hawks perch high in this tree...

Monterey pine is an evergreen conifer native to a small stretch of the central California coast and two islands off Baja California. In the wild, it occurs naturally near Año Nuevo, Monterey, and Cambria, where it grows on coastal terraces and inland slopes. It has been widely planted throughout California and around the world for timber and as a windbreak.

It typically reaches 50 to 100 feet in height. The trunk is often straight, with dark, deeply furrowed bark as it matures. Needles grow in bundles of three and are long, slender, and bright green.

Cones are asymmetrical, woody, and often remain attached to the tree for many years. Monterey pine can release seeds after fire or prolonged heat.

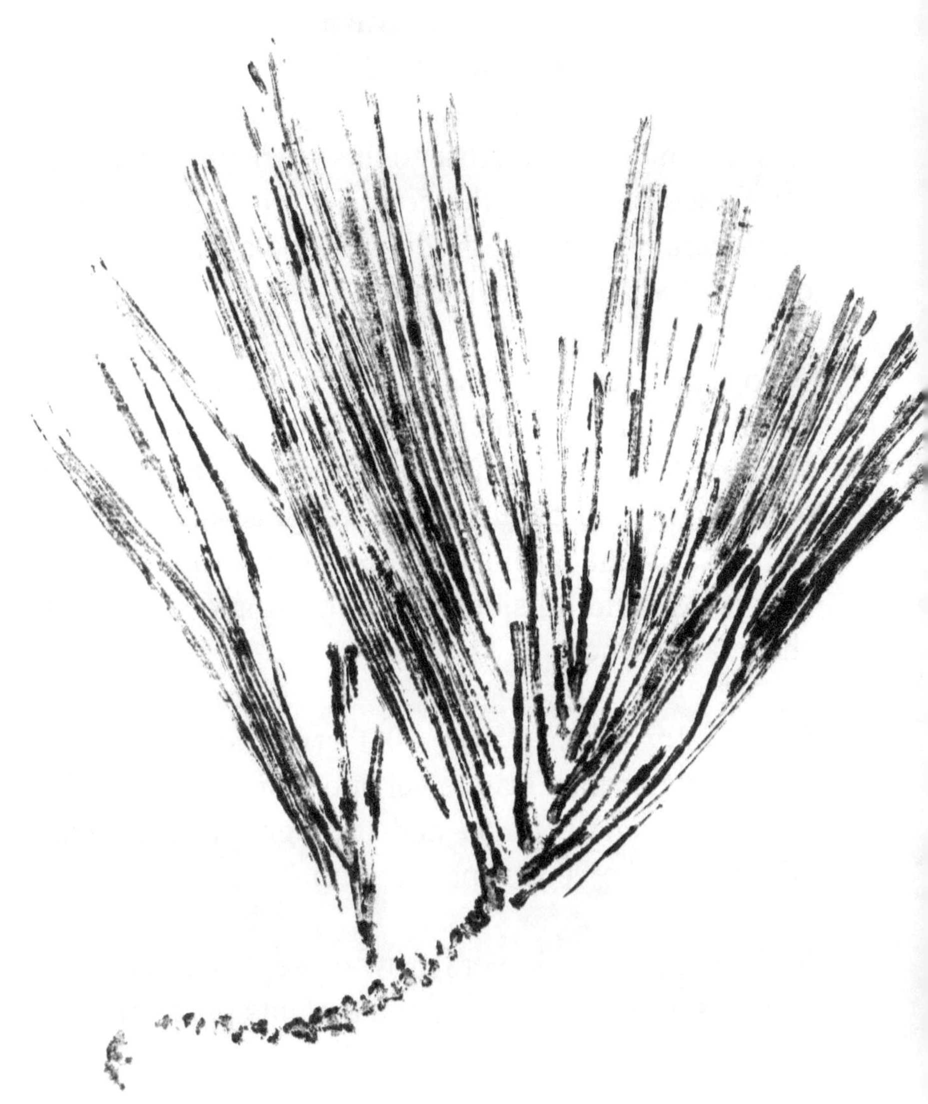

MEADOW

Coyote Bush
Baccharis pilularis

When you walk close to this bush, you will often see insects on the compact white flowers and small birds hiding in its foliage. Look for California quail as they dart underneath…

Also called coyote brush, coyote bush is an evergreen shrub native to coastal California and parts of Oregon. It is often one of the first plants to return to abandoned or disturbed coastal grasslands. At Sea Ranch, it is one of the most common shrubs on bluff tops and inland hillsides, often forming dense stands shaped by wind.

It typically reaches 3 to 10 feet in height, though coastal plants may stay lower and more compact. The leaves are small, thick, and dark green, often with slightly toothed edges near the tip.

Male and female flowers grow on separate plants. In late summer and fall, female plants produce clusters of small seeds attached to silky white hairs. These cottony seed heads give hillsides a silvery look when they catch the light.

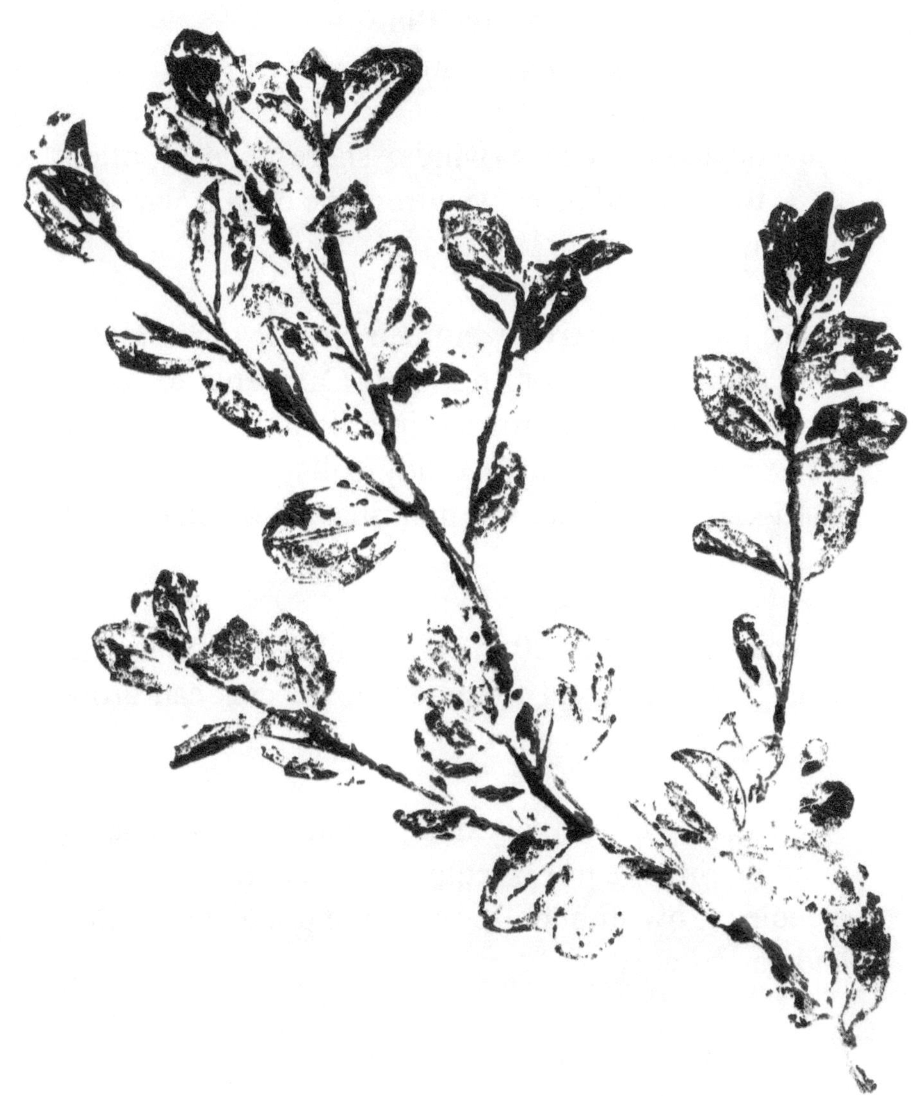

MEADOW

Shore Pine
Pinus contorta subsp. *contorta*

Adapted to ocean winds, shore pine is often twisted and bent away from the ocean. Nature's bonsai…

Shore pine is a native evergreen conifer found along the Pacific Coast from northern California to Alaska. In California, it grows primarily along the North Coast on coastal bluffs, sandy soils, and in foggy, wind-exposed habitats, often shaped by persistent ocean winds.

It typically reaches 20 to 50 feet in height along the coast, though inland forms of the species can grow much taller.

The trunk is often twisted or leaning in response to wind, giving the tree a sculpted appearance.
Needles grow in bundles of two and are short, stiff, and dark green.

Cones are small and woody, sometimes remaining closed on the tree for years. Some cones may open in response to heat, including fire.

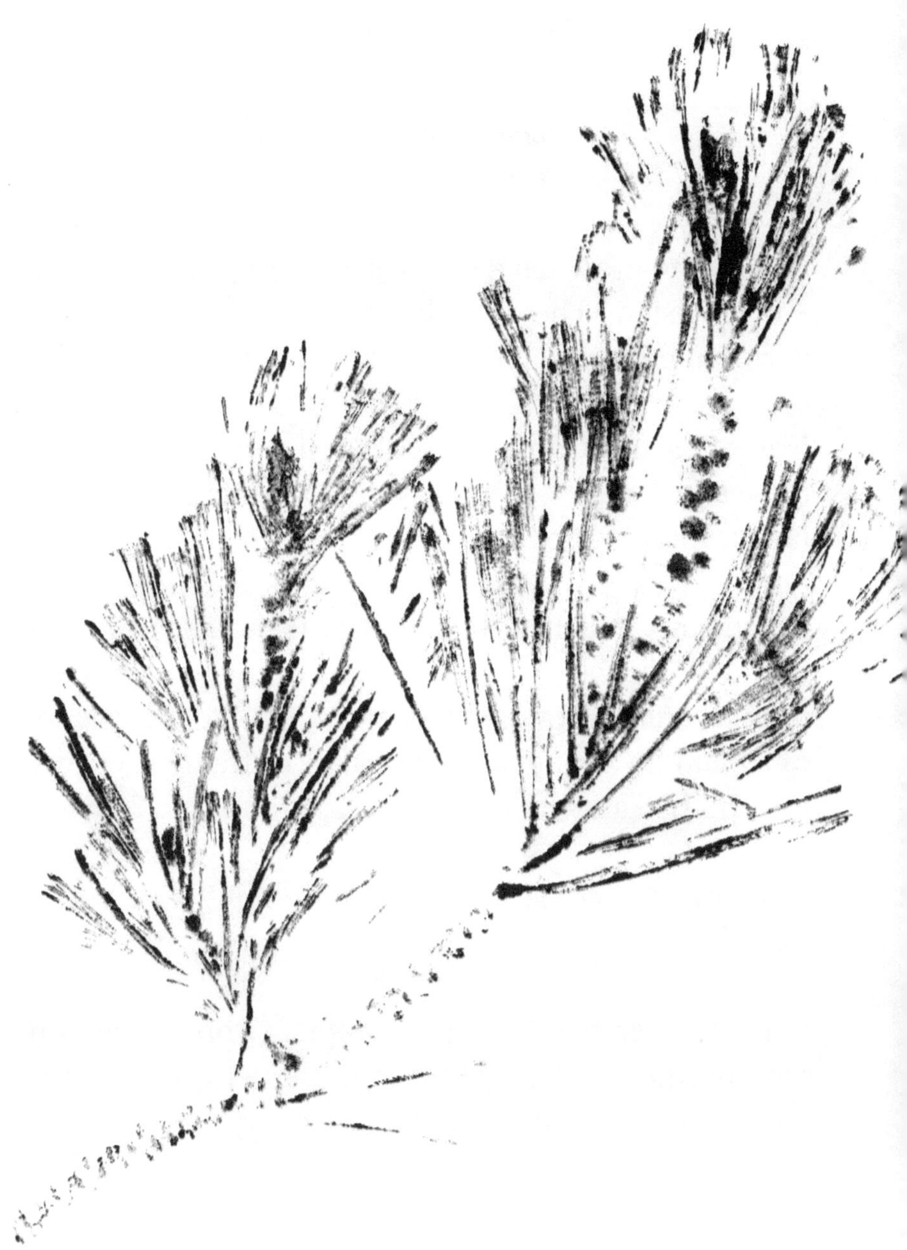

MEADOW

Coastal Bush Lupine
Lupinus arboreus

White-crowned sparrows gather in these shrubs. Listen. They perch on top singing and then dart into cover…

Native to the California coast. It appears on bluff tops and sandy terraces, often brightening spring landscapes with blooms.

It typically reaches 3 to 6 feet in height, forming rounded shrubs. The leaves are palmately divided into several narrow leaflets arranged like the fingers of a hand. In spring, upright spikes of fragrant yellow flowers rise above the foliage.

It tolerates wind, salt spray, and drought once established.

"Lupinus" comes from Latin lupus (wolf), based on the mistaken belief that lupines robbed soil of nutrients — the opposite of what they actually do.

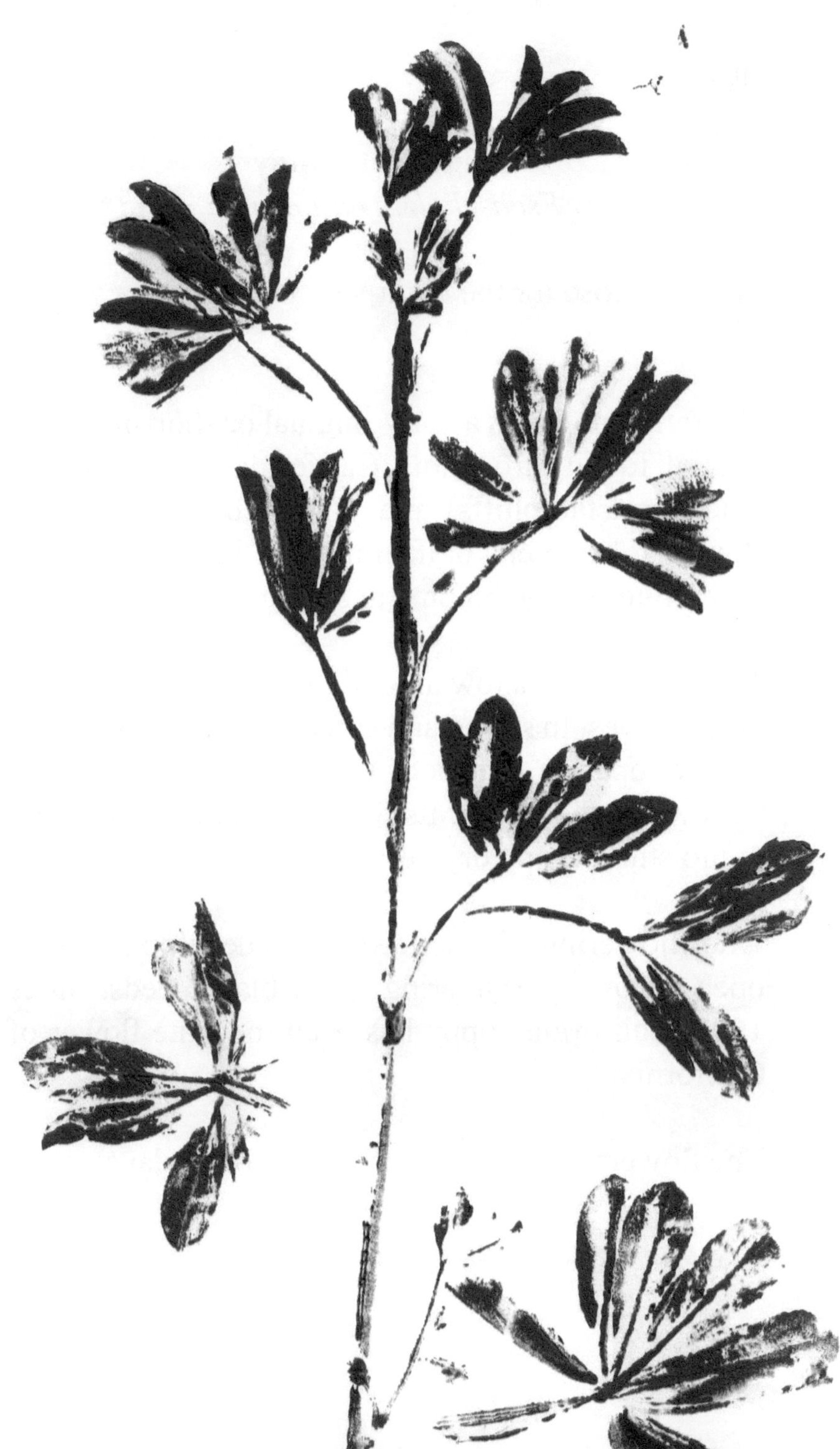

MEADOW

California Poppy
Eschscholzia californica

They close for the night...

California poppy is a native annual or short-lived perennial found throughout California in open grasslands, coastal bluffs, and disturbed soils. At Sea Ranch, it brightens bluff trails and inland meadows with vivid orange blooms in spring.

The plant forms a low mound of finely divided, blue-green leaves. In spring and early summer, cup-shaped flowers open in shades of bright orange, sometimes yellow or pale cream. Its deep taproot allows access to moisture during dry periods.

After flowering, slender seed pods develop and split open when dry, scattering small black seeds. Since 1903, California poppy has been the state flower of California.

The flowers close at night and on cloudy days.

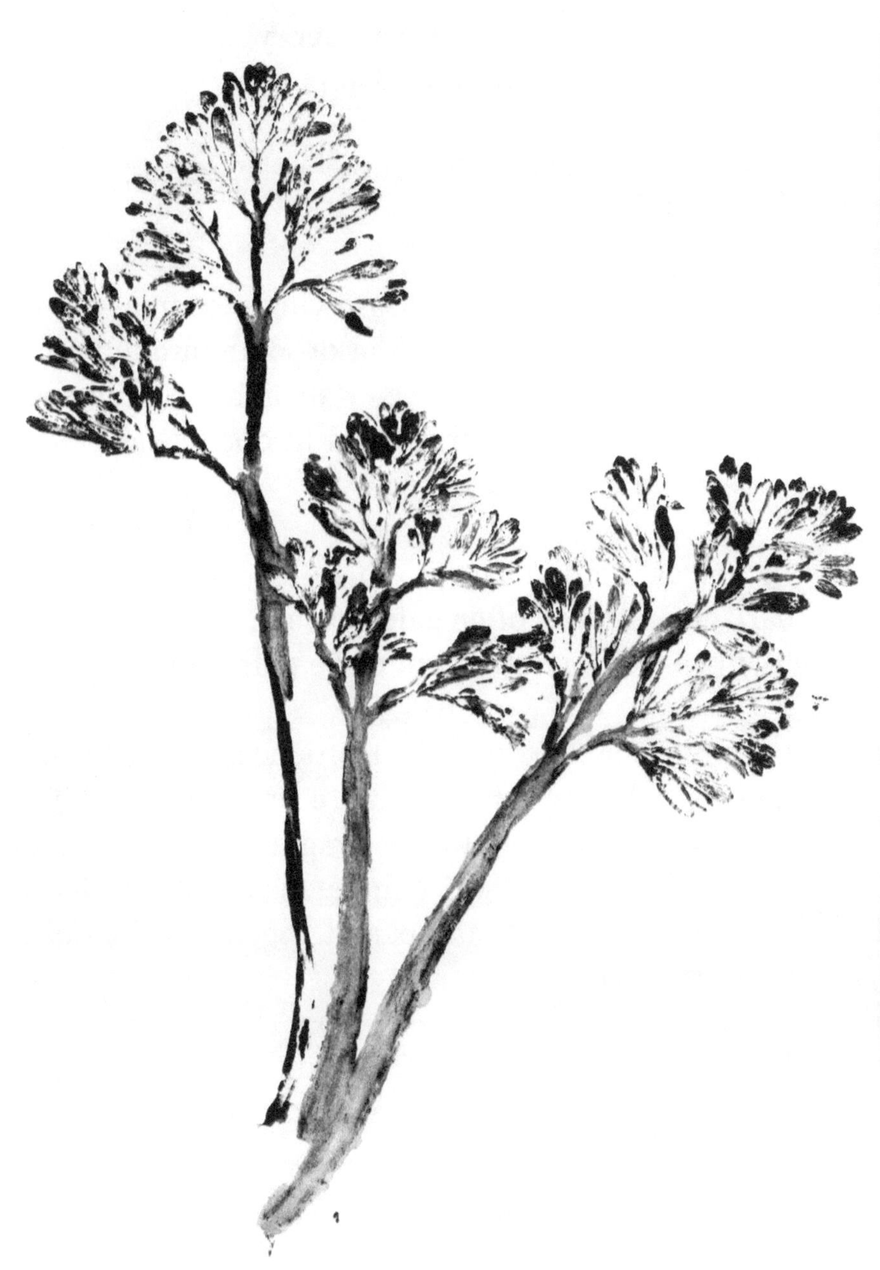

MEADOW

Beach Strawberry
Fragaria chiloensis

If any plant can be thought of as "cheerful," beach strawberry is the one…

Beach strawberry is a low-growing perennial native to the Pacific Coast from Alaska south through California and into Chile. At Sea Ranch, it forms spreading mats along bluff trails and in open sandy areas exposed to wind and salt spray.

Its leaves are divided into three leaflets, glossy and dark green above, often pale beneath. In spring, white five-petaled flowers bloom close to the ground.

By early summer, the plant produces small to medium-sized strawberries that are red when ripe. The berries are edible and often fragrant, though sometimes less sweet than cultivated varieties. Beach strawberry is one of the parent species of the cultivated strawberry.

Beach strawberry tolerates wind, salt spray, and drought. Its dense growth helps stabilize sandy soils.

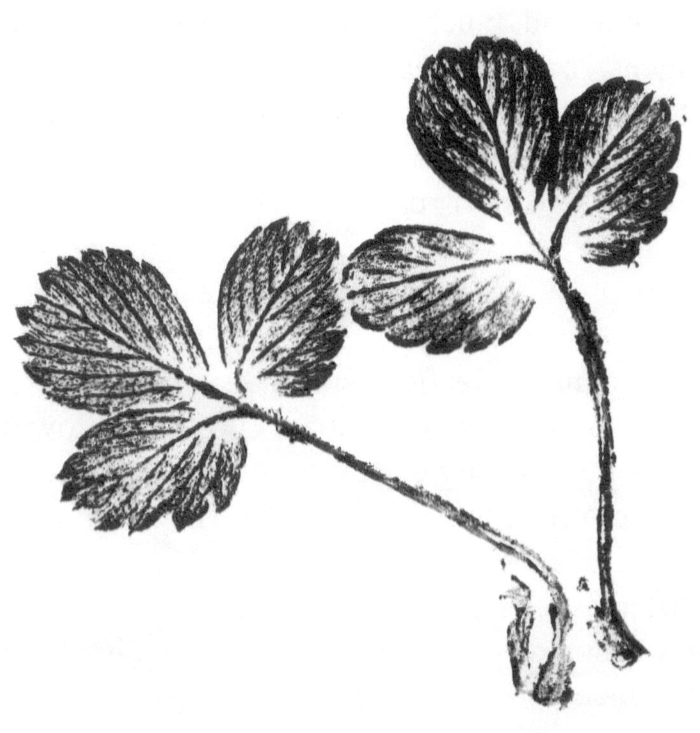

MEADOW

Ribwort Plantain
Plantago lanceolata

Ribwort plantain is a low-growing perennial native to Europe that is now widespread in California and much of North America. It grows in lawns, roadsides, pastures, and open fields, tolerating compacted soils and heavy foot traffic. At Sea Ranch, it appears along trails, in grassy clearings, and in disturbed soils near roads.

The plant forms a basal rosette of narrow, lance-shaped leaves with strong parallel veins. In spring and summer, leafless stalks rise above the rosette, each topped with a compact cylindrical flower head. Tiny flowers ring the head, with small white stamens that protrude in a delicate halo when in bloom.

After flowering, numerous small seeds develop and are easily dispersed by wind, water, animals, or passing feet.

It has long been used in traditional herbal medicine, particularly for minor wounds and respiratory ailments.

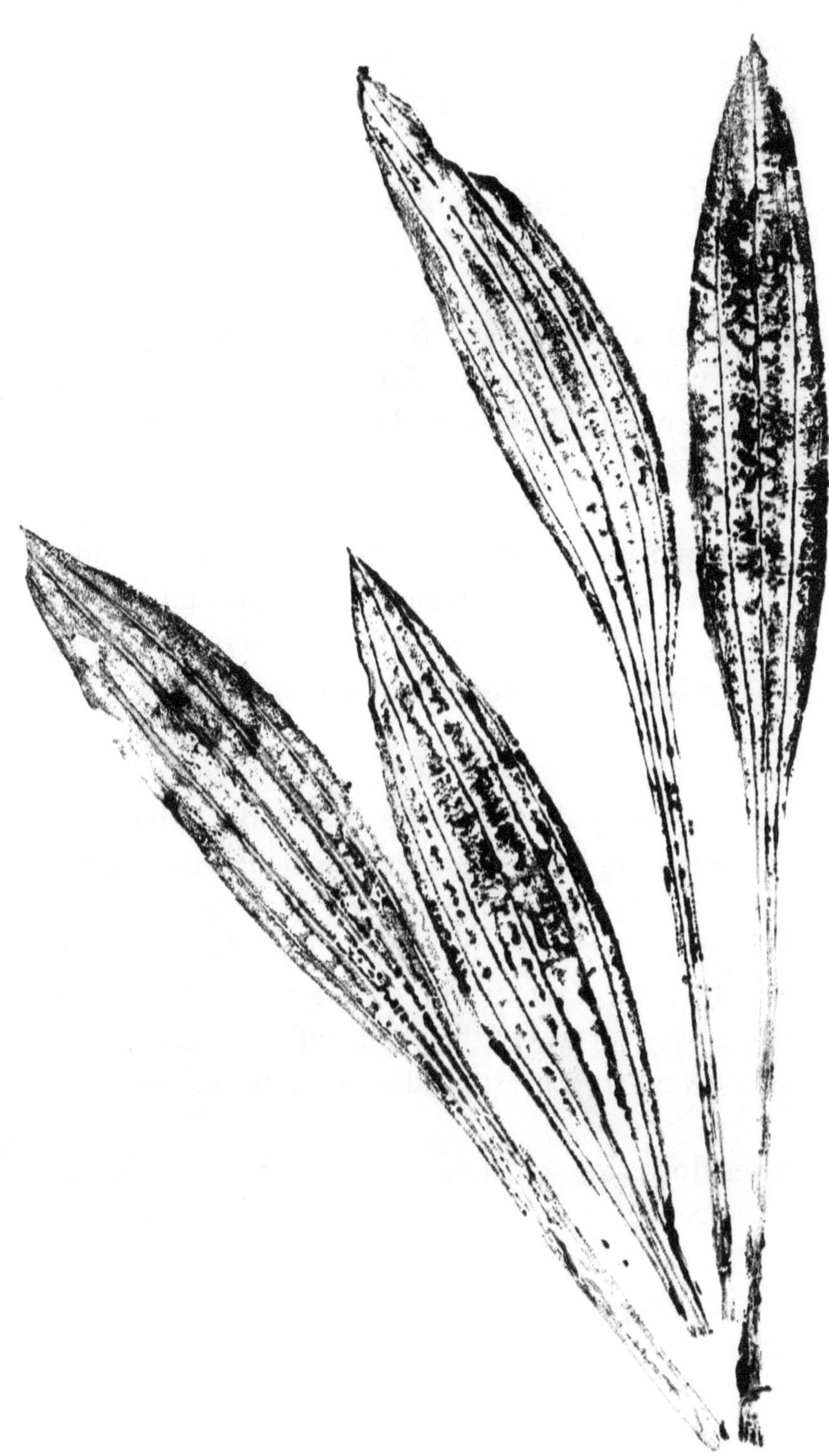

MEADOW

California Buttercup
Ranunculus californicus

Cheerful leaves and flowers in a buttery, waxy yellow. The name *Ranunculus* means "little frog," a nod to the damp places where many buttercups like to grow.

California buttercup is a native perennial found in grasslands, open woodlands, and coastal prairies throughout much of California. It thrives in full sun and well-drained soils, often blooming after winter rains.

The plant typically grows 1 to 2 feet tall, with branching stems. Its leaves are deeply divided into narrow segments, giving them a delicate, lacy appearance. In late winter through spring, the plant produces bright yellow flowers with five to many shiny petals. The glossy surface of the petals reflects light, making the flowers appear especially vivid in sunlight.

After flowering, clusters of small dry fruits develop at the center of each bloom.

Fresh buttercup plants contain compounds that can irritate the skin and are toxic if ingested.

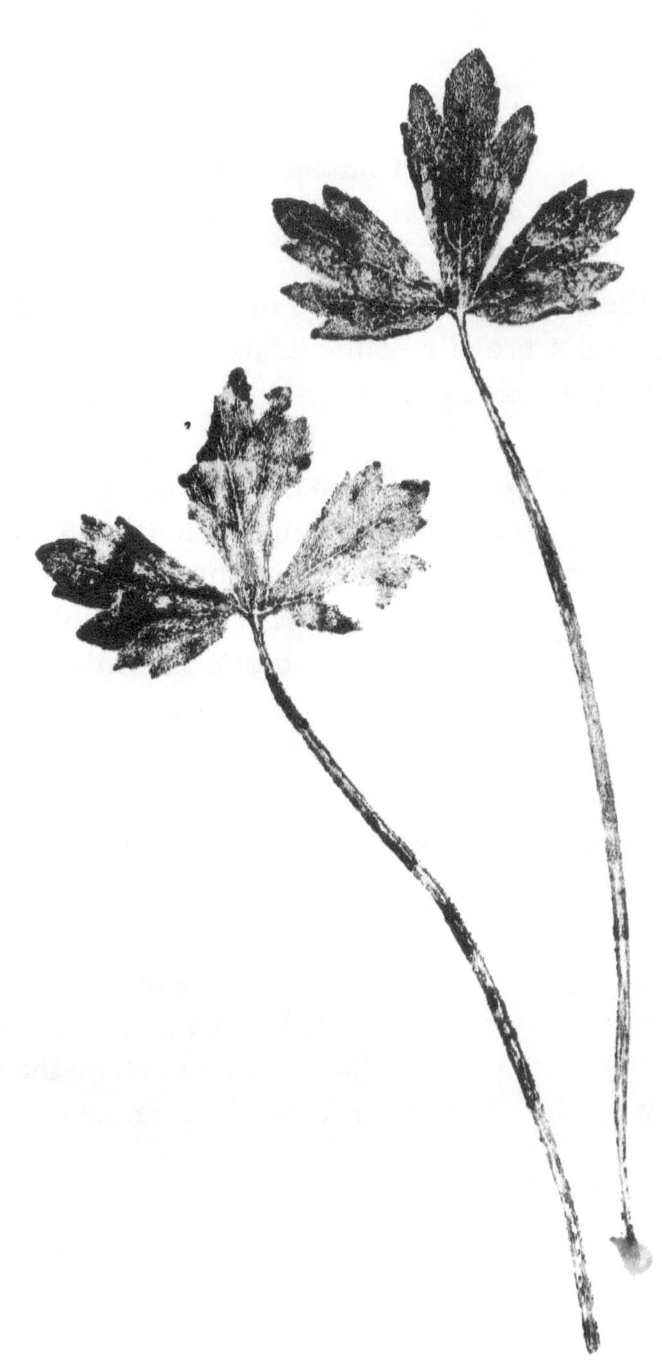

MEADOW

Tall Coastal Plantain
Plantago subnuda

The wide, ribbed leaves of this plantain, pressed into a broad rosette against the sandy cliffside, made a statement…

Tall coastal plantain is a native perennial found along the Pacific Coast from California north into Oregon. At Sea Ranch, it appears along bluff trails and in inland grasslands where winter rains keep soils moist. The plant forms a basal rosette of wide to lance-shaped leaves with strong parallel veins.

The species name *subnuda* means "almost naked," referring to its relatively smooth or sparsely hairy surfaces compared to related species.

In spring and early summer, tall, leafless stalks rise above the rosette. Each stalk bears a dense, cylindrical flower spike. Tiny flowers bloom along the spike, with small pale stamens extending outward when in flower.

After flowering, numerous small seeds develop and are dispersed by wind, animals, and foot traffic.

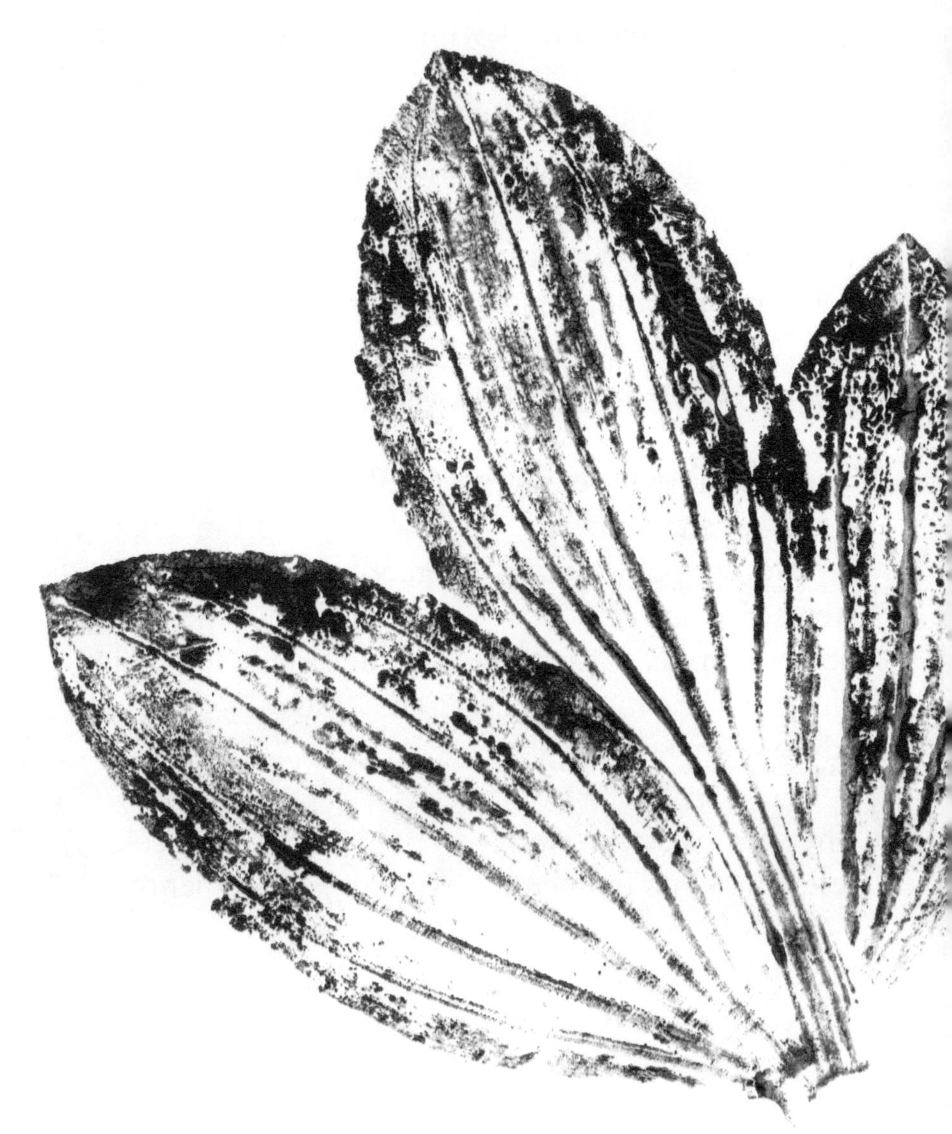

MEADOW

Alameda Thistle
Cirsium quercetorum

A prickly, old friend with an occasional flash of color…

Alameda thistle is a native perennial found in coastal prairies and open woodlands of central and northern California. It grows in grasslands, oak woodlands, and coastal scrub, typically in well-drained soils. At Sea Ranch, it is commonly found along the bluff trail, where it tolerates wind and salt spray.

The plant forms a basal rosette of spiny, deeply lobed leaves. It stays low and does not show off much, but in late spring to early summer, upright flowering stems rise and may reach 2 to 4 feet tall. The flower heads are pink to purple and borne singly or in small clusters at the tops of stems. The heads are surrounded by spiny bracts.

The species name *quercetorum* means "of the oaks," referring to its frequent growth in oak woodlands. After flowering, the plant produces seeds attached to fine, white hairs that aid in wind dispersal. It is also sometimes called Brownie thistle.

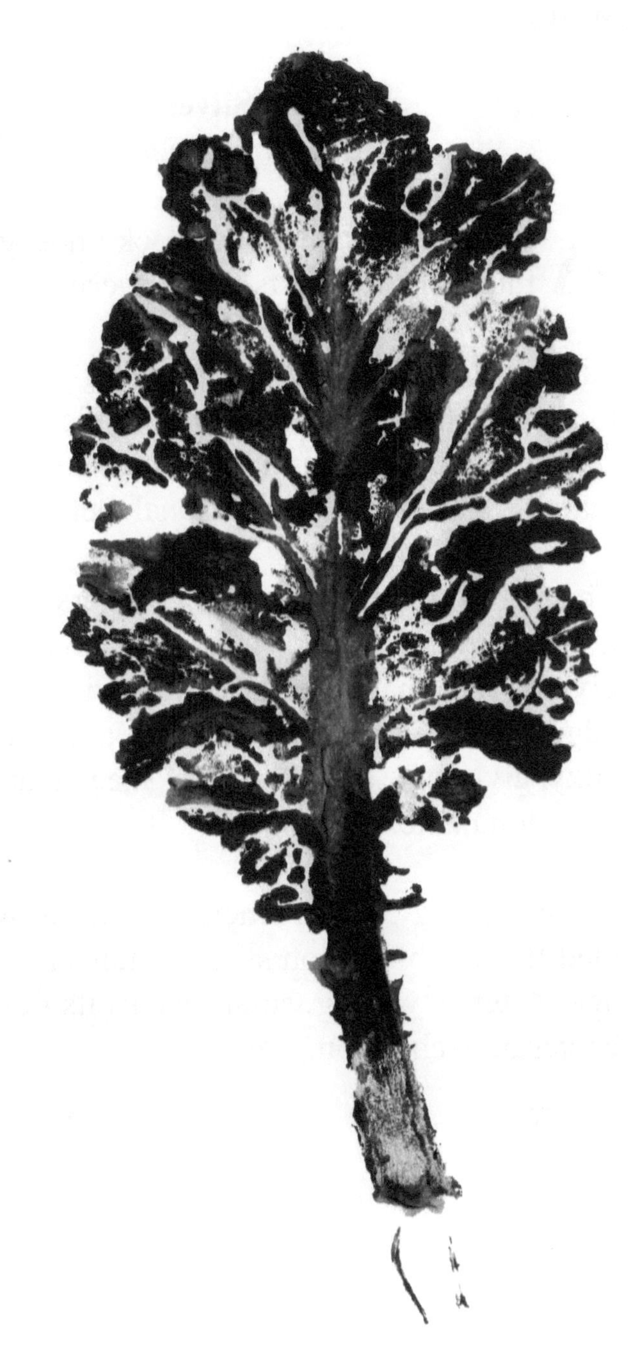

MEADOW

Pacific Silverweed
Argentina pacifica

After days of rain, I see Black Phoebes gathering mud for their nests near silverweed…

Pacific silverweed is a low-growing perennial native to coastal California and the Pacific Northwest. In California, it grows in moist coastal prairies, dunes, marsh edges, and along seasonal wetlands.

The plant spreads by creeping runners that root at the nodes, forming silvery mats. Its leaves are pinnate, divided into many small leaflets with finely toothed edges. The undersides of the leaves are pale and silky, giving the plant a silvery sheen that inspired its common name.

In late spring and summer, bright yellow, five-petaled flowers bloom on slender stalks above the foliage. After flowering, small dry fruits develop at the center of each bloom.

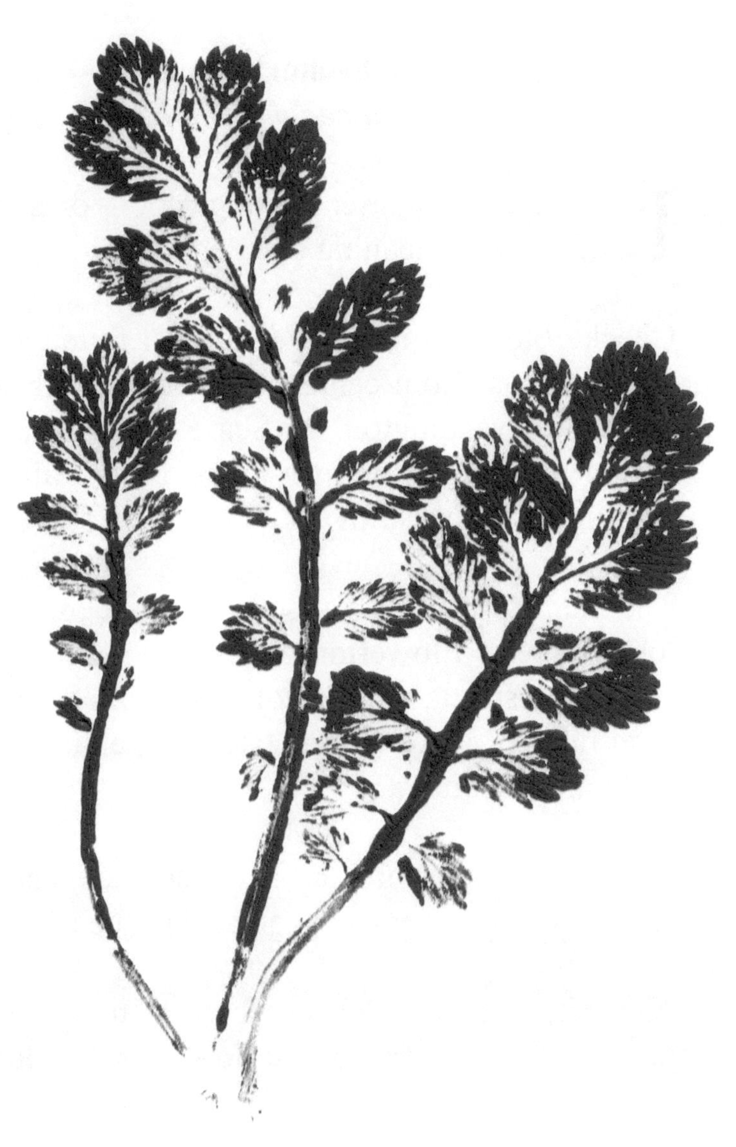

MEADOW

Checkerbloom
Sidalcea malviflora

L ike a three-quarter waxing moon, or the profile of someone leaning back and laughing…

Checkerbloom is a native perennial found along the Pacific Coast from central California north into Oregon and Washington. At Sea Ranch, it appears in spring and early summer along bluff trails and in open inland grasslands.

The plant forms a low rosette of rounded, shallowly lobed leaves. Flowering stems rise 1 to 3 feet tall, carrying a spring-surprise of showy pink to rose-colored flowers. Each flower has five petals, typical of the mallow family.

After flowering, small dry fruits develop, each divided into several segments containing seeds.

The common name "checkerbloom" may refer to the patterned appearance of the flower or the alternating arrangement of blossoms along the stem.

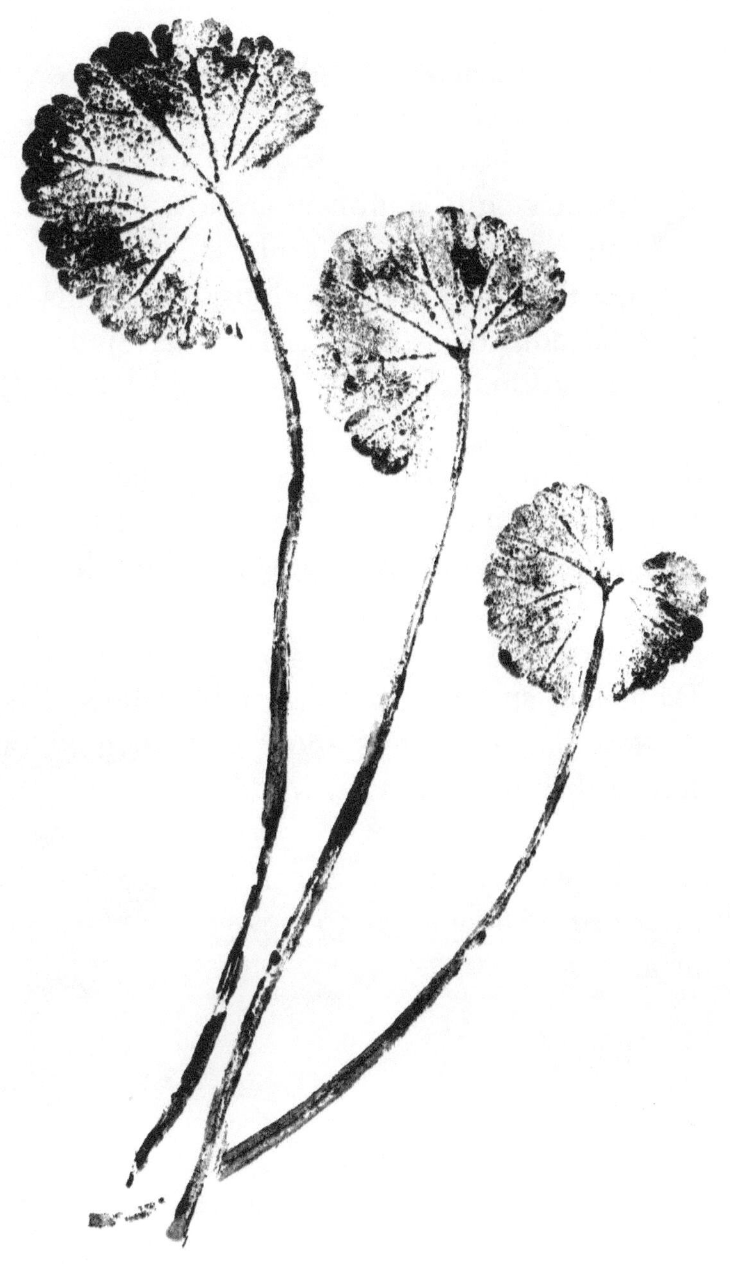

MEADOW

Seaside Woolly Sunflower
Eriophyllum staechadifolium

Seaside woolly sunflower is a low, spreading shrub native to coastal California and southern Oregon. At Sea Ranch, it appears along bluff trails and exposed headlands, where wind and salt spray shape its compact form.

The plant may reach 1 to 3 feet in height, forming rounded mounds. Its leaves are narrow and gray-green, densely covered with fine hairs that give the plant a soft, woolly sheen.

From late spring into fall, bright yellow daisy-like flowers rise in clusters above the foliage, blooming longer than many coastal wildflowers.

Seaside woolly sunflower can resprout from its base after fire, an adaptation to the cycles of coastal chaparral.

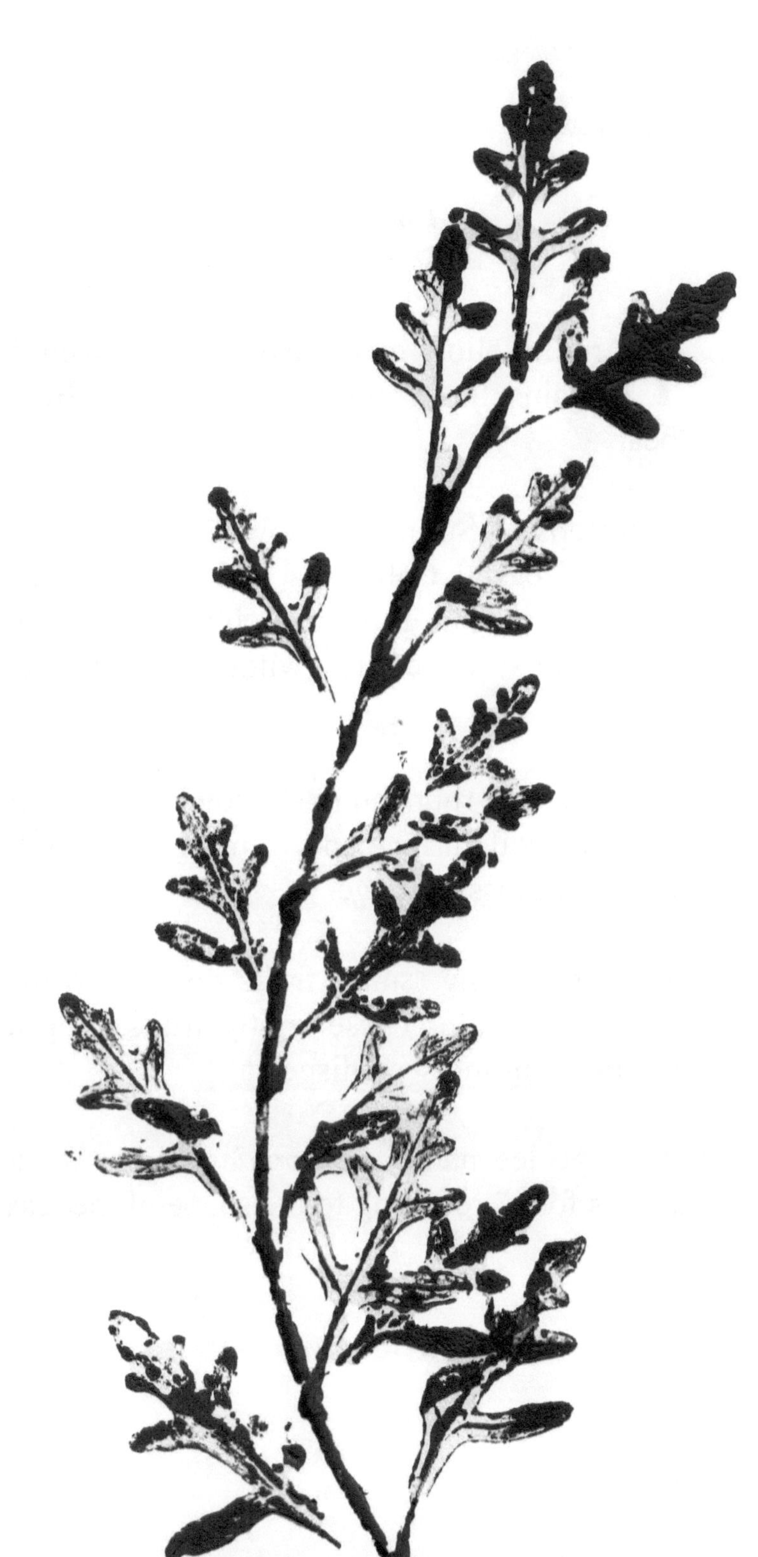

MEADOW

Footsteps of Spring
Sanicula arctopoides

Bright yellow-green leaves and flowers flattened against the ground, as if stepped on by a visiting bear…

Footsteps of Spring is a low-growing perennial native to coastal California and southern Oregon. It grows in coastal grasslands, bluffs, and open slopes and is one of the earliest wildflowers to bloom along the coast.

Its leaves are rounded to shallowly lobed, often hugging the soil surface and forming a compact rosette of thick, glossy foliage.

After flowering, small fruits covered with hooked bristles develop. These bristly fruits cling to fur or clothing, aiding seed dispersal.

The species name *arctopoides* means "resembling bear's foot," referring to the shape of the leaves.

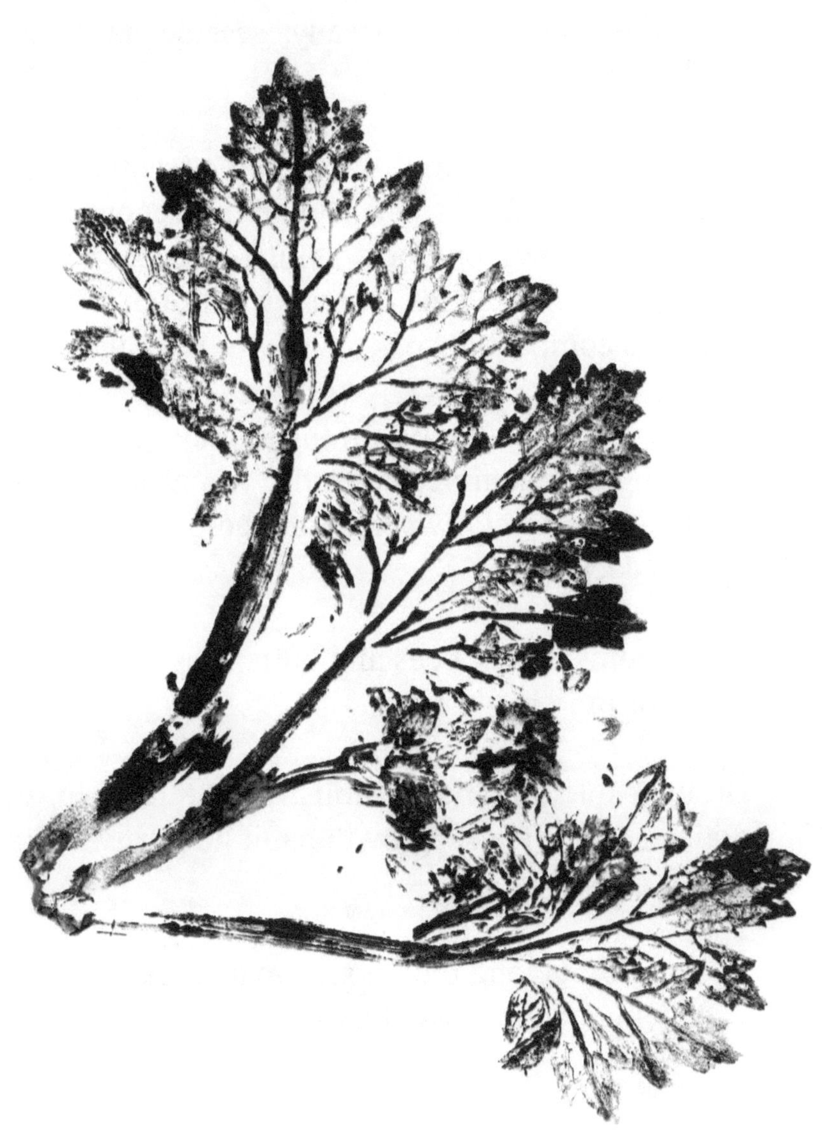

MEADOW

Seaside Daisy
Erigeron glaucus

When the wind is steady, seaside daisy holds fast…

Seaside daisy is a low, spreading perennial native to coastal California and southern Oregon. At Sea Ranch, it grows on rocky bluffs, coastal terraces, dunes, and cliff edges, where wind and salt spray shape its compact form.

It forms rounded mounds of thick, gray-green leaves. In spring and summer, lavender to purple rays surround a bright yellow center, the color ranging from pale to deep violet.

The blooms attract bees and butterflies and can continue for months.

Drought-tolerant once established, it thrives in well-drained soils. Its low growth habit helps it withstand strong coastal winds.

Because of its long bloom season and resilience, it is widely planted in coastal gardens.

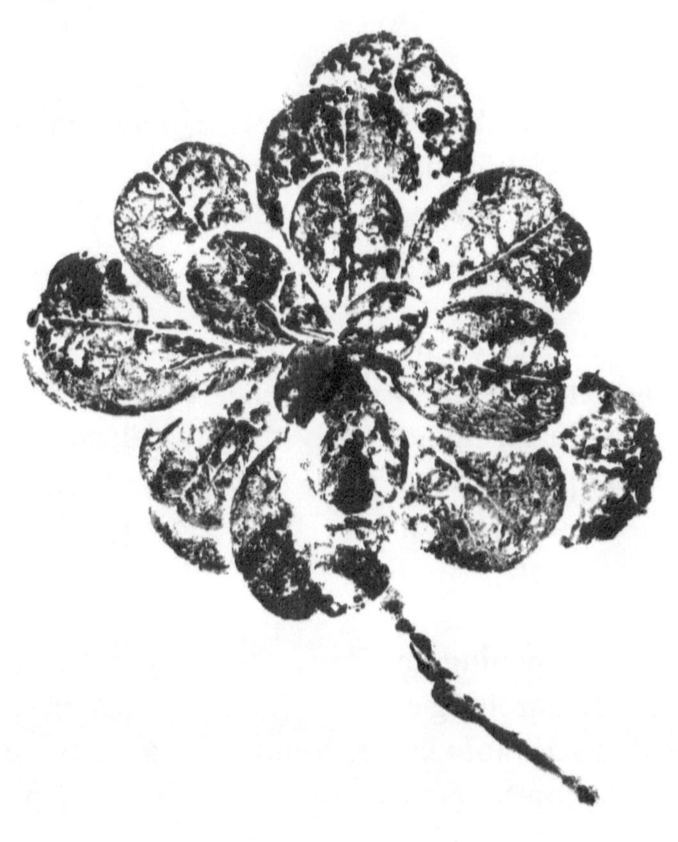

MEADOW

California Phacelia
Phacelia californica

L eaves lifted toward the light…

California phacelia is a native perennial found in coastal California and parts of the Coast Ranges. At Sea Ranch, it appears along bluff trails and at woodland edges.

The plant typically grows 1 to 3 feet tall, with branching stems. Its divided, fern-like leaves are often softly hairy. In spring and early summer, clusters of lavender to purple flowers rise at the tips of stems. Honey bees, bumblebees, hoverflies, and butterflies all love this flower.

Before opening, the flower buds curl into tight coils, slowly unrolling as they bloom — a pattern botanists call a scorpioid cyme, common in the borage family. Each flower has five rounded lobes and prominent stamens that extend outward.

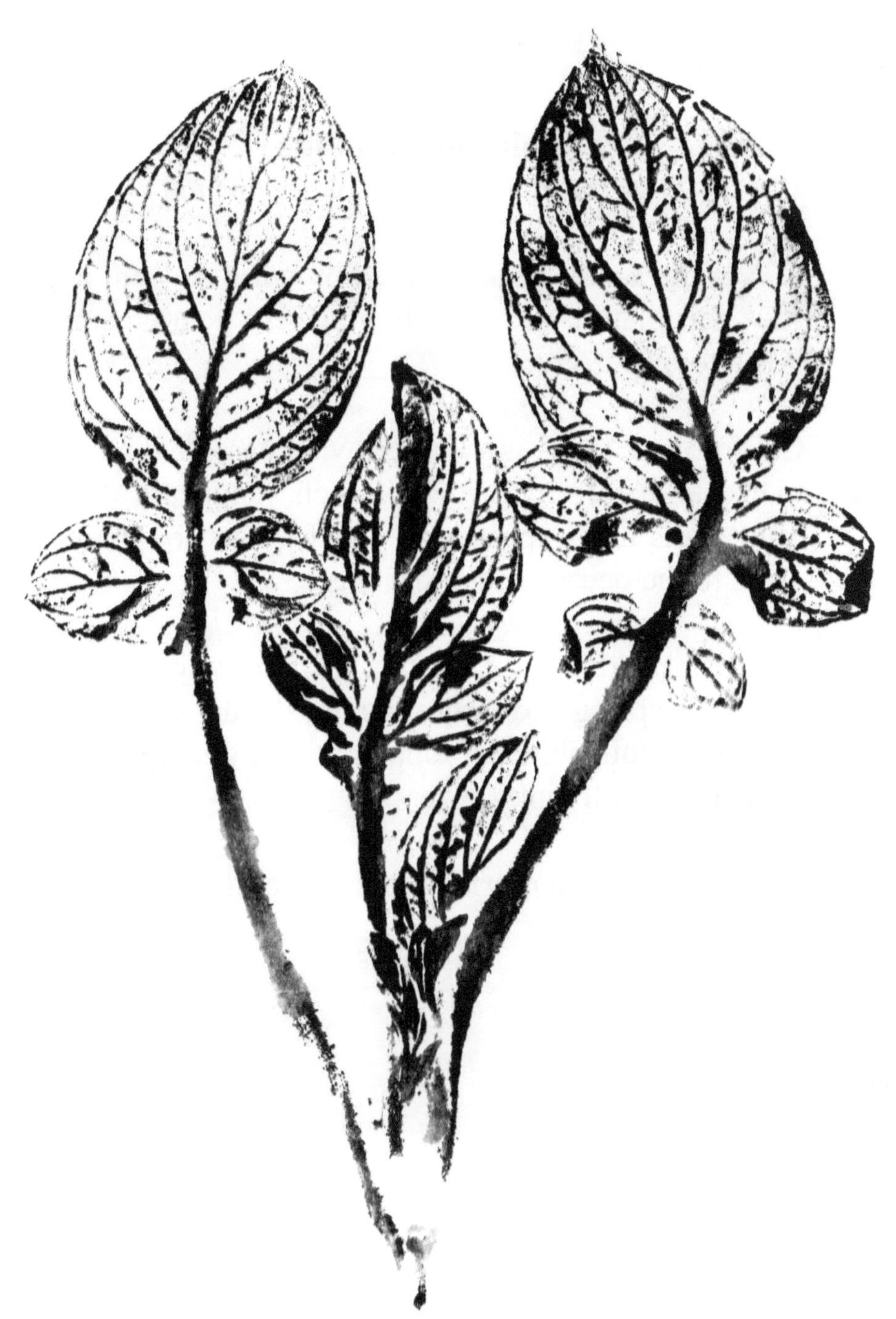

MEADOW

California Sea Pink
Armeria maritima subsp. *californica*

On the sandy bank battered by wind and salt air, this plant is at home. Even with a gentle name, it is a tough survivor…

California sea pink is a low-growing perennial native to coastal California. At Sea Ranch, it appears along bluff trails and exposed headlands, often blooming close to the ocean along cliff edges.

The plant forms tight clumps of narrow, grass-like leaves. In spring and early summer, slender stalks rise above the foliage, each topped with a globe-shaped cluster of small pink flowers.

The species name *maritima* means "of the sea."

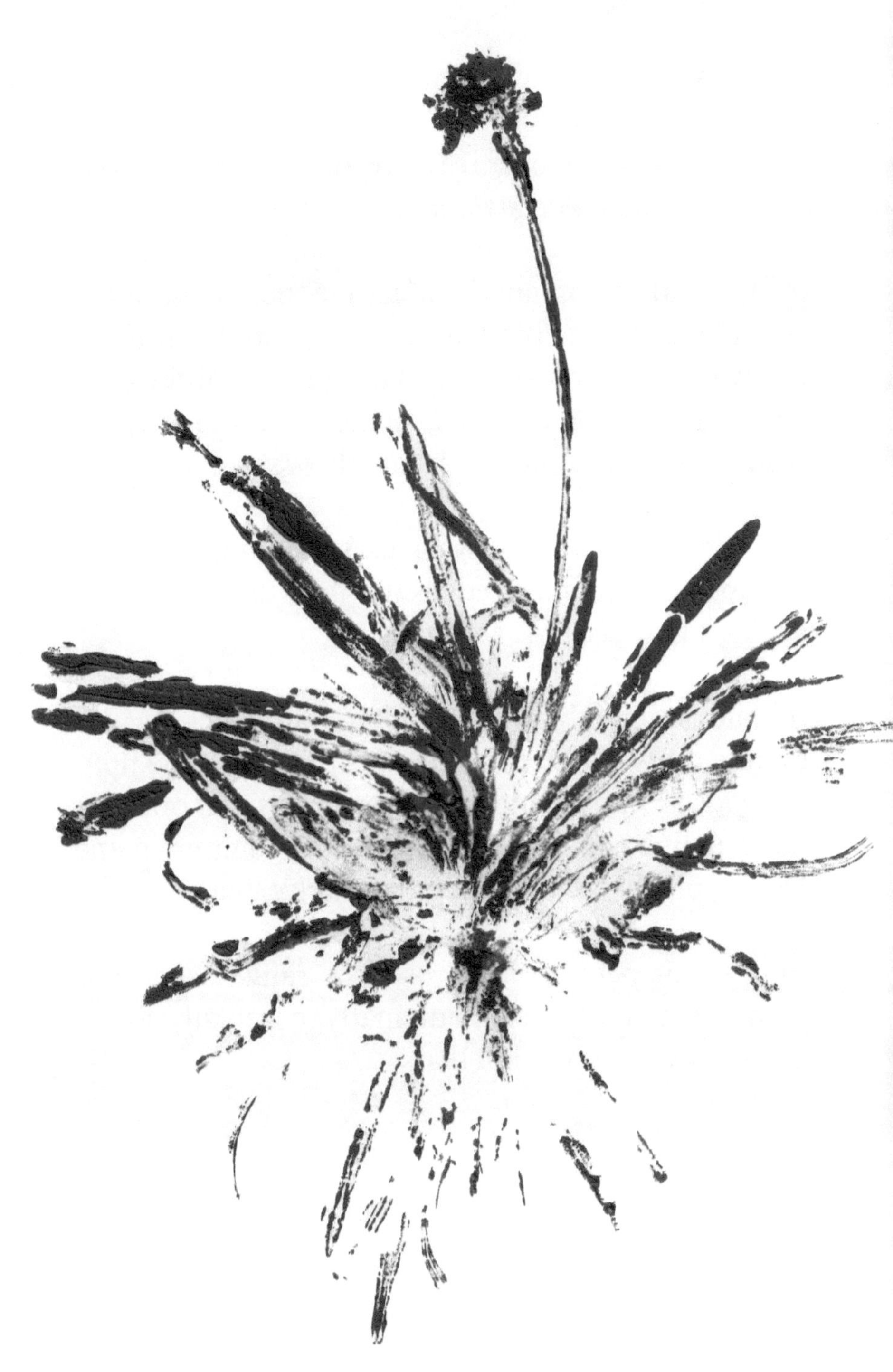

MEADOW

Coastal Gumplant
Grindelia stricta var. *platyphylla*

Coastal gumplant is a native perennial found along the Pacific Coast from central California north into Oregon and Washington. In California, it grows in coastal marshes, dunes, and moist grasslands, often in saline or seasonally wet soils.

The plant typically grows 1 to 3 feet tall, with sturdy, upright stems. Its leaves are thick and somewhat sticky, often clasping the stem.

In late spring through summer, large yellow daisy-like flowers bloom at the tops of stems. The flower heads are surrounded by green bracts that often exude a resinous gum, the source of its common name. Deer typically avoid eating this sticky plant.

Indigenous peoples in parts of its range used gumplant resin and leaves medicinally, especially for respiratory and skin ailments.

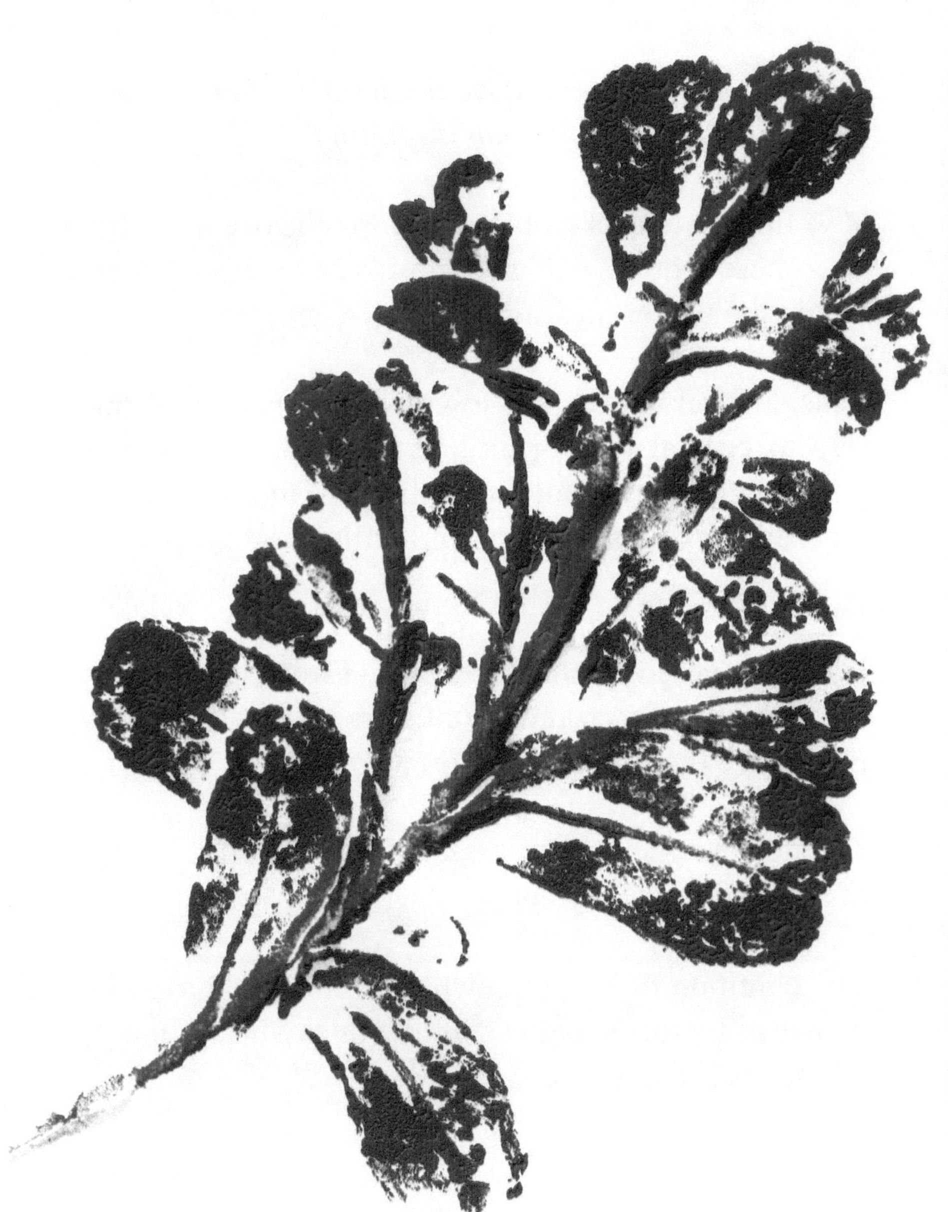

MEADOW

Seaside Buckwheat
Eriogonum latifolium

Clinging to rocky outcrops along the ocean bluffs, these sentries with soft gray arrow-shaped leaves watch the waves and sunsets…

Seaside buckwheat is a low-growing perennial native to coastal California and southern Oregon. At Sea Ranch, it grows along bluff trails and headlands, where wind and salt spray limit taller vegetation.

The plant forms compact mats of broad, gray-green leaves covered with fine hairs. From late spring through summer, rounded clusters of small flowers rise above the foliage on short stems.

The flowers open pale pink to white, often deepening to rosy tones as they age.

The common name "buckwheat" reflects the resemblance of its seeds to those of true buckwheat, though the plants are unrelated.

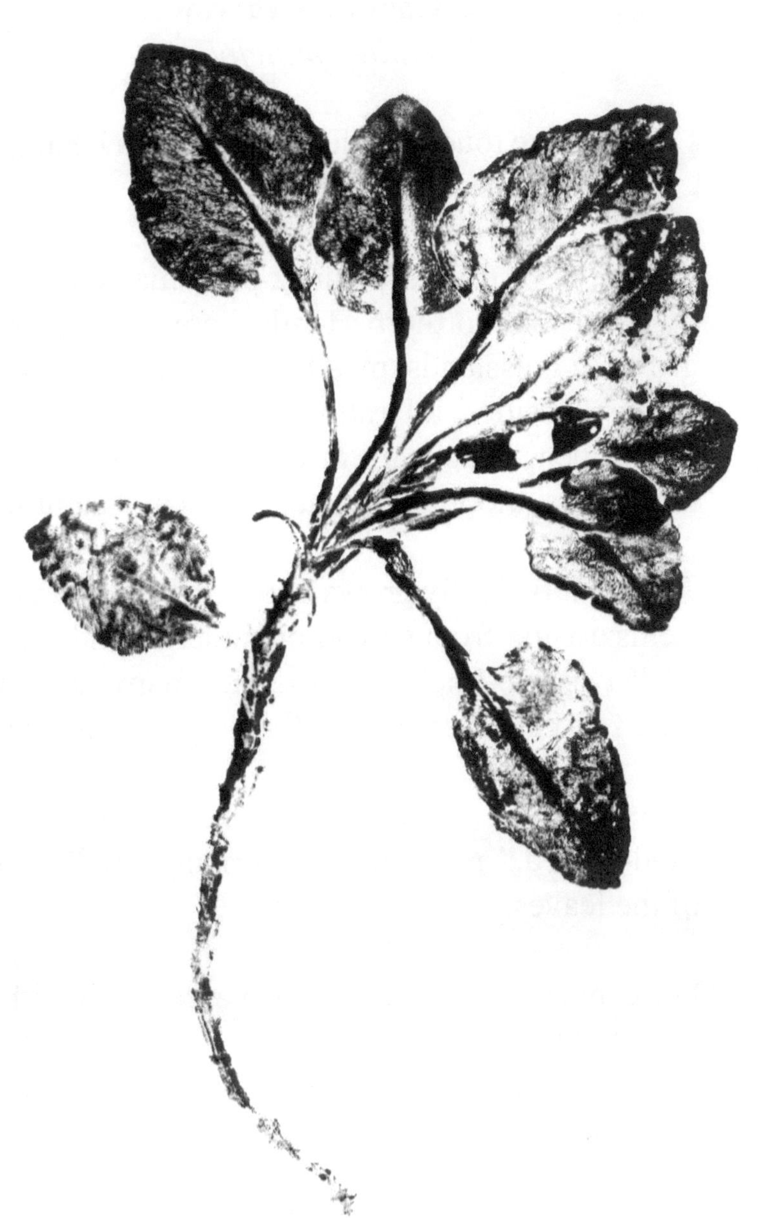

MEADOW

Common Yarrow
Achillea millefolium

S oft to the touch and long valued as a healing herb. This one is a dear friend…

Common yarrow is a hardy perennial found across much of the Northern Hemisphere. In California, it grows in grasslands, meadows, open woodlands, and along roadsides, tolerating a wide range of soils. At Sea Ranch, it appears in open meadows and along bluff trails, blooming in late spring and summer.

The plant typically grows 1 to 3 feet tall, with upright stems arising from spreading underground rhizomes. Its leaves are finely divided into many narrow segments, giving them a soft, feathery appearance.

The species name *millefolium* means "thousand-leaved," referring to the many small divisions of the leaves.

For centuries, yarrow has been associated with healing, divination, and protection in battle. The genus name *Achillea* honors the Greek hero Achilles, who was said to have used the plant to treat wounds.

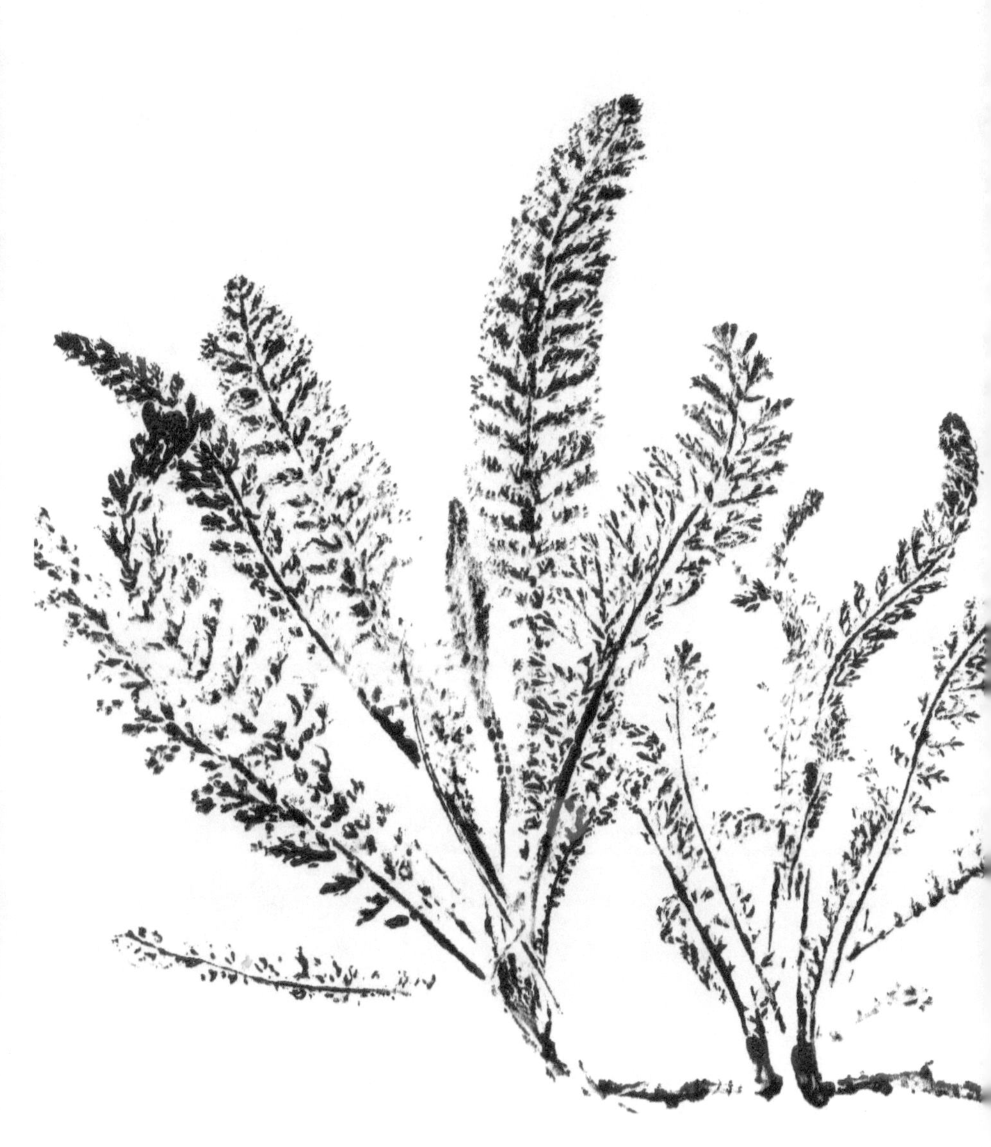

SELECTED GLOSSARY

Basal Rosette — A circle of leaves held close to the ground.

Bract — A small leaf-like part beneath or around a flower cluster.

Bristle — A stiff hair, sometimes helping seeds cling or travel.

Bristly — Covered with stiff hairs or bristles.

Bur — A prickly seed case that can cling to fur or clothing.

Canopy — The leafy roof formed by the branches and leaves of trees.

Catkin — A soft, often finger-like cluster of tiny flowers (common on willows).

Chaparral — Dry shrubland adapted to sun, drought, and fire.

Cleistogamous flowers — Closed, self-pollinating flowers that produce seeds without opening, ensuring reproduction when pollinators are scarce.

Cone — The seed-bearing structure of conifers such as pines and cypress.

Conifer — A cone-bearing tree or shrub such as pine, fir, hemlock, or cypress.

Crown — The upper branching part of a tree.

Deciduous — Dropping leaves seasonally.

Dioecious — Male and female flowers occurring on separate plants.

Disturbed Soils — Ground altered by people, animals, landslides, or grading.

Evergreen — Keeping leaves through the winter.

Female Catkins — Catkins that receive pollen and contain ovaries that develop into seeds.

Filament — The slender stalk that holds up an anther.

Forest Margins — The outer edge of a forest where light and shade meet.

Glabrous — Smooth—without hairs.

Headland — A point of land that juts out toward the sea.

Hedgerow — A planted line of shrubs or trees forming a living barrier.

Hooked Bristles — Small hooks on fruits that cling for

seed dispersal.

Lance — A long, narrow shape that tapers at both ends (short for lance-shaped).

Lobed — Leaves shaped with rounded or pointed sections along the edge.

Male Catkins — Catkins containing stamens that shed pollen.

Mallow — A plant family (the mallow family) that includes mallows and checkerbloom; flowers often have five petals.

Mats — Low, carpet-like growth that spreads across the ground.

Meadow — An open area with grasses and flowering plants.

Myrmecochory — Seed dispersal by ants, which carry seeds away from the parent plant.

Needles — A narrow conifer leaf, as in pines and firs.

Node — A point on a stem where leaves (or roots) can form.

Ovary — The part of a flower that holds seeds and becomes the fruit.

Palmately — Arranged like fingers from a hand (often describing leaflets).

Parallel Veins — Leaf veins that run side by side along the leaf.

Phylloxera — An insect pest of grape roots; resistance is one reason rootstocks matter.

Pinnate — Leaflets arranged along both sides of a central rib.

Pistillate — Bearing female flowers.

Pollen — Fine grains released by flowers as part of reproduction.

Ray — The petal-like outer florets on a daisy-type flower.

Rhizome — An underground stem that spreads and sends up new shoots.

Riparian — Growing along creeks and stream corridors.

Riparian Corridors — Streamside ribbons of wetter habitat.

Rootstock — The root system a grapevine is grafted onto.

Rosette — A circular arrangement of leaves, often

at the base.

Runner — A creeping stem that can root and form a new plant.

Saline — Slightly salty—common near the coast or in marshy soils.

Scale — A small plate-like part (as on cones), or a scale-like leaf.

Scorpioid cyme — A coiled flower cluster that slowly unrolls as the flowers open, resembling a scorpion's tail.

Scrub — A habitat of low shrubs, often on dry or coastal sites.

Spiny Bracts — Sharp bracts that form a prickly collar around some flower heads.

Spray — A branching cluster (often used for conifer foliage).

Spreading Mats — Low growth that spreads into a carpet.

Spring Ephemeral — A plant that grows, flowers, and dies back above ground quickly in early spring before the forest canopy fills with leaves.

Stamen — The male flower part (anther plus filament).

Stem — The main supporting structure that holds leaves and flowers.

Stigma — The pollen-receiving tip of the pistil.

Taproot — A strong central root that grows deep into the ground.

Tendril — A slender curling strand a vine uses to climb.

Terraces — Flat benches of land (often along coasts or hillsides) where plants can take hold.

Thicket — A dense stand of shrubs or small trees.

Toxic — Capable of causing harm if eaten; some plants are also skin irritants.

Umbel — A flower cluster whose stalks spread from one point like umbrella ribs.

Veins — The thin lines in a leaf that carry water and sugars.

Villous — Softly hairy, often with longer hairs.

Wetland — A place where soil stays wet for part or all of the year.

Woodland — Land with scattered trees and an understory.

SELECTED BIBLIOGRAPHY

Alaback, Paul. *Plants of Coastal British Columbia, Including Washington, Oregon, and Alaska*. Edmonton: Lone Pine Publishing, 1994.

Baldwin, Bruce G., et al. *The Jepson Manual: Vascular Plants of California*. 2nd ed. Berkeley: University of California Press, 2012.

Beidleman, L., and E. Kozloff. *Plants of the San Francisco Bay Region: Mendocino to Monterey*. Berkeley: University of California Press, 1994.

Elpel, Thomas. *Botany in a Day: The Patterns Method of Plant Identification*. Pony, MT: HOPS Press, LLC, 1996.

Gray, Beverley. *The Boreal Herbal*. Yukon, Canada: Aroma Borealis Press, 2011.

Hallowell, Anne. *Fern Finder*. Rochester, VT: Nature Study Guide, 1981.

Johnson, R. L., S. Foster, L. Dog, and Kiefer. *National Geographic Guide to Medicinal Herbs*. Washington, DC: National Geographic, 2010.

Keator, Glenn. *Complete Garden Guide to the Shrubs of California*. San Francisco: Chronicle Books, 1994.

Kruckeberg, Arthur R. *Introduction to California Soils and Plants*. Berkeley: University of California Press, 2006.

Lyons, K., and B. Cuneiform-Lazaneo. *Plants of the Coast Redwood Region*. Arcata, CA: Shoreline Press, 1988; revised ed. 2003.

Mahaffey, Elaine. *Wildflowers of the Sea Ranch*. Santa Rosa, CA: Bookcrafters, 1990.

Murie, Olaus. *Animal Tracks. Peterson Field Guide Series*. Boston: Houghton Mifflin Company, 1954.

Noss, Reed F. *The Redwood Forest: History, Ecology, and Conservation of the Coast Redwoods*. Washington, DC: Island Press, 2000.

Pavlik, Bruce, et al. *Oaks of California*. Los Olivos, CA: Cachuma Press, 1991.

Sawyer, John O., Todd Keeler-Wolf, and Julie M. Evens. *A Manual of California Vegetation*. 2nd ed. Sacramento, CA: California Native Plant Society Press, 2009.

Sinclair, W. A., H. H. Lyon, and W. T. Johnson. *Diseases of Trees and Shrubs*. Ithaca, NY: Cornell University Press, 1987.

Stuart, John D., and John O. Sawyer. *Trees and Shrubs of California*. Berkeley: University of California Press, 2001.

Wessels, Tom. *Reading the Forested Landscape*. Woodstock, VT: The Countryman Press, 1997.

Whitney, Stephen. *Western Forests (The Audubon Society Nature Guides)*. New York: Knopf, 1985.

Online Resources (2026):

Calflora. "Calflora: Information on California Plants for Education, Research and Conservation." Berkeley, CA. **https://www.calflora.org**

iNaturalist. "An online social network of people sharing biodiversity information." **https://www.inaturalist.org/**

Jepson eFlora. University of California, Berkeley. Jepson Flora Project (eds.) 2026. **https://ucjeps.berkeley.edu/eflora/**

INDEX

About the Author

Karen Cairn Kreisel studied ornithology and forest ecology at the University of Montana and Eastern Washington University, but never let her advanced degrees get in her way. A lifelong observer, she is drawn to the mysteries of the natural world and the beauty that is waiting for us to notice. She lives on the coast in Northern California, as well as in the mountains of Western Montana.

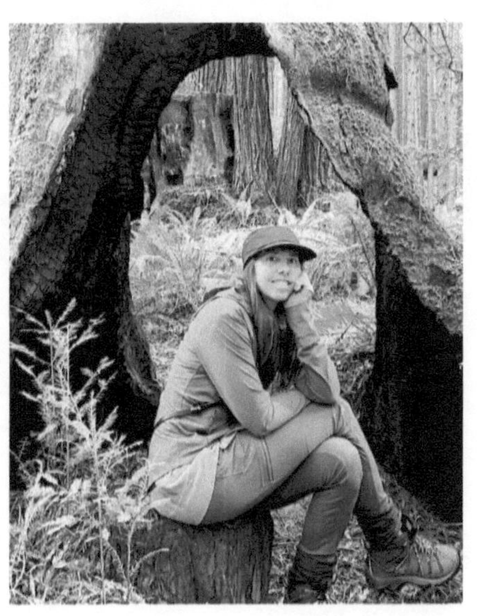

Follow on Instagram, @SeaRanchImpressions and write to SeaRanchImpressions@gmail.com

If you enjoyed this book, *please* leave a review on Amazon (where reviews now have the most reach) and encourage your local bookstore to shelve *Sea Ranch Impressions*.

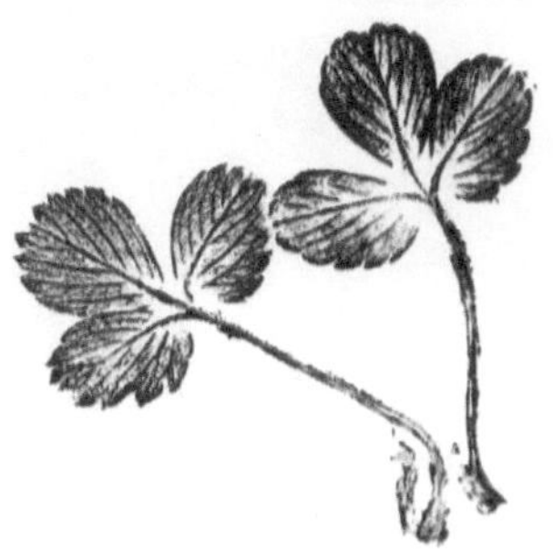

www.ingramcontent.com/pod-product-compliance
Lightning Source LLC
Chambersburg PA
CBHW030906060726
47591CB00005B/1435